MBC
7/00

# Expansion, war
# and rebellion

## Europe, 1598–1661

*For my wife, Liz*

PUBLISHED BY THE PRESS SYNDICATE OF THE UNIVERSITY OF CAMBRIDGE
The Pitt Building, Trumpington Street, Cambridge, United Kingdom

CAMBRIDGE UNIVERSITY PRESS
The Edinburgh Building, Cambridge CB2 2RU, UK        http://www.cup.cam.ac.uk
40 West 20th Street, New York, NY 10011-4211, USA     http://www.cup.org
10 Stamford Road, Oakleigh, Melbourne 3166, Australia
Ruiz de Alarcón 13, 28014 Madrid, Spain

© Cambridge University Press 2000

First published 2000

Printed in the United Kingdom at the University Press, Cambridge

Text design by Newton Harris Design Partnership

*Typeface* 10½pt Minion     *System* QuarkXPress®

*A catalogue record for this book is available from the British Library*

ISBN 0 521 58616 X     paperback

The cover shows a painting of the Officials of the Company of Bowyers of St Sebastian at Amsterdam, 1653 (oil on panel) by Bartolomeus van der Helst (1613–70), Louvre, Paris, France / Peter Willi / Bridgeman Art Library.

ACKNOWLEDGEMENTS
Graphische Sammlung Albertina, Wien: p.122*br*; theartarchive/Kunsthistorisches Museum, Vienna: p.5, theartarchive/Prado Museum, Madrid: p.75, theartarchive/The British Library: p.135; *Portrait of Galileo Galilei* (1564–1642), by Ottavio Mario Leoni (*c*.1578–1630), Biblioteca Marucelliana, Florence, Italy/Bridgeman Art Library: p.160; *Aurora*, 1613–14 (fresco), by Guido Reni (1575–1642), Casino Pallavicini-Rospigliosi, Rome, Italy/BAL: p.121; *Madonna of Loreto* (1604–05), by Michelangelo Merisi da Caravaggio (1571–1610), Chiesa di San Agostino, Rome, Italy/BAL: p.122 *tl*, *Albrecht Wenzel Eusebius von Wallenstein*, Duke of Friedland and Mecklenburg, Prince of Sagan (1583–1634), by Ludwig von Carolsfeld Scnorr (1764–1841), by Sir Anthony van Dyck (1599–1641)(after), Heeresgeschichtliches Museum, Vienna, Austria/BAL: p.126; *Portrait of Armand-Jean du Plessis, Cardinal Richelieu* (1585–1642), by Philippe de Champaigne (1602–74), Louvre, Paris, France/Peter Willi/BAL:

p.38; *Philip IV of Spain* (1605–65) *c*.1628, by Diego Rodriguez de Silva y Velasquez (1599–1660), Prado, Madrid, Spain/BAL: p.78; by permission of the British Library: pp.11 *r*, 166 *l* & *r*; Mary Evans Picture Library: pp.118, 145 *tl* & *bl*, 161; by kind permission of the Earl of Leicester and the Trustees of Holkham Estate: p.9 *b*; Hulton Getty Picture Collection: pp.56, 144; National Gallery, London: pp.122 *tr* & *bl*; Roger-Viollet Agency Photographique: pp.9 *t*, 40, 55 *t* & *b*, 59, 145 *r*.

We have been unable to trace the copyright holders of the material on pages 11 *l*, 137,138, and would be grateful for any information that would enable us to do so.

Picture Research by Sandie Huskinson-Rolfe of PHOTOSEEKERS

# Contents

# Introduction: was it all doom and gloom?

Seventeenth-century Europe was a very different world from our own. The landscape was emptier and greener. People and places smelt more pungent. The climate was cooler; winters were more frequently long and hard. The seventeenth-century English philosopher **Hobbes** said that for most people life was 'nasty, brutish and short'. For many, life was indeed hard and lacked the comforts that most people take for granted three centuries later. Life became even harder for most Europeans during the period in question, and that was the cause of numerous revolts in the middle of the century. Making a living, surviving even, was a difficult business. Caught up in wars, revolutions and witch-hunts and living in an age of constant discovery, seventeenth-century people lived in a hazardous but stimulating environment.

There were many wars in this period. The largest of them was the Thirty Years' War. This devastating conflict was fought out in central Europe but involved almost all the great powers – France, Spain, Sweden, Denmark and the **United Provinces** (see Map 1 on page 4). For this reason and because of the complexity of some of the issues, the Thirty Years' War is considered late in the book. War and witch-hunting were two of the darker sides of life in this period.

Not all was doom and gloom. Holland was prospering. Dutch merchants and engineers helped to develop the rest of Europe. Progress was achieved through economic development and overseas trade – a blueprint for Europe in later centuries. For the Dutch war was often involved too, but most of the leading people in the United Provinces looked to conditions of peace to achieve their goals. In most other states for most of the time the majority of the leading politicians and heads of state saw war as the best way to advance their interests. To think in the Dutch way was a refreshing novelty.

Science as we would recognise it today was also developing, not just in Holland. Though the process was slow, superstitious beliefs were declining as modern science developed. Between the limited scientific knowledge of the Middle Ages and the boom in research of a more modern kind in the eighteenth century came the invention of the superstitious quasi-science of demonology, which reached its climax in the first half of the seventeenth

**Thomas Hobbes** (1588–1679) was an English political philosopher. He is best known for *Leviathan* (1651), a defence of absolute sovereignty.

**The United Provinces** (1581–1795) were the northern provinces of the Netherlands; sometimes inaccurately known as Holland, the dominant province.

century. Most scientists lived in cities and frequented universities. Most Europeans lived in the countryside, where the pace of change was hardly noticeable. It is to life as it was experienced by the rural masses that we shall first turn.

# 1 The people divided

**Focus questions**

- ◆ In what ways was their environment different from ours?
- ◆ How far did ethnic differences create divisions?
- ◆ How did social class, gender and age affect your chances?
- ◆ What was the quality of life?

## Overview

Seventeenth-century Europe was sparsely populated; large towns and cities were few and far apart. Life was hard for most people, linked to the seasons and confined to the countryside. They survived in a climate that was colder than today's and were without modern comforts.

People were sharply divided in several ways. There were many ethnic groups. Minorities were more often persecuted than appreciated for their different qualities, though people from different ethnic backgrounds rubbed shoulders with each other in many fields of activity, especially commerce and the armed forces. The divides between rich and poor, and men and women, were also very great. Life for many children, though, was not much different from adult life. This was because poor families – most of the population – needed the contribution of the whole family to survive. The poor became poorer and more numerous in many parts of Europe in the first half of the seventeenth century. Even some of the rich struggled to retain their position, especially those who relied on rents paid to them by the poor. In between, the middle classes were growing in importance.

Whether rich, poor or in between, ill-health, appalling medical care and an inadequate diet affected everyone, though in different ways. There were opportunities for fun and light relief from an arduous life, but for many people low and declining standards of living ruled out any chance of lasting improvement.

## In what ways was their environment different from ours?

It is easy to imagine that we know a great deal about seventeenth-century Europe already. In reality, almost everything about the way people lived – even the climate – was different.

### Population distribution

Today, Europe's population is over 500 million. At the end of the sixteenth century it was a little over 70 million. Most Europeans lived in villages or isolated farms. The most densely populated regions were the coastal areas of France, north and west Italy, the west and south of Germany, Austria, the southern Netherlands, south-east England and central Ireland. Scandinavia, Spain and eastern Europe were very sparsely populated. The largest cities – mainly outside the most populous regions – were Paris, London, Naples and Constantinople, each with about 200,000 inhabitants. People moved around Europe more than might be imagined, though doing so was difficult because land communications were extremely poor. A galloping horse provided the fastest means of transport. Huge tracts of Europe were still densely forested and ice cover in the high mountain passes added to the problems.

> Which were the most densely populated regions of Europe? Which cities were the largest?

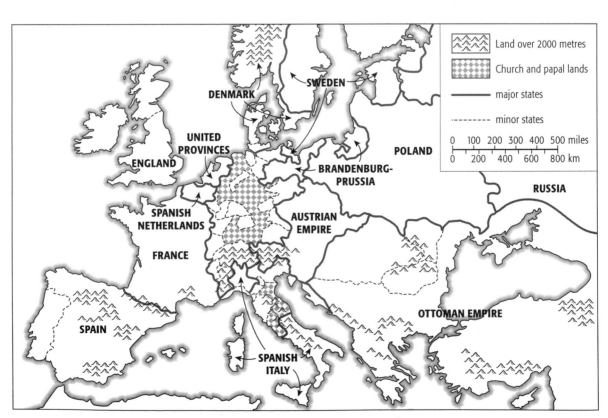

Map 1: The major states in the early seventeenth century.

### The mini Ice Age

Most people were peasant farmers, renting little plots of land and living in small bare cottages. Getting enough to eat was their main concern. Without central heating, they were cold for much of the year, not helped by the fact that Europe was experiencing the last stages of a mini Ice Age that had started in the thirteenth century. In northern Europe winters were often hard, with lakes and rivers frozen. Outdoor skating, frequently shown in pictures from the time, was one of the few fringe benefits. Spring came late and the growing season was shorter than it is now. The working day was long, varying with the seasons but generally from dawn to dusk. On the other hand, so few worked in industry that there was no factory clock to dictate a rigid day.

How did the winters at this period differ from those three centuries later?

*Hunters in the snow* by Pieter Bruegel the Elder (1565). Big freezes like the one shown were common in the sixteenth and seventeenth centuries.

## How far did ethnic differences create divisions?

With most of Europe loosely divided into several large empires – those of Spain, Sweden, Poland, Russia, Austria and the **Ottomans** – there were many ethnic minority groups in each state, as the table on page 7 shows. Linguistically Europe was more varied than it is today. There were, for example, proportionately more speakers of Breton and Catalan. Religiously it was just as diverse as today and, with many more people actively religious, the differences were more obvious. Rulers and ruling elites were often part of ethnic minorities in their own states. One might imagine that such a situation

**The Ottoman Empire** (in Europe, Asia and Africa) lasted from the late thirteenth century to the end of the First World War.

would lead to the break-up of the great states. However, most of them had experienced little fragmentation by 1661.

What kept these multicultural states going for so long was chiefly the determination of their rulers to hold on to scattered lands, lands which had been acquired through centuries by marriage settlements and wars. The borders of many states were unstable, as new rulers tried to extend and consolidate their inheritance. Since they lacked the manpower and the means to organise strong national armies and powerful national industries, they tended to prefer flexible arrangements for defence and commerce. By the end of the seventeenth century armies were becoming more national in composition, but most states continued to rely on mercenaries. These were drawn from every corner of Europe. It was not unusual to find Scotsmen fighting for the tsar of Russia or Irishmen for the emperor of Austria.

Commerce also helped to mix ethnic groups. The Dutch were leaders in the field of commercial colonisation. Dutch entrepreneurs, for example, dominated the economic life of Scandinavia and Ireland. Dutch, Germans and English were particularly sought after by rulers of east European states, who offered merchants, craftsmen and farmers incentives to settle. Holland itself was open house to persecuted minorities from elsewhere in Europe.

Multicultural societies they may have been, but they were rarely harmonious. The situation of many of the ethnic minority groups was extremely difficult, and things became harder in the seventeenth century. The persecution of the **Huguenots** in France is one example. When the religion of the minority group was different from that of the ruling elite or that of the majority population, persecution was often the norm. Jews and gypsies were often expelled from places where they had settled. Sometimes – like the Jews in Poland – they had come originally come to those places by invitation. Poland's Jews became victims of a seventeenth-century holocaust during the Ukrainian **Cossack** revolt of 1648–51, when popular leaders inspired hatred against Jews and other 'outsiders'. Jewish chroniclers estimate 100,000 were put to death and 300 communities destroyed, twice the number of people executed in witch-hunts over the 90-year period 1560–1650.

Other regions of Europe were just as intolerant. By the end of the sixteenth century the Spanish had decided on a policy of expulsion for their Moorish population; in 1609 Spain deported 300,000 Moors to Africa, splitting apart mixed-race married couples in the process. Copying his Habsburg cousins in Spain, the Austrian emperor Ferdinand II suppressed Czech Protestants in the 1620s; some 150,000 left **Bohemia** to escape persecution. In this period 'ethnic cleansing' was no less common and no less drastic than it has been in the twentieth century.

How did the rulers keep control in their widely spread territories?

The **Huguenots** were the French Protestants, who were influenced by John Calvin, a reformer from Geneva.

The **Cossacks** were warrior horsemen from the Ukraine who fought for the tsars of Russia.

**Bohemia** was an independent kingdom in central Europe from the ninth to the thirteenth century, inhabited by the Czechs.

Which ethnic minorities suffered most in this period?

| Table 1: Ethnic breakdown of the major states | | | |
|---|---|---|---|
| Empires/states in 1600 | Language and religion of ruling elite | Main linguistic minorities + number of others | Main religious minorities |
| Spain | Spanish Catholic | Italians, Catalans, Portuguese, Dutch, Moriscos + 6 | Islam, Jews, Protestants |
| France | French Catholic | Bretons, Provençals, Basques | Protestants (Calvinist) |
| United Provinces | Dutch Protestant (Calvinist) | Jews (Ladino) | Jews, Catholics |
| Denmark | Danish Protestant (Lutheran) | Norwegians, Swedes, Dutch + 3 | Jews, Catholics |
| Sweden | Swedish Protestant (Lutheran) | Finns, Karelians, by 1650 + 5 | Catholics, Eastern Orthodox |
| Poland | Polish Catholic | Jews (Yiddish), Ukrainians + 3 | Jews, Calvinists, Eastern Orthodox |
| Russia – European only | Russian Eastern Orthodox | Jews (Yiddish), Ukrainians + 3 | Jews, Tatars |
| Austria | German Catholic | Czechs, Italians, Hungarians + 5 | Protestants |
| Ottoman – European only | Turkish Islam | Greeks, Italians, Albanians, Jews + 6 | Christians, Jews |

# How did social class, gender and age affect your chances?

## Social class

The question 'What was life like for people in the seventeenth century?' cannot be answered without asking 'Life for whom?' Society was rigidly stratified and social class was, in most situations, the most vital of divisions. It was immediately apparent to which social class you belonged, for dress instantly gave it away. Though not as rigidly kept to as in medieval times, dress regulations dictated what was proper for each social class. In France young nobles could wear silk stockings but young men of lower social standing only cotton ones. Social behaviour was regulated too; in France it was an offence for men of different rank to use the same washing bowl after eating. There was a kind of social 'apartheid'. Most societies were legally divided into 'Estates'. In France, for example, there were three, the first being the clergy, the second the nobility and the third everyone else.

| Table 2: The social classes | | |
|---|---|---|
| **Income band** | **Social class** | **Relationship to others** |
| Rich | Monarchy<br>Aristocracy<br>Top churchmen<br>Lower nobility | Landowners |
| 'Middle sort' | Top merchants<br>'Middle-class' professionals<br>Small shopkeepers, artisans<br>Top peasants | Independent and employers |
| Poor | Most peasants<br>Industrial workers,<br>Fishermen<br>Servants<br>Beggars, vagrants | Mostly tenants of landowners and at their beck and call |

It says much for the growing importance of money over inherited power that contemporary writers often preferred to refer to the 'rich', the 'poor' and the 'middle sort' rather than the 'Estates'. A Spanish proverb said that there were only two families in the world: the Haves and the Have-Nots. The contrasts were striking: the showy luxury of the few was in stark contrast to the poverty of the 'rabble', the numerous beggars who were merely the tip of an iceberg of poverty. A child's access to schooling, to good food, to future prosperity, even to life itself, was largely dependent on social status.

Although the social classes are placed in clear divisions in Table 2, there was in reality a good deal of overlap between 'rich' and 'middle' and between 'middle' and 'poor'. Within a noble family there could be a lot of variation between the oldest son, who would inherit, and the youngest, who would not. Social position was not completely fixed, but by modern standards it was rigid. Though the feudal Estates were beginning to crumble, few made it from the bottom to the top. Those at the top did their best to stop them. **Richelieu** was typical of his class in believing that men of noble birth were, by nature, bound to have greater talents than those of low birth. Those at the bottom not only had very little money, they had no power at all. A poor person's life was not their own. The poor were often subject to their landlord, to the rules of the church and, in some states, to military service. They had neither a direct place in public decision-making nor access to the law.

**Cardinal Richelieu** (1585–1642) was a French statesman who strengthened the power of the crown in France and the influence of France in Europe.

Why was it difficult for the poor to improve their situation in the seventeenth century?

*Left:* An engraving of noble and peasant in seventeenth-century France, by J. Lagnier.
*Below:* Contemporary earl and his estate staff, Holkham Hall, Norfolk, in a painting by Andrew Festing (1993).

## The rich, 'old' and 'new'

In the seventeenth century the 'old' rich were mostly the aristocracy and the 'new' the most successful merchants, high clerics, generals, top government office-holders and financiers. Many of the new rich were of non-noble birth; that is to say, not belonging even to the lesser nobility. This caused a great stir amongst their contemporaries, but the process was not new and they remained the minority. Merchant numbers actually declined in Spain and only in the province of Holland and in Venice did they have political power equal to their economic importance.

An aristocrat's household was modelled on the court life of the monarch. He had his house extended to palatial dimensions, filling it with the finest furnishings and surrounding the whole building with the latest fashion in gardens. He was expected to live up to his position. He had to entertain extravagantly and he had to look right, choosing the correct wig for the occasion from several different types and maintaining a wardrobe that had to grow each year to cope with fast-changing male fashions. What did the aristocracy contribute in return? In 1600 the Spaniard Martín Gonzalez de Cellorigo complained that the rich 'loll at ease' (*Memorial*, 1600). There had undoubtedly been some loss of public function since the Middle Ages and aristocratic lives increasingly revolved around private concerns. For the majority, estate management, the upkeep of property, collection of **feudal dues** and management of estate staff was their only work and much of this was in the hands of **stewards**. Their real function declined. In many states flattering the monarch replaced the former role of the top aristocracy, that of adviser. Fencing and hunting replaced service as officers in the army. An excess of money and an abundance of free time combined to lead many to a life of gambling and adultery. The arranging of profitable marriages became a much more important occupation for them than the search for better productivity and income from their estates.

**Feudal dues** were duties owed by a tenant to his lord.

**Stewards** managed estates on behalf of their owner.

How did the role of the aristocrats at this time differ from what it was earlier?

### The 'middle sort'

Contemporary observers of society talked about the 'middle sort' rather than the 'middle class' – the word 'class' came into use for social distinction in the nineteenth century. The 'middle class' in most European states was a tiny proportion of the population, the exception being the United Provinces. There was a hierarchy within the middle class, with lawyers and high financiers at the top and doctors, some men of law, municipal officers, merchants and industrialists next. Slightly below came lesser financiers, bankers and tax-collectors. At the bottom came lawyers' clerks, shopkeepers, ordinary priests and school teachers. Despite having many different occupations the middle class was small outside the towns, even in the United Provinces.

Like their social superiors, middle-class people across Europe were preoccupied with status, making them the butt of many jokes. They were a favourite target for comic playwrights like **Molière**, speaking here through Monsieur Jourdain in *Le bourgeois gentilhomme* (*The self-made gentleman*), first performed in 1670 (from G. Gravelly, trans., *Six prose comedies of Molière*, 1968):

**Molière** (1622–73) was a popular French comic playwright.

> I am going for a little walk in the town to show off my fine clothes. Follow me, and remember, both of you [lackeys] to walk close at my heels, so that everyone may see you belong to me . . . [later on] I show my good sense in frequenting with the aristocracy. It's better than hobnobbing with shopkeepers.

## The poor

Some 80 per cent of the population were poor, in the sense that they were regularly below the absolute **poverty** line, the level needed to provide sufficient food, shelter and heating to ensure survival. Only 10 per cent of the peasantry were in a position to feed their families adequately.

Contemporary definitions of poverty were usually relative. The poor were labelled, either as 'undeserving': beggars, the homeless, casual and nomadic labourers; or as 'deserving': artisans, labourers and peasants who had fallen on hard times, generally through sickness or old age. **Vauban** classified 10 per cent of the French population as beggars and 30 per cent as near-beggars in the late seventeenth century. Even the relatively affluent United Provinces had about the same proportion of beggars and near-beggars. Almost a quarter of the population in Overijssel, one of its rural provinces, owned no property.

The absolute definition of poverty will be the one used here. It reminds us both of the gulf separating the mass of the people from the middle and upper classes and also of the enormous level of absolute poverty during this period. Poor families lived much as they had done throughout the medieval period – in small, cramped households, often shared with a cow, a sheep and poultry. Usually there was only one room, with the cowshed separated from it by a partition. The floor was beaten-down earth. Typical furniture consisted of one feather bed, a straw mattress for the children, a table and wooden chairs.

**Poverty** can be measured 'absolutely' as here; or 'relatively', when comparisons are made with the average living standards and expectations of people at the time.

**Vauban** (1633–1707) most famous as a military engineer, also commented on faults in the government of France.

*Left:* A contemporary engraving of a street-seller of food. *Right:* An engraving of a water-carrier by J. Bonnart.

Clothes, usually made from coarse wool or linen, were often cast-offs from other family members or bought second-hand.

Poverty increased in the late sixteenth and seventeenth centuries over most of Europe, particularly in Italy, Spain, France and Germany. The population was growing and states that were geared to war failed to keep pace with the increase. In the countryside more and more peasants become landless labourers, thanks to their mounting debts. Dispossessed in this way, they lost the food grown on their own plots. In towns, particularly in southern Europe, the collapse of traditional woollen textile industries caused unemployment. Many towns had doubled or trebled in population in the sixteenth century. Prices rose with the increase in demand and wages bought less. Not surprisingly, the level of violence and crime increased as desperate people struggled for survival. Mugging, pick-pocketing, aggressive begging, banditry, rioting, smuggling and prostitution were the resort of many of the 40 per cent loosely classified as beggars or near-beggars.

> What evidence is there that poverty increased in this period?

## Life for women

For a woman life's most significant event was usually marriage. Her social and economic status depended on the man she married. As divorce was virtually impossible, marriage lasted until the death of one of the parties. Having children was considered to be the main purpose of marriage. In sermons and illustrations, whether Catholic or Protestant, the ideal woman is shown sitting with her children, listening to a sermon or reading the Bible. Church and state encouraged large families. Typically, a baby would be born every two years during a woman's fertile years. The price of maternity was high. One in twenty women died in childbirth.

> What was a woman's role in life in this period?

In marriage, as in all things, the woman was subordinate to the man. Religion, science, popular literature and economic changes all reinforced that inferior status. The law said that a wife's first duty was to obey. A married woman could not sue, make contracts, or go to court for any reason without her husband's approval. The husband had complete control over his wife's property. Women were classified alongside peasants and the simple-minded as not legally responsible for their own actions. Many parts of Europe introduced male guardians for unmarried women and widows. The law punished the sexes differently: female adultery was considered to be a serious, punishable crime; while male adultery was pardonable. Women were excluded from all aspects of religious life in the Jewish and Islamic faiths. The scientific revolution (see Chapter 11) left almost unchallenged long-held notions about the unequal capacities of the sexes, based on the **humours**. Men were believed to be hot and dry, women cold and wet; heat was superior as it rose towards the brain and towards the heavens.

> Scientists believed the body contained four **humours**, fluids corresponding to the four elements, as follows:
>
> | Humour | Element | Quality |
> |---|---|---|
> | black bile | earth | cold and dry |
> | phlegm | water | cold and moist |
> | blood | air | hot and moist |
> | yellow bile | fire | hot and dry |

Those women with ambitions to make a career in any of the higher-status jobs found that men were turning one occupation after another into a 'closed shop' for themselves. Society was increasingly male dominated in this period. Women were rarely heads of state; few of those who were had full powers. Public positions of any importance were held by men, and occupations such as midwifery and care of the sick as well as the legal profession and the artisan trades were increasingly denied to women. The education system and property and inheritance law all reinforced male dominance. 'Masterless' women were perceived as a danger to the social order. There were women who tried to improve the status of their sex, but they were few in number and their claims were modest by modern standards. One such was the Spaniard **Maria de Zayas y Sotomayor**, born about 1590 into an aristocratic family. Maria entered into a convent, perhaps after an unsuccessful marriage, but her main passion was for reading and writing. Men, she said in the introduction to her *Novels*, published in 1637, had produced more scholars only because they had been educated; women with an equal education would be as capable of filling demanding professional jobs as men. In most of her stories men are cruel deceivers and the heroines reject married life, preferring to enter the convent either before or after 'tying the knot'.

'Women have the same soul, abilities and feelings as men': **Maria de Zayas y Sotomayor**, *Novels*, 1637.

The women who are known to have been exceptions to the rule in the seventeenth century were from upper-class backgrounds. Lower-class women were not only saddled with the heavy roles of housewife and mother but were generally expected to do paid work as well. The commonest areas of employment for women were domestic service, farm work, selling and textiles. Domestic service was probably the largest field of employment. In France, 1 in 12 of the population was a servant and two-thirds of servants were female. In farming many jobs were carried out by women. In regions where textiles were big business, women were favoured for employment. Wages were low in spinning, and the authorities encouraged women to work in large workshops under male supervision.

In what ways did men increasingly dominate in the world of paid work?

### Children: the emergence of a distinct childhood

Many a modern family home is adorned with photographs and other reminders of children at each stage in their childhood. This has not always been the case. Childhood was given a low priority in the medieval and for most of the **early modern** period. There were no novels for or about children and nothing equivalent to comics. However, things were beginning to change. The concept of a distinct period of childhood was emerging, although mainly for upper-class boys. Portraits of children shown separately from their parents, a rarity until the end of the sixteenth century, were to become commonplace at the beginning of the next one. The boy was shown dressed

'The **early modern** period' is a useful tag for the period from the Renaissance to the Industrial Revolution, c. 1450–1750.

**Swaddling bands** were broad strips of material wrapped tightly round the body of an infant to create a tight cocoon.

distinctively as a child, wearing ribbons, robes and false sleeves. In medieval times as soon as a child had been taken out of **swaddling bands** they were dressed like a miniature adult.

The emergence of childhood, particularly amongst upper-class boys, was linked to a growing social trend, attendance at school. School prolonged the period of separation between infancy and adult life. The curriculum emphasised biblical instruction, Latin and Greek, arithmetic, modern languages, history, geography, writing, speech and physical education. Teaching methods relied heavily on learning by heart and corporal punishment – even up to the age of 20. In the eighteenth century such discipline was used less frequently. Force was not entirely on the schoolmaster's side; boys as young as 5 might arrive at school armed with swords and guns. As one might expect, colleges had rules requiring disarmament on arrival, but even when disarmed pupils could be violent. In 1661 at Beaune in France an Oratorian father was beaten up by his pupils. On occasion staff had to cope with armed student mutinies. In France these continued to occur until the end of the seventeenth century.

Lower-class children rarely went to school and often worked from an early age. Boys were expected to become self-supporting at the age of about 15 and if they came from poor families the line was generally drawn at 12. Many children from poor or orphaned backgrounds began work at the age of 7 or even 6. Seven-year-old children at La Charité orphanage in Lyons rose at 5 a.m. and worked at silk-making until dark in winter and until 6 p.m. in summer. Daughters were expected to work in the home and learned to sew, cook and to take care of the domestic animals from the earliest age possible. Schooling for girls was confined to the rich. Expected to behave as adults, children of the lower classes wore the same style of clothes as those worn by their parents.

## What was the quality of life?

Music, drama, fine art, reading, study and travel were significant sources of pleasure for a minority, mainly though not exclusively the rich and 'middle sort'. However, then as now, the extremes of pleasure or pain were physical in nature and these experiences were universal.

### Ill-health and medicine

If you were poor, there was a 50–50 chance that you would not survive childhood. In the first half of the seventeenth century those strong enough to resist disease were fewer in number than in late medieval times. This was because a big population increase in the previous century had put too much pressure on food supply. The poor were in a permanent state of malnourishment, which left them vulnerable to disease. When the economy went through depressions, when harvests failed or epidemics struck, the death rate rose sharply. Shortage of food was the main cause of years of exceptionally high mortality. The situation worsened in France, Spain and Italy throughout the century before slowly and sporadically improving in the eighteenth century. There were crises in many parts of Europe in the 1590s and 1640s. At such times, the most desperate people ate anything: poor-quality bread, human nail clippings, entrails of animals. By doing so they risked adding infections to their existing deficiency diseases.

Epidemics – usually of bubonic plague, but also of typhus – were the second main cause of peaks in the death figures. Epidemics did not always coincide with bad harvests, but were often associated with war and revolt since soldiers and refugees carried infections. This was the cause of severe plagues in Spain and central Europe in 1629. By the late seventeenth century plague was less widespread and less frequent, probably thanks to a reduction in the virulence in the disease strain. However, there continued to be many deaths from bronchitis, pneumonia, flu and food-poisoning – diseases that a fit, well-nourished population would have withstood. People had too little knowledge to avoid the risks. Many people, even rich people, were pockmarked by small-pox and their teeth were foul with infections and abscesses. Many were lame and twisted with gout. Hump-back conditions were not uncommon. Many poor children were potbellied from malnutrition. Most people were considerably shorter then people are today.

What diseases threatened people in the seventeenth century?

Physicians (doctors) were notoriously bad. Those people with enough money turned to one in desperation, often with a good deal of justified cynicism about the likelihood of relief or cure. The dying Louis XIII complained that he had had the unhappy lot of all prominent men – to be committed to the care of physicians. Treatment was inadequate largely because biological knowledge was poor. Lacking anaesthetics, antiseptics and antibiotics – the big three breakthroughs of the last two centuries – the unlucky patient was usually doomed. Though their numbers were growing, physicians rarely practised outside towns or armies or treated anyone who was not rich. Apothecaries (chemists) were widely consulted about common ailments like ringworm, sprains, cataracts and infected sores. However, most people relied on the herbal cures known to the local 'wise woman'. Herbal medicine often offered a better chance of a cure than the more drastic remedies of the physicians. In the absence of reliably effective cures, there was much resort to spells and charms, incantations and amulets. These belonged to the spectrum of religious and quasi-religious practice that ranged from respectable Christian pilgrimages to unlawful witchcraft. Catholics made wax and metal images of eyes, breasts and limbs for their shrines.

Why was there so much ill-health in this period?

## Food: vegetarians – but not from choice!

Out of necessity the poor person's diet was largely vegetarian. Grains were the basis of most meals. The commonest meal was bread floating in a thin vegetable soup. Fresh meat was a luxury, eaten perhaps a dozen times a year. Butchers were only to be found in sizeable towns and their prices were high. Milk, eggs and hard cheese were expensive and the poor urban dweller probably never tasted them. Even chicken and geese were becoming costly items, and if the poor country dweller wanted game they had to risk severe punishments for poaching. Fishing rights and most of the catch from rivers and lakes belonged to monastic and noble households. Ironically, modern thinking considers the peasant diet to have been marginally healthier for the heart than the grossly fatty and meat-centred diet of the rich. However, there simply wasn't enough nutrition in those vegetable soups. The diet lacked calcium for good bones (no cheese) and fat and protein for muscular growth, tissue repair and quick energy (almost no fish, meat and nuts). High prices and scarcity were behind what peasants chose to eat.

At any suitable occasion – a wedding, a death or the bringing in of the harvest – the common people threw caution to the wind to indulge in an orgy of eating and drinking. The indulgence of the rich was imitated, one meat course following another. The church and many governments attacked these occasions, seizing on the violence, illness and bastardy to which they sometimes gave rise as evidence of the effects of the **deadly sin** of gluttony. Attempts were made to limit the number of dishes at wedding feasts and other celebrations.

Eating for the middle and upper classes was a very different matter. Their quality of life was enhanced by two factors. The first was the greater availability of meat. A growth in livestock rearing and trade in north-west Europe widened urban access to meat and dairy products. The second was the introduction of new products from overseas. In the middle of the seventeenth century, tea, coffee and chocolate were introduced and sold in coffee houses, providing a new kind of social entertainment. As trade with the East and the Americas increased, the price of sugar fell. The middle classes began to enjoy sugary puddings. However, it was to be many decades before this enjoyable source of energy came within the price range of the poor. Tea and coffee were also beyond their reach. Alcohol, in the form of 'small beer', provided a cheaper source of calories. With 150 to 200 calories a pint, up to three pints of good home-brewed beer provided a significant part of the daily diet of all but the youngest children of poorer families in northern and central Europe.

## Sex: pressure grows for a relaxation of puritanism

The alleged misuse of sex was a major concern of Christian moralists throughout the period. The Reformation and Counter-Reformation brought

The seven **deadly sins** that the church identified were pride, covetousness, lust, envy, gluttony, anger and sloth.

Thomas Muffat, an Englishman writing in 1655, quoted this popular saying of the day: 'The Spaniard eats, the German drinks and the English exceed in both.' How reliable is this comment about national eating habits at this time?

a return to the sexual puritanism of the early church fathers. Pope Paul IV (1555–59), who ordered the naked figures of Michelangelo's Last Judgement in the Sistine Chapel to be modestly covered in loincloths and robes, was extreme, but he was certainly not alone. Although sex was no longer to be seen as altogether sinful a century later, it was still only for married couples. Extra-marital sex was wrong, being regarded as 'against nature'.

In addition to prohibiting sex outside marriage, the church specified acceptable and unacceptable sexual positions and frequency within marriage. Women should adopt a passive and subordinate position because this was their God-given nature. Sex for the pursuit of pleasure was unnecessary and sinful. Sex more than once a week was wasteful. Masturbation, the 'sin of Onan', and coitus interruptus, the crudest form of contraception, were among the most serious of sexual sins, classed alongside homosexuality and bestiality.

Social and economic trends generally worked in the opposite direction from church teachings. During medieval times, only 5 per cent of Europe's population had remained single. In the seventeenth century, the figure was near 15 per cent. Furthermore, in northern, central and north-western Europe the 85 per cent who eventually married often left it until their late 20s, so that they could save enough to set up an independent household. As marriages were rarely contracted out of romantic love, adulterous affairs were quite frequent, particularly amongst people of the upper class. It was not surprising that by the late seventeenth century there was a more relaxed attitude to sex, at least to sex within marriage. The new message in books on sex published in the second half of the century was that it was perfectly acceptable within marriage, even for purposes other than reproduction.

## Occasions for enjoyment: rites of passage and festivals

Births and marriages were above all occasions for enjoying yourself, a brief escape from the trials of daily life. In many communities even death was an opportunity for a wake, for over-eating, drunkenness, music, dancing, practical jokes and fighting.

The high death-rate made the marking of deaths, marriages and births more frequent occasions than they are today. However, they were too irregular to provide much release from the struggle for survival. This was an age without holiday periods. Work, which for most people was linked to the seasons, might have its lighter periods but it was rarely avoidable for more than a day at a time. **Religious festivals**, either in celebration of a local saint or of a major event in the religious calendar, provided other short breaks. The main ones – Ascension, Corpus Christi, St John's Eve and St Bartholomew's Day – were celebrated with plays and floats, fireworks and noisy music, food and drink. Even though the official reason for celebration was religious, some

Major **religious festivals** Ascension was celebrated 40 days after Easter, Corpus Christi in late spring, St John's Eve on 23 June and St Bartholomew's Day on 24 August.

representatives of the church disapproved of it. Here is a Lutheran pastor in Estonia describing the celebration of St John's Eve: 'Around these bonfires people danced, sang and leaped with great pleasure and did not spare the bagpipes . . . Many loads of beer were bought . . . what disorder, whoring, fighting and killing and dreadful idolatry took place!' (quoted in J. Hale, *The civilisation of Europe in the Renaissance*, 1993, p.506). The worries of some churchmen were not completely without foundation; a major revolt in Catalonia in 1643 began at a celebration of Corpus Christi.

Why did both church and civic authorities generally disapprove of popular celebrations?

Some amongst the governing classes took a more relaxed and long-sighted view about such festivals. Writing in 1604, a French lawyer familiar with Lyons – a town often associated with popular revolts – argued that it was 'sometimes expedient to allow the people to play the fool and make merry, lest by holding them in with too great a rigour, we put them in despair' (Hale, 1993, p.506).

Groups of young workers and apprentices organised their own entertainment clubs. Club leaders were given such names as 'Prince of Pleasure', 'Prince of Youth' and 'Abbot of Misrule'. They would get drunk and rush through the streets, sometimes carrying out commissions to cause a disturbance – perhaps at the home of a remarried widower or a notorious adulterer. Outside the victim's house they would shout obscenities, bang on saucepans, ring bells and blow horns. Apart from providing amusement and creating bonds within working groups, such clubs probably provided an outlet for pent-up hostility to the authorities that could not be directly expressed without great risk. The officers of the club of under-officials in the French town of Royan, for example, included 'Bishop Meany', 'Duke Kick-Ass' and the 'Grand Patriarch of Syphilitics'.

## Summary questions

1   Describe any *two* factors that affected the quality of life in this period.

2   For discussion or a full essay:
    To what extent was quality of life linked to social class?

3   For discussion:
    Was the quality of life restricted by the church moralists' preachings on the place of sex?

# 2 Powers and faiths

◆ Which were the most powerful states?

◆ Apart from emerging nation-states, what else commanded loyalty?

◆ When and why did Christianity start to be divided?

## Significant dates

**1530s** The first states defy the authority of the pope (head of Catholic Church) and become Protestant (Lutheran).

**1555** Peace of Augsburg agreed within the Holy Roman Empire, accepting the existence of Lutheran Protestant states but not Calvinist ones.

**1560s** Calvinism – a new form of Protestantism – wins many converts, including large numbers in the Netherlands, the northern part of which starts fighting to win independence from Spain.

**1648** The United Provinces and the Confederation of Switzerland are acknowledged as fully independent. Protestant Bohemia fails to break free from Austria. Portugal continues its war of independence from Spain.

## Overview

With the exceptions of those in the Holy Roman Empire and Italy, the states of Europe were larger and more compact than they had been in medieval times. Almost all were monarchies, with their royal families often inter-related. Some of the states that were to dominate in later centuries – France, Austria and Russia – were becoming prominent. Others, particularly Spain, were over-grown empires and were showing signs of breaking down. However, the nation-state was the great organising force of the future. For the time being, both the smaller loyalties of region and the bigger ones of religious faith continued to be important.

Christian Europe was divided between Catholic and Protestant states by the end of the sixteenth century, with the Protestant ones further split between

Lutheranism and Calvinism (see pages 28 and 29). After losing out in the early stages of the Protestant Reformation, the remodelled Catholic Church, working with ambitious Catholic monarchs, was winning back people to Catholicism as the seventeenth century began.

## Which were the most powerful states?

### The rise of nation-states

A **nation-state** is a block of territory based upon national identity (one dominant language and culture) under the authority of one government.

Popular identification with the nation-state did not take off until the early nineteenth century, but ambitious rulers were increasingly attracted to the idea of forming nations in the sixteenth and seventeenth centuries. Rather than acquiring more outlying, unmanageable pockets of territory, they wanted to round off their dominions. It was better for defence, administration and justice to have a definite frontier. In the seventeenth century the great **nation-states** – France, Austria–Hungary, Britain and Russia – were slowly emerging. There was little that was inevitable about the rise of these particular states to greatness. At the start of the fifteenth century Europe comprised some 40 identifiable states, all of them small and many broken into pockets of territory separated by land belonging to other states. By the early sixteenth century the number had almost halved. They then included two new imperial great powers, Spain and the Ottoman Empire, and two extensive but relatively weak powers, Denmark and Poland. What is remarkable is that none of these four was to dominate Europe after the early seventeenth century. The first half of the seventeenth century was a turning point in their fortunes.

The European map of the eighteenth century shows about 20 states of note. This simple fact disguises some important changes. Four of the great powers that were to dominate in the nineteenth century were now sizeable and consolidated: France, Russia, Austria–Hungary and Great Britain. Only Germany's later great-power status was still hard to predict. The second half of the seventeenth and early decades of the eighteenth century was a major period of growth for all of them.

**Why did rulers want to create nation-states?**

### A survey of the major states

**Which factors contributed to European disunity in this period?**

Connections were developing between the western and southern regions of Europe (ruled by the French Bourbon and Spanish Habsburg royal dynasties) and the eastern and northern ones (Swedish and Polish Vasa dynasties). The mountains of the Vosges, Alps and Balkans formed a physical barrier between these two, while the splintered nature of the Holy Roman Empire and Italy created a political division. The difficulty of overland travel also emphasised the divide between eastern and western Europe.

No state was a parliamentary democracy in the modern sense, with free elections in which the entire adult population participated. In most there were regional and national parliaments, which were usually monopolised by the privileged classes: the nobility and clergy.

The major states in the early seventeenth century.

## Western and southern Europe

*Spain, Spanish Italy and the Spanish Netherlands*

In 1598 Spain was the leading power in Europe. Through its vast overseas empire it was also supreme in the world. By marriage alliances, conquests and a good measure of chance the Spanish Habsburg monarchy had, some forty years earlier, inherited a European empire that stretched from Amsterdam in the north to Naples in the south-east and Lisbon in the west. In addition, they had a world empire that ranged across four continents. In our period parts of this empire were breaking away, including the northern Netherlands (United Provinces). Still mighty, but wracked with internal problems and external threats, the Spanish Empire was declining in strength. Spain is discussed in more detail in Chapter 5.

*France*

At the end of the sixteenth century France was the largest state in western Europe, with a population of about 17 million. At times in the Middle Ages it had been one of Europe's greatest powers; it was less important at this point. With fertile land and a temperate maritime climate in many areas, good ports and easy access to the mineral wealth of the interior of the continent, its potential was tremendous but largely untapped. It was still troubled by the noble, peasant and religious revolts that had crippled it in the late sixteenth century. However, through strong and sometimes ruthless royal government (Louis XIII and Richelieu, Mazarin and the young Louis XIV) it was re-emerging as one of Europe's leading powers. France is discussed in more detail at the start of Chapter 3.

*The United Provinces or Dutch Republic*

Sometimes referred to as the Dutch Republic, the seven breakaway United Provinces formed Europe's newest state at this time and one of its smallest. In practice it was already independent from Spain, but this was not made official until 1648. The northern provinces had had to fight desperately hard to achieve independence and the southern ones had failed in the attempt. The province of Holland was the mainspring of the success of the rebellion against

Spain. It dominated the new union, providing more revenue than the rest of the provinces put together. With the most dynamic economy in Europe, in economic terms the United Provinces was powerful in spite of its small area. The United Provinces is discussed in more detail at the start of Chapter 7.

### 'Germany' excluding Habsburg Austria

The German principalities were small, religiously divided and nearly all land-locked and vulnerable to invasion by virtue of their location on a great plain. Only language and a fine-sounding title – The Holy Roman Empire of the German Nation – gave any meaning to 'Germany' in this period. The empire was rather like Europe on a small scale, divided by religion and containing a number of strong, aggressive states alongside smaller, more vulnerable ones. There was potential for one or two of the more dynamic states to play on the weakness of neighbours to increase their own size and power. Some states had a head start as they had the status of electorates. This meant that their sovereigns, or electors, were allowed to vote in the choice of the Holy Roman emperor and had some rights of participation in imperial decision-making. The electors of Brandenburg, one of these states, were to play for dominance of the chessboard that was northern Germany, making small but strategically vital advances in the seventeenth century.

What made some German states more powerful than others?

### 'Italy' excluding Habsburg Spain

Long settled, densely populated and by the standards of the time exceptionally urbanised, Italy was still far from unity. This was in spite of its being, like the Holy Roman Empire, a single, large linguistic area. The situation was complicated by the existence of the papacy. The pope possessed territory, the Papal States, that was practically invulnerable to absorption by neighbouring states by virtue of his special status as a world religious leader. Venice, with ancient commercial colonies in the eastern Mediterranean, was the most successful of the other non-Habsburg powers in Italy. However, its position was increasingly challenged by the Ottoman Empire.

Which were the rising powers in western and southern Europe in c.1600? Which states were experiencing problems and why?

## Eastern and northern Europe

### The Ottoman Empire

With a population of between 25 and 30 million in 1600 and territory spanning eastern central Europe, the Balkans, Asia Minor and Africa, the Ottoman Empire was a considerable European power as well as a Middle Eastern one. The Ottomans were widely feared in Christian Europe but treated as any other European power when it came to diplomacy. France, in particular, was willing to use alliance with the Ottomans as a southern counterweight to the Austrian Habsburgs, who were a greater power.

The empire was ruled by a royal family or sultanate and a first minister, the grand vizier. The capital was Constantinople, the former Christian capital of ancient times and the Ottomans' most famous conquest. Cultural differences from the rest of Europe not only included religion – the Ottomans were Muslims – but a social and economic system that was partly based on plunder and slavery.

Under Suleiman the Magnificent (reigned 1520–66) the Ottoman Empire had made spectacular advances into Christian Europe. In 1600 they were poised to make further inroads.

## Poland–Lithuania

To the north of the Ottoman Empire were the extensive territories of Poland–Lithuania, a product of empire-building through dynastic marriage alliances. Nicknamed the 'royal republic', Poland had a reputation as a haven for landowning nobles. Traditionally it was a state where monarchs did not impose too much authority or demand too much taxation from their nobility. This did not mean that the peasants also enjoyed a good life. The situation was quite the reverse, for they were subjects of a particularly privileged and demanding nobility.

Another unusual feature of this state was that its kings were elected. In 1572 a successful Polish dynasty had come to an end and the practice of electing non-Polish outsiders as kings began. This could have the advantage of adding new territories to Poland, but it also had its dangers. The dangers were illustrated when in 1587 the throne passed to Sigismund III of the Swedish royal family, who subsequently became king of Sweden but was deposed and had no option but to stay on as king of Poland. Under Sigismund, Poland became a strictly Catholic state. **Jesuits** were given full support in their work of ridding the state of Protestants.

Poland's vast territories were vulnerable to invasion, raids and mass migrations since there were no natural frontiers along most borders. In 1657 Poland lost East Prussia and soon after that a large part of the Ukraine – both valuable territories.

The **Jesuits** are members of the Society of Jesus, a Roman Catholic order set up to work as missionaries and to defend their church against the Protestant Reformation.

In what ways was the Polish state built upon weak foundations?

## The Austrian Habsburg Empire

To the north-west of the Ottomans, Habsburg Austria was the dominant power in central Europe. By the end of the sixteenth century the Austrian Habsburgs were the leading German dynasty and were invariably elected to hold the position of emperor. Through inheritance they had acquired a patchwork of territories. Austria itself, with its capital Vienna, was sandwiched between Bohemia to the north and Styria to its south. There was little sense of unity in these lands, which had a great variety of languages and cultures and high levels of local control. The territory consisted of mountains and rivers whose upper reaches were not navigable. However, there was a lot of mineral wealth and industry in Silesia and Bohemia. Prague prospered as the capital of Bohemia, a relatively densely populated region with 4 million people.

As well as physical and linguistic disunity, the Habsburgs faced two more great problems, one internal and the other external. The internal problem was that of religious disunity. Bohemia included many Protestants but most of the territories making up the empire were fervently Catholic, as were the Habsburgs themselves. Inspired by their Spanish cousins, they began to enforce the Counter-Reformation with increasing firmness. The external threat came from the Ottomans, who had pushed their frontiers to within 70 miles of Vienna. As the seventeenth century began the Austrians were in the middle of a 15-year war against the Ottomans in Upper Hungary (modern Slovakia).

What were the main strengths and weaknesses of Austria at the start of the seventeenth century?

### Russia

Russia, or **Muscovy** as it was often referred to by contemporaries long after it had grown well beyond the status of a city-state, was the most rapidly expanding state in Europe and the Near East. In spite of rapid expansion, it was in several respects a weak state at the start of the seventeenth century. In some ways it was similar to Poland, with powerful nobles electing their king – the tsar – and therefore dominating decision-making. The powerful nobles, known as boyars, were given a free hand to do as they wished with their peasants, nearly all of whom were **serfs**. In the early part of the century it looked for a time as if Russia might be absorbed into the gannet-like Polish state. However, religion was a powerful force, forging national identity in Russia. Most Russians proudly followed the Eastern Orthodox Church, which they believed to be the truest form of Christianity. Poles who were Eastern Orthodox had fled to Russia, consolidating the cultural divide between the two states.

**Muscovy** was a Russian principality from the thirteenth to the sixteenth century. Moscow was its capital.

The **serfs** were people who were tied to the land – if an estate was sold, the serfs would be passed on with the property.

### Sweden

Although it covered all of eastern Scandinavia, including Finland, Sweden had a total population of only 2 million in 1600. Settlements were widely scattered and there were few towns. Nevertheless the Swedish state was a significant military power, often led by ambitious, capable and war-loving monarchs. The most famous of these in this period was Gustavus Adolphus (reigned 1611–32), the Protestant hero of the Thirty Years' War. Swedes were proud defenders of the Lutheran Protestant faith, which most had embraced in the sixteenth century. In spite of under-population Sweden was to emerge as the leading power in Scandinavia by 1600, with colonies on the southern shores of the Baltic Sea that alarmed the other powers.

The Swedish nobility was comparatively small and poor by European standards. Although Swedish peasants were no better off than those elsewhere in economic terms, they were freer than peasants in most of Europe outside England and had political representation in the national parliament, the Riksdag. In this respect at least, they were uniquely privileged in Europe.

### Denmark

Sweden's great rival in the Baltic was Denmark, which possessed Norway at this time and had once dominated the whole region. Until a series of crushing defeats in the 1620s, both the Danes themselves and most of the outside world considered Denmark to be the leading Baltic power. Socially the state had more in common with Eastern Europe than Sweden. In the countryside the nobles were powerful, holding a high proportion of their peasants as serfs.

Which were the rising powers in eastern and northern Europe in c.1600? Which states were experiencing problems? Why?

## Apart from emerging nation-states, what else commanded loyalty?

National identity and national loyalties meant far less to seventeenth-century Europeans than they do today. The nation-state emerged gradually. Many borders were fluid, with the people living in those areas changing from one state to another almost every generation. National flags and national teams were unheard of. Except in times of national emergency, most people identified with their region, town or lordship rather than with the nation-state. The educated and the upper classes – which were overlapping groups – were increasingly more widely travelled and more cosmopolitan in their attitudes. Some of them identified with social, religious, intellectual or dynastic communities that were wider than the nation-state. The escaping Charles Stuart of England fled to exile with the French royal family. Ferdinand II of Austria recruited Catholics from as far afield as Ireland and Scotland to replace his displaced Protestant Czech nobility. Scientists and philosophers from all over Europe wrote to each other in Latin.

### Bigger than the nation-state

### Religious allegiances

An appeal to defend Christendom was the rallying cry of those latter-day crusaders who called for international action against the infidel Muslim Turks. More often than not in our period, this call fell upon deaf ears. This was partly because of the growing importance attached to the pursuit of national and dynastic interests, and partly because Christendom was itself divided between Catholic and Protestant. In the late sixteenth and early seventeenth centuries commitment to the rival Christian faiths (or denominations, as they came to be known) had more meaning than allegiance to Christendom. In the civil wars in France and the Netherlands dedicated Calvinists from all corners of Europe fought against Catholics from several states in a war of ideas – an ideological war.

Apart from the Papal States, the embodiment of the idea of an international community of faith was the Holy Roman Empire of the German Nation. It had been created under **Charlemagne** in 800 to sustain Christian influence and authority north of the Mediterranean when the Roman Empire broke down – a new Christian 'Roman Empire' for central Europe. Even though it was a relic from a much-earlier period, the Holy Roman Empire still had some importance in European affairs. Officially it continued to represent the common interests of hundreds of states, with a population in 1600 of about 20 million. It still had some of the trappings of a state, with an imperial Diet (parliament) and an elected emperor retaining feudal rights to oversee territory within the Empire. However, it was increasingly fragmented because the many principalities within it adopted different Christian faiths and their leaders pursued their own ambitions. Weakened in this way, it was vulnerable to dismemberment by its most powerful neighbours: Sweden, France and Austria. The Holy Roman Empire and the important question of its relationship to Austria is given further attention at the start of Chapter 7.

### Royal dynastic states

Most of the larger states of Europe in this period are sometimes described as 'dynastic' states, territories amassed by one royal dynasty over several generations. The Spanish, Austrian and Polish Empires are those most commonly referred to in this way. As Table 3 on page 27 shows, the royal families were inter-related through marriage alliances. These allowed ambitious monarchs to lay claim to parts of other states or even to whole states. A lot of time and energy went into seeking out the best marriage connections. There is little evidence that many people other than the royal families, their agents and servants felt much loyalty to dynastic states such as those possessed by the Habsburgs. However, for the royal families themselves these conglomerations of territories, usually acquired through marriage and inheritance, were as familiar as the grounds belonging to a favourite palace. As a child, Louis XIV was educated in a study in which all the antique family claims of the Bourbons were marked on a map showing France and surrounding states. Though dynastic concerns continued to be of great importance, the disentanglement of the Spanish from the Austrian Habsburg lands in the sixteenth century was a major step towards the displacement of the dynastic state by the

**Charlemagne** (?742–814) was king of the Franks from 768 and Holy Roman emperor from 800.

In this period tombstones often recorded ancestry and heraldic books featured genealogical tables of the kind shown. Why were monarchs and nobles obsessed with genealogy?

nation-state. The independence struggles of the Dutch Republic and Portugal took that process a step further.

## Table 3: The royal families of the major states

Dates in brackets are those of the reign unless otherwise stated.

A. The Habsburg–Bourbon–Stuart link

B. The Vasa–Brandenburg link

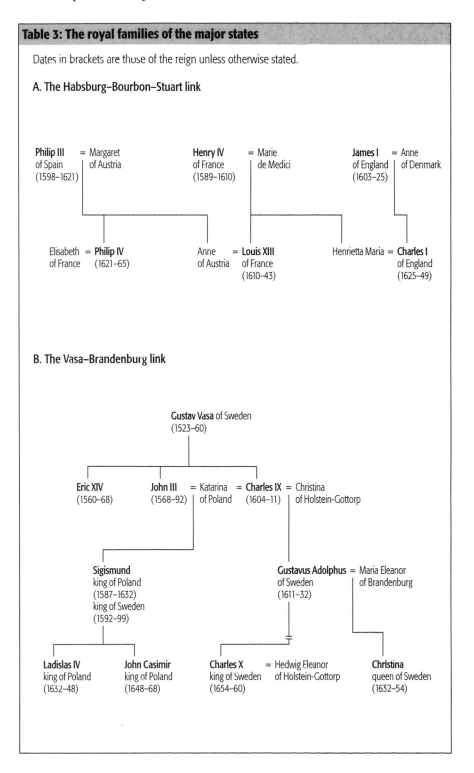

## Smaller communities

Probably more important for most people than the nation-state, the dynastic state or the community of faith was their identification with the town or province in which they lived. Since it took as long to travel around the little duchy of Luxemburg as it does to cross the length and breadth of England today, it was not surprising that many people referred to their county as their 'patria', their country. Provinces and major towns possessed far more independent powers than they do today. Though the great age of the city-state was passing, each town controlled its own **tolls** and regulations. Seville and Antwerp largely ran their own affairs within the Spanish Empire. There were still 50 imperial free cities in the Holy Roman Empire. Genoa and Venice, though reduced in size and influence, were still independent states. Towns and provinces were more frequently the subject for historical and geographical writers in this period than nation-states. Most of the many revolts were confined to provinces or cities – only rarely were they national affairs.

**Tolls** were payments levied by local authorities, for example for using a bridge or operating a market stall.

# When and why did Christianity start to be divided?

It is essential to go further back than 1598 to appreciate the religious situation between 1598 and 1661. This was a time of turmoil in the Christian world.

## The Protestant Reformation

Protestantism was the greatest of many break-away movements in Christianity. At the start of the sixteenth century the translation of the Bible from Greek, Latin or Hebrew into the living or vernacular languages of Europe had opened up debate about the meaning of the Gospels. All Protestants agreed that to hold such a debate was a basic right. They also held the view that no pope or priest had the right to preach anything that could not be supported by the Bible. To different degrees all Protestants felt that priests were not required for direct contact with God; many of the new Protestant faiths involved men (but not women) who were not ordained as priests in their internal government. Protestants objected to the continued corruption and wealth of the Catholic Church. Protestantism took hold in communities across the length and breadth of Europe in the period from the 1530s to the 1560s.

Protestants soon came to be divided amongst themselves. They looked at things in the Bible differently and started to make arrangements for worship in different ways. **Anabaptists**, the most radical and most persecuted, insisted that adults be baptised and aimed to introduce Christian social values and a belief in peace. **Zwinglians** held services in bare whitewashed rooms without music. **Lutherans** had an almost Catholic style of church organisation, with a hierarchy of bishops and priests. They also sought the full backing of heads of

**Anabaptists** rejected infant baptism. The **Zwinglians** were founded by the Swiss Ulrich Zwingli (1484–1531). The **Lutherans** were founded by the German Martin Luther (1483–1546). The **Calvinists** were followers of John Calvin (1509–64), a Swiss preacher.

state. **Calvinists** despised Lutherans and annoyed many other Protestants with their belief in predestination: that God had already chosen to save some people and to damn others eternally even before they were born. As early as the 1520s the German Luther and the Swiss Zwingli led different groups. In the course of the next thirty years two further splits had created Anabaptism and Calvinism. By the beginning of the seventeenth century the Calvinists were themselves divided between Original Calvinists and Arminian Calvinists.

The last decades of the sixteenth century were difficult ones for Protestants. This was mainly because from the mid-1580s the self-styled 'Catholic Emperor' **Philip II** of Spain chose to increase pressure on the Protestant rebels in the Netherlands and France.

However, by this stage at least as serious a problem for the Protestants was their increasing division. In the German lands Lutheran rulers felt as threatened by the continued growth of Calvinism as they did by the continuing presence of neighbouring Catholic states. They thought they had achieved security by the Peace of Augsburg in 1555, which permitted Protestant rulers to choose only Lutheran Protestantism for their state. Religion was fast becoming an excuse for rivalry between ambitious young neighbouring rulers.

However, there was much more to conflict between Protestants than the rivalries of monarchs. Though propaganda exaggerated the differences, there were real distinctions between different varieties of Protestant theology. When a Lutheran writer in the German lands declared that 'the Calvinist dragon is pregnant with the horrors of Mohammedanism [Islam]' (in C. V. Wedgwood, *The Thirty Years' War*, 1938; this edn 1962, p. 42) there was some factual basis to his propaganda; both Calvinists and Muslims emphasised the idea of an all-powerful god determining the future.

It is worth exploring how the key Protestant belief that the Gospels could and should be interpreted afresh led to more and more radical views. Some free-thinking individuals went much further than any of the faiths to which they nominally belonged. The playwright Christopher Marlowe (1564–93) was a shadowy figure who may have fought with the Dutch rebels against the Spanish and worked as an English spy in a Catholic Jesuit college in France. The day before his death, allegedly in a pub brawl, Marlowe was faced with accusations of atheism and blasphemy. According to Richard Barnes, an obscure character who was later hanged, Marlowe believed that Christ was a bastard and his mother dishonest, and, in similar vein to Karl Marx three centuries later, Marlowe argued that the first beginning of religion was to keep men in awe.

Such radical challenges were not confined to free-thinking writers like Marlowe. Young artisans, concerned to rid the church of idolatory, engaged in

When and why did Christianity start to be divided into two great opposing groups? What was the appeal of the Protestant faith?

**Philip II** said: 'Before suffering the slightest damage to religion I would lose all my estates . . . because I do not wish to be the ruler of heretics' (in J. Kilsby, *Spain: rise and decline*, 1986, p.61).

Why were Protestants internally divided?

assaults on church property in the Netherlands. Some of the princes who took up Calvinism could be equally hot headed, though usually making use of the brute force of the armies at their command rather than their own hands. Frederick IV, the Elector Palatine, demonstrated his disbelief in 'transubstantiation' – the Catholic belief that in mass or communion the bread and wine become Christ's body and blood – by jeering and tearing the bread into pieces. The ruler of Hesse–Cassel, another German principality, had the toughest bread provided for the communion so that his people should be quite aware of the material nature of what they were eating.

Why did the Protestant approach to religion lead to different views about the true message of the Bible?

## The Catholic revival

By the end of the sixteenth century the Catholic Church had regained some of its former dynamism and strength. It helped that it seemed to have become less hypocritical. When Luther had denounced it in the early sixteenth century the moral standards of some of the Catholic clergy at all levels were bad. Too many popes, cardinals, bishops, monks and parish priests were thoroughly worldly; the priests were frequently drunk, ignorant and far removed from celibacy (living without sexual relationships); the top leaders were more interested in power and wealth than Christian conduct. A number of new spiritual movements which were critical of the low moral standards of the papacy and the cardinals were started at this time. There were echoes in this of Protestant dissent and it seemed for a time that the Catholic Church might disintegrate.

A century later, thanks to a programme of internal reform, standards were higher. A succession of popes between 1534 and 1590 improved the governing body or 'curia' of the church. They also gave their support, albeit grudging, to the Tridentine reforms, reforms recommended by the **Council of Trent** between 1545 and 1563. Many of these reforms were answers to the revolutionary doctrines of Protestantism rather than arising from a genuine desire for change. Nevertheless, they helped to reform the church by reaffirming a set of clear beliefs and practices for Catholics. God's message, they insisted, was communicated in many ways, not just through the Bible. All seven sacraments were confirmed, including the 'miracle of transubstantiation'. Outward signs of the worship of Christ and the Virgin Mary, such as holding idols aloft in processions, were deemed acceptable. Some reforms were directed at moral improvement; there was a new stress on the celibacy of the priesthood and the need to build up merit by living a good life. These helped the church authorities to insist on higher standards amongst those in holy orders. The Jesuits were increasingly active in the late sixteenth century, bringing a new vitality to the church through their stress on the life of Christ as a model for all Christians. Catholic mystics like **Filippo Neri** and new religious orders such as the Capuchins, Ursulines and Theatines were also inspirational but, with the

The **Council of Trent** was a council of the Roman Catholic Church that reaffirmed traditional Catholic beliefs and drew up the principles of the Counter-Reformation.

**Filippo Neri** (1515–95) was an Italian priest who founded the Congregation of the Oratory in 1564.

exception of the Ursulines in France after 1604, they exerted an influence only within certain regions.

The reformed Catholic doctrine had considerable appeal, combining charity, emotional security and morality with colourful pageantry. Catholics in religious orders – especially friars, monks and nuns – became more and more involved in the wider community as charitable workers. Catholics were able to get on with their everyday lives, leaving the priest, the monk or the nun to mediate with God and to interpret his holy word. Catholics could enjoy colourful religious art and exuberant Baroque architecture, music and processions. They could worship figurines of Mary and the saints, outward tokens of faith and shared belief. They might find evidence of salvation and the promised life after death though the occurrence of fresh 'miracles'. With so much on offer, unquestioning acceptance of the church's theology was a price worth paying in a world where dissent or heresy seemed to bring war and ruination.

What was the appeal of the revived and reformed Catholic faith?

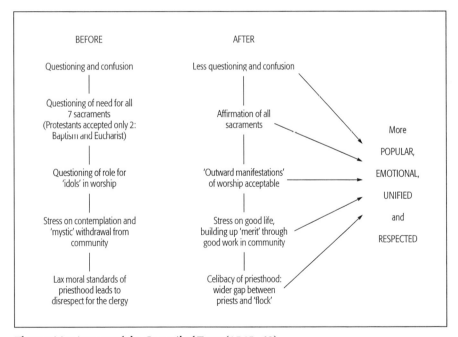

The positive impact of the Council of Trent (1545–63).

By the end of the sixteenth century Catholic reform had reached its limits. By then the trend was clearly away from the new liberal spiritual movements and mystics and towards the uncompromising Jesuits. Typical of the stricter atmosphere was the insistence that the nuns in the Ursuline order take vows, wear uniform and abandon life outside the religious community. The Jesuits, once regarded by Pope Paul IV as an international organisation too independent and too closely linked with Spain and France, became loyal and admired disciples of the papacy. By the middle of the seventeenth century the Austrian Empire, the region of the Jesuits' greatest triumphs, had moved to a strict and intolerant version of Catholicism (see p. 114).

## Summary questions

1  (a)  Christian Europe was religiously divided by the start of the seventeenth century.
        How did any *two* factors contribute to the growth of divisions?

   (b)  Explain which one problem was the most important cause of discord.

2  For discussion or full essay:
   What united and what divided Europeans c. 1600?

3  (a)  To what extent was the nation-state the basis of the European state system by the start of the seventeenth century?

   (b)  Why did the idea of a nation-state appeal to rulers?

# 3 France: Richelieu

## Focus questions

◆ Why did monarchs often rule through powerful favourites in this period?

◆ What were Richelieu's aims?

◆ How far did Richelieu achieve his aims?

## Significant dates

| | |
|---|---|
| 1617 | Louis XIII assumes full powers as king, ending the minority. |
| 1622 | Louis XIII directs campaign against Huguenot revolt. The government side is successful, but La Rochelle holds out.<br>Richelieu is made a cardinal, with support of the queen mother. |
| 1624 | Richelieu is appointed leader of the Royal Council, the first minister. |
| 1625 | France attacks Genoa, an ally of Spain, to stop Spanish troop movements through the Valtelline Pass in northern Italy. |
| 1626 | Treaty of Monzón produces compromise over Valtelline.<br>'New France' founded by French trading company in north-east America.<br>Start made by Richelieu on creation of a navy. |
| 1627 | Huguenot risings in south of France and La Rochelle combine with English expedition to support them. Louis and Richelieu eventually prevail. |
| 1629 | The Edict of Alais is imposed on the Huguenots. Their armies are to be disbanded and fortresses destroyed.<br>French troops led by Louis and Richelieu attack Savoy. |
| 1631 | Franco-Swedish and Franco-Bavarian alliance. France agrees to subsidise Sweden's army in their campaigns against Austria. |
| 1632 | Army of rebellious duke of Montmorency defeated. |
| 1634 | Post of intendant created. Intendants begin job of overseeing extra tax collection for the wars. |
| 1635 | Direct French military intervention in Thirty Years' War begins. |
| 1636 | Austrian and Spanish forces invade France. French army under Louis only just holds them back by recapturing Corbie. |
| 1642 | Cinq-Mars plot to assassinate Richelieu and end the war uncovered; Cinq-Mars executed. Richelieu dies. |

# Overview

France had the potential, in terms of human and natural resources, to be a great power. However, its greatness was to lie in the future. In the early seventeenth century, France was beset with problems. Though far from unique, these were formidable.

- Economically, its great resources were largely untapped and most of its people desperately poor.
- Socially, its nobility were self-absorbed and lacking in loyalty to the state.
- Religiously, it was divided between the Catholic majority and Protestant (Huguenot) minority. An uneasy peace prevailed.
- Politically, monarchs and noble-dominated parliaments disputed power while France remained vulnerable to a Spanish Habsburg takeover.

If France's rulers could solve these problems, their state might become one of the leading powers of Europe. It is worth looking at each aspect in a little more depth before seeing later in this chapter how Richelieu attempted to overcome some of the difficulties.

## Problems that beset France

### The economy

Economic success was the foundation of Dutch achievement in this period. Economic failure was the underlying cause of French stagnation.

France tended to look within itself and towards its landward neighbours rather than towards the sea. It was large enough and sufficiently fertile to provide for most of its own needs. This bred a complacency not found in smaller, less well-resourced states like the United Provinces, Genoa and Venice. **Sully**, Henry IV's chief minister, had observed that animal husbandry and pasturage were the twin pillars of the French economy. France was well provided with food and textiles, the basics required for self-sufficiency. Every province had its own regional centre of trade. Paris, the only large city, was supplied with all its wheat by Brittany. Exports were chiefly in fabrics and wheat and were small compared to the more lucrative manufactured hardware that Holland and England were producing at this time. Roads were in a bad condition and there were too many customs dues and tolls on roads and rivers. There was expansion in industrial enterprise between 1595 and 1620, but it was mostly in luxury and artistic products. The potential for economic success was there; France had excellent iron and coal resources and the advantage of coastlines not only on the Mediterranean but also on the English Channel and the increasingly profitable Atlantic. Richelieu was keen to imitate the Dutch economic success, but his expensive foreign policy inhibited any significant development (see pp. 46–47).

**Sully** (1560–1641) was a French statesman who helped to restore the finances of France.

## Society

French society reflected its economy, with some additional negative features. This was an overwhelmingly rural society, with poor peasant farmers comprising the bulk of the population. The peasants in the countryside were ruled by a landowning nobility happy to depend on peasant rents for their income. Commercial activity was thought to detract from noble status. Lawyers and merchants aspired to become land-owning nobles. These attitudes, which contrasted strongly with the approach of the Dutch, discouraged innovation. The nobility invested very little in new enterprises on their lands, such as mines and canals. The number of people in the merchant class was small. The striking contrast of society in France and Holland is discussed in more detail in Chapter 7 (pp. 104–105).

## The religious divide

The sixteenth-century Protestant Reformation and Catholic Counter-Reformation brought prolonged and bitter civil wars – nine so-called 'wars of religion' over the last 40 years of the century. The economy, and therefore the people, suffered. Henry IV's succession to the throne in 1589 helped pacify much of the country. His conversion from Protestantism to Catholicism helped unite France. His settlement of 1598, the **Edict of Nantes**, allowed Protestants and Catholics to co-exist. However, this infuriated many Catholics; the king was assassinated by a Catholic fanatic in 1610. Over the next century religious civil war came to be restricted to the south and west (where most of the Huguenot strongholds were located – see Map 2 on page 36). Broadly successful 'carrot and stick' policies for dealing with the Huguenots were pioneered by Richelieu.

The **Edict of Nantes** granted religious and civil liberties to the French Protestants.

## Political strengths and weaknesses

Powerful noble rivals to the French monarchs had used the opportunities offered by religious civil wars to seek possession of the crown. During the reign of Henry III in the 1570s and 1580s, internal strife had come close to unravelling France and allowing the Spanish Habsburgs to take over in the guise of defenders of the Catholic cause. However, earlier stronger kings like Louis IX (1226–70) and Francis I (1515–47) had built up royal power and Henry IV was able to reinstate most of the crown's lost authority. The French recovery was so successful that just before his assassination Henry was preparing to challenge Spain in the Rhineland and Italy.

Study Maps 2 and 3 on pages 36 and 70. What political strengths did France possess compared with Spain?

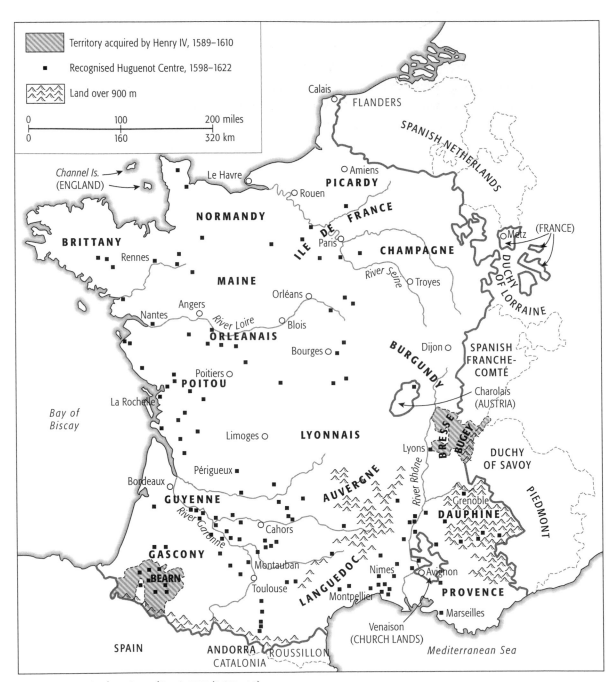

**Legend:**
- ▨ Territory acquired by Henry IV, 1589–1610
- ■ Recognised Huguenot Centre, 1598–1622
- ⌇ Land over 900 m

0 ——— 100 ——— 200 miles
0 ——— 160 ——— 320 km

Channel Is. (ENGLAND)

Calais
FLANDERS
SPANISH NETHERLANDS
Amiens
PICARDY
Le Havre
Rouen
NORMANDY
ILE DE FRANCE
Paris
CHAMPAGNE
Metz (FRANCE)
DUCHY OF LORRAINE
BRITTANY
Rennes
MAINE
River Seine
Troyes
Orléans
Angers
Nantes
River Loire
Blois
ORLEANAIS
Dijon
SPANISH FRANCHE-COMTÉ
BURGUNDY
Bourges
Charolais (AUSTRIA)
Poitiers
POITOU
La Rochelle
BRESSE
BUGEY
Bay of Biscay
Limoges
LYONNAIS
Lyons
DUCHY OF SAVOY
Périgueux
AUVERGNE
River Rhône
Grenoble
DAUPHINE
PIEDMONT
Bordeaux
GUYENNE
River Garonne
Cahors
GASCONY
Montauban
BEARN
Toulouse
LANGUEDOC
Nimes
Avignon
Montpellier
PROVENCE
Venaison (CHURCH LANDS)
Marseilles
SPAIN
ANDORRA
CATALONIA
ROUSSILLON
Mediterranean Sea

**Map 2: France in the reign of Louis XIII (1610–43).**

## The early 1620s: France on the eve of Richelieu's coming to power

Henry IV's assassination brought a return of many of the political problems of the late sixteenth century. Since Henry's son, Louis, was still too young to rule (a minor), he was succeeded by Henry's wife, **Marie de Medici**, who ruled as regent on behalf of her son from 1610 to 1617 (a period known as the minority). Regencies during minorities were never welcomed in this period. Though this particular one was far from disastrous, it brought with it renewed worries about a Catholic/Spanish takeover. Marie abandoned the anti-Habsburg foreign policy. Spain's profile in the French court once again increased. The Spanish first minister Lerma proposed a dynastic alliance with France, which was agreed in 1612. In 1615 Louis married Anne of Austria, Philip III of Spain's daughter. However, this was as far as the drift towards Spain went. Leading nobles began to rebel when effective power started to pass to a court clique led by Marie's childhood friend Leonora Galigari and her husband Concino Concini, a Florentine adventurer. Nobles started to make common cause with Huguenot rebels and only outbreaks of plague and a hard winter persuaded them to compromise.

The young Louis was a strong figure. In April 1617 he had Concini assassinated. In October 1617 he declared himself of age. Subsequently, he put Leonora on trial and placed his mother under house arrest. It is said that on hearing of Concini's death he leapt onto a billiard table shouting 'Now I am king! Now I am your king!' Some of his Parisian subjects, moved by a hatred for foreign favourites, dug up Concini's corpse and mutilated it. Concini's ghost would later haunt the French royal family; Mazarin, the young Louis XIV's first adviser, was Italian and owed much of his unpopularity to comparisons with Concini.

The French Counter-Reformation, which had been proceeding steadily and peacefully since the Edict of Nantes, was given a new combativeness by Louis XIII's determination to regain properties acquired by the Huguenots. In 1617 he started a campaign for their restoration. This provoked a new religious war. Though the crown had a good war, after three years of fighting the Huguenot fortress of La Rochelle could not be taken. In Languedoc, in the deep south, Huguenot forces still held control in 1622 and were preparing to hold the mountainous Cévennes and the towns along the coast from the Rhône valley to Toulouse. At this point the king called upon a young but tough and capable nobleman called Richelieu to lead a new assault on La Rochelle.

In this period, monarchs and their first ministers worked in close cooperation. Richelieu's aims were to increase royal power, keep disloyal nobles in check, impose one religious faith and, above all, finance almost constant war. Wars were fought on the basis of attack being the best form of defence, each side claiming – with some justification – that they needed to strengthen

**Marie de Medici**
(1573–1642), a princess from the ruling family of Florence. She angered Louis XIII and Richelieu, whose potential she had first spotted, by her later plotting against them. She was exiled by Richelieu in 1630.

A painting of Cardinal Richelieu by Philippe de Champaigne (seventeenth century). Full-length portraits of kings, queens and major political figures were designed to put across clear messages.
What impression of Richelieu was the picture intended to give?

themselves against predatory neighbours. In France's case this was against Habsburg Spain and Austria. In exchange for his diligence in pursuing these aims Richelieu was amply rewarded, becoming one of the richest and most powerful men in France. Other aristocrats and lesser nobles were not so lucky, while the peasantry shouldered almost all the tax burden. Resentment grew.

Royal powers were increased and opponents, noble and religious, were subdued. There were some military successes but there were failures as well, including an invasion in 1636 that brought the armies of Austria and Spain to within 80 miles of Paris. These policies were both costly and unpopular and Richelieu had no effective ideas for promoting sustained economic growth. Although he did not live to see it, his policies contributed to the deep mid-century crisis known as the **Fronde**.

The two '**Frondes**' were rebellious movements in the early years of the reign of Louis XIV, the first a true revolution and the second a civil war inspired by ambitious nobles.

## Why did monarchs often rule through powerful favourites in this period?

Government by royal favourites was nothing new in the early seventeenth century, nor was the practice unique to France. What was new was the extent of the powers granted in this period: to Richelieu in France, Olivares in Spain (see Chapter 5), Buckingham in England and Oxenstierna in Sweden.

Richelieu acquired new titles, several of his own creation, including 'principal minister of state'. Olivares, already a count, was also made a duke. Buckingham became the first non-royal English duke for 50 years. Oxenstierna was given almost unlimited powers. Ruling through favourites was a risky strategy for monarchs. The favourites amassed personal fortunes and promoted their relations and clients, causing resentment not only amongst other high aristocrats but also within royal families. Jealous factions plotted the favourite's downfall.

Why were monarchs, generally kings of sound mind, prepared to run such risks? Part of the answer is that Spain and France were becoming too large and complex to be ruled single-handedly by a monarch. **Philip II of Spain** had attempted to do this but the tremendous burden had almost defeated him. Besides, the rulers need not be slaves to their positions; they had the power to enjoy their privilege. Louis XIII of France enjoyed his hunting and falconry, Philip IV of Spain pursued all kinds of hobbies – anything to avoid confronting the thorny problems of public policy. If things went wrong the favourite would deflect the unpopularity of unpalatable decisions. Real executive power to have the final say still rested with the monarch. It is important to remember that in spite of the enormous power given to the favourite, in all vital matters of state final decisions were almost always taken by the monarchs.

Throughout Europe the first half of the seventeenth century was a difficult period as far as the relationship between monarchs and their subjects was concerned. Serious political and economic problems – major wars, revolts, clashes over taxation and economic depression – came together in the 1640s. What was happening in France under Richelieu was far from unique. The unrestrained pursuit of war was leading to similar problems in Spain, Sweden, Russia, England, Denmark and Brandenburg. Monarchs put their faith in favourites, increasing their powers to the maximum so that they could do everything possible to obtain the increased funding the rulers required. This generally involved pushing firmly against noble-dominated parliaments and resulted in considerable unpopularity.

## What were Richelieu's aims?

Richelieu had his own objectives, ambitions and distinctive ways of working. However, to a great extent his aims were set by King Louis XIII – his employer or patron. Above all, the aim of both men was to increase royal power.

### King Louis XIII and Richelieu

**Louis XIII** was a hard-headed king and Richelieu an ambitious aristocrat. This was to prove the basis for an effective partnership. Louis retained

**Philip II of Spain** (1556–98) handled all government papers himself. Dealing with up to four hundred documents a day, be became depressed by the burden of work. Delays and ill-advised decisions were often the result.

Why did monarchs often rule through powerful favourites in this period?

**Louis XIII** as high and mighty monarch: 'To your knees, little man, before your master' (to the president of the Bordeaux parliament). 'You are here only to judge Master Peter and Master John, and I intend to keep you in your place: if you continue your machinations I will cut your nails to the quick' (to a deputation of parliamentarians, 1632) (quoted in R. Wilkinson, *France and the cardinals*, 1995, pp. 62–63).

Richelieu when others were pushing for his resignation, while for his part Richelieu remained loyal to the king.

Louis liked to spend his time in hunting, falconry and warfare. He disliked his wife, the blameless **Anne of Austria**. He was shy, mistrustful and vindictive. He was also prudish; for Louis swearing and blaspheming were serious social problems. A devout Catholic who firmly supported the Counter-Reformation, he took his royal obligations seriously. He lived in the shadow of his famous father, Henry IV, whom he considered to be his superior. He had what today would be called an inferiority complex. Richelieu found his master difficult to handle.

Richelieu is shown in his portraits as a tall, grave, lightly bearded man robed in the fabulous red silks of a cardinal (see page 38). However, it is helpful to separate the man from what was the most famous of the many posts he held. In taking a high ecclesiastical post he was following one of a number of avenues open to the nobility for the achievement of privilege and power. He acquired for himself many other high offices, and was the first minister of the country. At this time, when the Counter-Reformation was at its height and France's Protestant minority was still seen by many in the majority Catholic community as a threat, the church was one of the best routes to the top, and the post of cardinal was one in which a powerful impression might be made. It was no coincidence that Richelieu's successor as first minister, Mazarin, was also a cardinal.

**Anne of Austria**
(1601–66), daughter of Philip III of Spain. Obliged to marry Louis XIII at the age of 14, starting a loveless marriage. As regent between 1643 and 1661 for her son, Louis XIV, she relied on Cardinal Mazarin to do the ruling.

A painting of Richelieu in La Rochelle by Henri Motte. From time to time Cardinal Richelieu discarded his church robes in favour of armour, leading military campaigns.

Richelieu came from an old aristocratic family, one of the so-called 'sword' nobility. His father was marshall of Henry III's court, responsible for organising provisions and procuring prostitutes. His mother came from a family of Parisian lawyers. At the age of 9 the young Richelieu was sent to Paris to study for a military career, following in his brother's footsteps. In Paris he learnt to fence and to dance. There too he contracted gonorrhoea, a sexually transmitted disease. He might well have gone the same way as his brother, who became a respected soldier and was later killed in a duel. It was purely by chance that he emerged from this distinctly unchristian background to become a high ecclesiastic. The post of bishop of Luçon, which was a Richelieu family inheritance, had become vacant and someone was needed to fill the position. Richelieu was chosen from amongst his brothers, even though he had no natural inclination to enter the church. At the age of 22 he took up the job. This new post did not fill him with any joy. He described Luçon as a poor and dirty backwater and, in keeping with his background and his personality, he took an unyielding, militaristic approach to his duties. For example, he simply demolished a Huguenot church that he judged to be too near to his cathedral. Such toughness was clearly appreciated by his masters in the church.

How did Richelieu's background prepare him to rule France?

In 1622, at the age of 37, he was promoted to the high rank of cardinal. This was as a reward for sorting out a potentially damaging quarrel between Louis XIII and his mother, Marie de Medici, concerning an attempted coup in which Marie had been involved. Marie had been his patron up to this point. Richelieu needed to walk a tightrope, keeping the support of both the king and the queen mother. He managed to do this remarkably well. In 1624 he was admitted to the royal council and within months was promoted to the new post of first minister.

## Richelieu's handling of the plots against him

As the king's first servant, a richly rewarded favourite and the instigator of unpopular policies, Richelieu soon became the target of plots to overthrow him. The conspirators represented three interest groups. First, and perhaps most dangerous because they possessed regional power-bases, were powerful nobles such as Vendôme in Brittany, Montmorency in Languedoc and Guise in Provence. Sometimes described as **noble magnates**, these men flaunted their independent military power. When the royal government defied Languedoc's traditional rights by making new tax demands, Montmorency rose in revolt in 1632.

There was a second group of plotters at an even higher level of society, members of the royal family, conspirators who were after the king no less than his first servant. Louis XIII's younger brother, Gaston of Orléans, was always plotting, always ready to join forces with any other interested party. Spain gave

Richelieu feared that **noble magnates** would plunge France back into the chronic civil wars of the previous century, with religion as the excuse to take up arms.

The **Chalais conspiracy** of 1626 was hatched in the court by Gaston, the queen and the Duchesse de Chevreuse. The idea was to assassinate Richelieu and perhaps the king himself. Gaston was spared, but Chalais, a fellow conspirator, was painfully dispatched with a rough execution.

him financial backing in his last plot. Marie Medici, the queen, was another plotter. She was influenced by the extreme Catholic and pro-Spanish 'dévots'. The mis-named **Chalais conspiracy** was the first of two major conspiracies centred around the queen, both of which were outwitted by Richelieu, largely thanks to the work of efficient spies.

A third group of plotters were based around the finance minister, the politically acute figure of Marillac. He was more sincere than Montmorency or Gaston in his attacks on the policies of Richelieu. Marillac argued that Richelieu's foreign policy was ruinously expensive to the country and a diversion from greater needs (see Source 1, p. 49). On 10 November 1630, 'The Day of Dupes', Richelieu outwitted Marillac and the queen, who had once more seized an opportunity to gamble for power. It seems that one reason for the cardinal's success was that he simply professed his devotion to the king more exuberantly than his rivals. Marillac paid with his life. Richelieu always dealt with lesser plotters ruthlessly, while avoiding severity when members of the royal family were involved.

### Richelieu's aims in religion – the Huguenot issue

Above all, Richelieu wanted a people and a church loyal to the monarchy. It was by praising the queen mother's toughness in handling the Huguenots that Richelieu first found favour. Richelieu wrote at the time of his coming to power that the Huguenots shared the kingdom with the monarch. They were a distraction from the need to strengthen frontiers against the Habsburg powers. His main aim was to eliminate the independent power of the Huguenots. He saw them as a continuing focus for civil war. However, he was not himself a Catholic fanatic or **dévot**. In his dealings with the Huguenots, he displayed the same mixture of ruthlessness, combined with the knack of knowing when to compromise, that had served him so well earlier. In 1627 he led a siege of La Rochelle, the Huguenot stronghold on the western coast. The siege was carried on for so long that 24,000 of the town's 30,000 inhabitants died from starvation. Some accounts of the siege relate episodes in which Richelieu apparently displayed great cruelty. One says he was joyful on learning that a large number of Huguenots had been drowned by the accidental capsizing of a raft, another how he ordered the execution of a rebel and the exposure of his head on a lance to make his fiancée die of grief.

Pro-Spanish Catholic fanatics, the **dévots**, wanted the Huguenots eliminated by all-out war. Richelieu's eventual compromise with the Huguenots and his support for Protestant powers in the Thirty Years' War angered the 'dévots'. In response, Richelieu suppressed the writings of the extreme Catholic critics.

In what ways did Richelieu treat opponents to Louis XIII?

However, in his arrangements for a peace treaty to follow the siege he showed himself ready to compromise in order to achieve a lasting settlement. The Edict of Alais removed all Huguenot military power, but it also confirmed freedom of worship and granted a general amnesty to all except the rebel leaders. This was so effective that in the desperate years of the 1630s a number of prominent Huguenots actually lent their support to Richelieu's campaigns in the Thirty Years' War.

## What inspired Richelieu?

Richelieu expressed great admiration for Machiavelli, the fifteenth-century political theorist. He employed hack writers to write defences of **Machiavelli** and summaries of his best-known work, *The prince*. All Machiavelli's arguments find echoes in the cardinal's own writings and actions. For both men military strength and internal discipline were favourite themes. Richelieu appreciated the value of propaganda and was one of the first statesmen to make great use of it, employing pamphleteers to present his actions in a favourable light.

Richelieu wrote that he expected to be rewarded with great wealth for his loyal services to the king and there is little doubt that, faithful servant of the state though he was, he was also strongly motivated by self-interest. Like a medieval pope, he amassed a vast personal fortune and he looked after his own family and clients, appointing relatives to top commands. His fortune grew to over 20 million **livres**. His average annual income was 750,000 livres, equivalent to 1 per cent of the national income. He owned four châteaux, including the palace of Fontainebleau.

Richelieu gave a convincing public account of his motivations, as we might expect. He claimed that he acted only in the interests of France and the king. Machiavelli had said that a ruler's preoccupations should be his country's security and future glory and Richelieu made these his priorities too. Richelieu managed to combine enormous personal ambition with devotion to the interests of state. After his death he became a hero amongst French historians, who regarded him as the greatest of patriots.

## What were Richelieu's foreign policy aims?

Most rulers in this period sought to expand their territories, though always declaring that they were acting in a purely defensive way to strengthen themselves against attack from menacing neighbouring powers. They usually did so for a mixture of motives, ranging from the need for stronger frontiers and economic benefits to pure ambition and the pursuit of fame and honour in warfare. Richelieu argued that France needed stronger, more consolidated land frontiers because the state was threatened everywhere by Habsburg power: Spanish to the north and south, Austrian to the east. There was some justification because the Spanish had invaded France during the course of the religious wars in the late sixteenth century. The case against the Austrians was flimsier. However, Richelieu's critics felt he was addicted to war and his declaration that there was no nation in the world less inclined to war than France seems hard to take seriously. Both his readiness to commit France to wars – in northern Italy in the mid-1620s, in Germany in the 1630s – and his statements about the virtues of war indicate that he was not telling the whole truth (see Historical sources B).

**Machiavelli** was secretary to the war council of the city-state of Florence, 1498–1512. Memorable quotes from Machiavelli: 'Men are more prone to evil than to good'; '[The populace can be] brought to realise what is bad and what is good for it by someone in whom it has confidence'; 'One should admire those who know how to govern a kingdom, not those who actually govern one' (*Discourses on Livy*, 1513–18, trans. L. J. Walter; *Dedication to Buondelmonti and Rucellai*).

The **livre** was the French unit of money at the time, equal to 1 pound (0.45 kg) of silver.

What did Richelieu himself gain in exchange for his loyalty to Louis XIII?

Such a warlike foreign policy affected his domestic policy. Wars were costly, so taxation had to be heavy and the economy strengthened. Nobles and religious minorities needed to be subjected to the royal government, so that there was no distraction from the pursuit of war. Richelieu fumed at the constant revolts that distracted from his foreign policy and gave openings for enemies, both internal and external, to attack the government (see Historical sources B).

Considerations of religious loyalty – the greater good of the Catholic Counter-Reformation – did not enter into his foreign policy. In 1631 France gave financial backing to the Protestant Swedes in the Thirty Years' War, considering the Swedish campaigns against the Austrian Habsburgs to be more important than loyalty to co-religionists. The French church was anyway determined to show its **Gallican** independence within the Catholic world. Four years later French armed forces took up the cudgels from the overstretched Swedes. For similar reasons, a French subsidy was given to the Dutch in their war against Spain in the 1630s.

## How far did Richelieu achieve his aims?
### To what extent was an absolutist state established?

The conventional answer to this question is that a drive towards **absolutism** was started by Richelieu. Some historians have disputed this, arguing that there simply were not enough royal administrators to enforce the royal will throughout the country. Faced with practical problems of this kind and the continuing power of aristocrats in the provinces, Richelieu found himself able to succeed only by giving ground.

Several political theorists of the time, including Richelieu and **Lebret**, argued that unrestrained monarchy would be a good form of government. Lebret said that monarchs had the right to rule because it was God's will and that they were responsible only to God. Since kingship was their 'divine right' they were not to be held to account by their subjects. It was for the king to make laws, to declare war and decide when it was time to make peace. The only limitation to the king's authority was that he did not own his subjects' property. In his own writings Richelieu argued that absolutism was the only alternative to lawlessness, that the people were fools and that repression and heavy taxation were good for them.

As well as wealth, Richelieu accumulated power by accepting several offices of state. He used these extra powers to ensure the passage of laws that he wanted. He quickly put his own appointees on the royal council, and the **parlement** of Paris was reduced to the role of registering his decrees. In 1624, two years after becoming France's first principal minister of state, he made

---

**How did Richelieu's foreign policy affect his domestic policies?**

The **Gallican** movement among the French Roman Catholic Church aimed to restrict papal power and achieve greater independence for the French church.

**Absolutism** is royal government without legal or parliamentary restraint.

**Lebret** was one of Richelieu's propagandists.

**Why did Richelieu favour absolutism?**

The '**parlements**' (parliaments) were courts whose main function was to register royal decrees. They were made up of magistrates from the nobility. There were parliaments in Paris and in 10 provincial centres.

himself grand master and superintendent general of commerce and navigation, traditionally a job reserved for a member of the ancient nobility. Lesser posts were taken on according to his needs or whims. Following an objection to an action of his, on the grounds that only the governor of Brittany was allowed to supervise shipping, Richelieu himself took on the post. However, comparisons with twentieth-century **dictators** must be made cautiously, for France was not a democracy before this period and the cardinal ruled alongside a king who sometimes overruled him forcefully.

The Paris parliament and the provincial parliaments frequently clashed with Richelieu. They were invariably the losers. When he wanted to bypass them he set up new bodies. Richelieu created extraordinary judicial commissions to try important state prisoners, up to this point a responsibility of the Paris parliament. In 1631 he set up a special court, the Chambre d'Arsenal, to punish political offenders. This court became notorious for its midnight arrests and executions. In the ordinary courts he enforced his will by removing any judges he did not like. In 1626 the Paris parliament was informed that it had no right to interfere in affairs of state when it protested about his handling of the Chalais conspiracy (see page 42). On meeting parliamentary resistance to higher tax demands in 1635 and 1637, Richelieu created 24 new parliamentary posts. In 1641 the Paris parliament was told to confine itself to judging criminals and to give advice on political matters only when asked. In short, instead of developing into the kind of political debating chamber that England had by the eighteenth century in its London parliament, the Paris equivalent was sidelined.

Popular revolts, of which there were many, were dealt with ruthlessly. The poor peasants and the **nu-pieds** rose up in revolt in Normandy in 1639 because of excessive taxation. This was handled ruthlessly by Richelieu without recourse to compromise. However, in spite of his toughness in handling resistance, Richelieu often compromised when his opponents were of high social standing. He allowed the nobles to retain their dominance in offices of church and state, partly because he wanted the church to be 'Gallican' in its outlook and partly because he was saving his fire for those who held the powerful post of provincial governor. He exiled a considerable number of governors and stopped the ancient nobility's right of inheritance to this office. By the time of his death in 1642, Richelieu had either failed to replace, exiled, imprisoned or executed three-quarters of the original 16 provincial governors.

Richelieu's will did not always prevail. He attempted to reduce the influence of the provincial aristocracy by imposing government tribunals or 'elections' on the local parliaments or Estates. But in the face of fierce resistance from vested interests, such as the wine growers, he backed down in nearly every

In what ways did Richelieu increase his personal power?

A **dictator** is a person with complete authority, especially one who suppresses or succeeds a democratic government.

How did Richelieu reduce the power of the provincial nobility?

How did Richelieu overrule the parliaments?

The **nu-pieds**, the 'barefooted', rebelled against rises in the salt tax; a local tax official was murdered and the peasants formed a militia with support from local clergy and nobles. The revolt ended with the reimposition of order.

case. Only Protestant Dauphiné lost its parliament. His attempt to put a stop to duelling proved unenforceable despite the sanctions of exile and death. His authority was frustrated on other occasions too. For example, when he wanted the conspirator Cinq-Mars to be tortured after his trial, he was overruled by the judge. This evidence has been used to argue that he was far from being either a dictator or even the man who was most responsible for taking France in the direction of absolute monarchy.

## Results of Richelieu's foreign policy

### Territorial

In spite of the near collapse of French campaigns in northern Italy in 1630, the near-total defeat after the invasion of France in 1636 and the continuing poor quality of the army, Richelieu's foreign policy aims were largely achieved. France became a little stronger. His foreign policy was continued by Mazarin and there were eventually some small but solid territorial gains that strengthened the frontiers with 'Germany' in 1648 and with the Spanish Empire in 1659. Richelieu's persistence produced the occupation of Lorraine, Rousillon and Breisach by the time of his death as well as the start of a navy, and he deserves half the credit for strengthening France's borders. Looking at the situation from a French point of view, a little more of a barrier had been created against potential aggressors. Seen from the Spanish, 'German' and Austrian points of view, France now had launchpads for further expansion into what had been their territories.

How did Richelieu's foreign policy strengthen France?

### Economic consequences

Like most of his counterparts across Europe, the cardinal admired the Dutch economic miracle and would have liked to improve the economy of his own state. He was unable to imitate their success. Taxation of the peasants was too heavy for an internal market to develop in France. Peasants were too poor to invest in agricultural improvement. Their landlords, who had the money, preferred to use it for buying honorary posts, a policy encouraged by a government desperate for funds. As commerce was also subject to heavy taxation, there was little incentive for industrial development.

Richelieu's greatest success in this area was the creation of a navy. This stimulated ship-building and encouraged trade. However, by the mid-1630s wars which he had promoted had driven his own merchant ships from the sea. Much has been made of his support for overseas colonisation and trade. He founded trading companies and supported the precarious new colonies of Quebec (founded 1608) and New France (modern Nova Scotia, founded by Frenchmen and re-taken from the poaching English in 1632). However, the French emigrants soon became unhappy, complaining that he was more interested in spending money on the building of a convent than in pressing for measures to improve their physical well-being and security.

## Political consequences

There was a heavy political price to be paid for the foreign policy successes. For his last seven years of power, Richelieu was immensely unpopular because of the suffering caused by the cost of a policy of ceaseless war. Military expenditure more than doubled between 1624 and 1642, to 38 million livres. New government officials called intendants were appointed to ensure that the tax was paid. Taxation was raised in three ways, none of which was new, efficient or free from corruption: personal taxation, from which the nobility remained exempt; indirect taxation of commerce; and extraordinary taxation – borrowing and selling government bonds and offices. In spite of the tax burden there was never enough money to pay or supply the troops, who lived off the land by extortion and looting. This caused much resentment in the countryside.

## Richelieu as a controversial figure

Historians take different views about Richelieu's achievements. Some point to the eventual success of his foreign policy, arguing that the need for security from foreign enemies justified the expense. Internal enemies, chiefly in the shape of the Huguenots, were also brought into line.

Other historians argue that the cost was too great – the point of view that has mainly been offered here. In general, the modern view is that Richelieu had a number of short-term successes, but the collapse of France into the Fronde a few years after his death should lead one to ask whether in the long term he was more of a failure than a success.

> What were Richelieu's most successful economic policies?

> How was the general population affected by Richelieu's foreign policy?

> Taken as a whole, was Richelieu's ministry successful? You may want to consider this question along the lines of 'Successful for whom?'

---

### Historical sources

## A  Richelieu's relationship with Louis XIII

We can never be quite sure who was the dominant partner. Some historians have accepted the verdict of Source 3, while others say that the king was the key figure. The evidence from Richelieu himself seems to point in different directions.

## 1 Recognition for services rendered

Great princes normally for reasons of their grandeur and well-being allow those who hold the most important offices of their State and have their confidence to make an honest fortune. Such princes allow <u>their servants</u> to leave office after receiving due recognition of their services, which displays the magnificence of their masters. The king by his generosity has made me wealthier.

Source: Richelieu to King Louis XIII, 13 January 1629 (from R. Bonney, *Society and government under Richelieu and Mazarin*, 1988, p.11).

## 2 Advice on how to become a greater king

Now that La Rochelle has been captured, if the king wishes to make himself the most powerful monarch in the world . . . he must consider his personal behaviour and reforms for his State.

The king is good, virtuous, secretive, courageous and a lover of glory, but in truth one must say that he is extremely easily aroused, suspicious, jealous.

At all costs the <u>heretical rebellions</u> must be destroyed . . . We must act in such a way that the king will be completely obeyed by great and small alike.

Source: Richelieu to King Louis XIII, 13 January 1629 (from Bonney, 1988, p. 9).

## 3 An allegation that Richelieu ruled, not Louis

Today it is generally accepted that it is just to imprison anyone because of the slightest wish of <u>a favourite</u> (for all know that these acts do not come from the king). Every suspicion is cause for imprisonment; every imprisonment is authorised by the judges. Every pretext is a crime; every crime is subject to condemnation; every condemnation is for not less than life. Whoever displeases a favourite is put in prison, and whoever is in prison must be executed to justify the act of him who causes him to be imprisoned.

Source: A pamphleteer working for Marie de Medici (quoted in R. Wilkinson, *France and the cardinals, 1610–61*, 1995, p. 59).

## Historical-source questions A

1　Explain the references underlined in Sources 1, 2 and 3.
2　What do the three sources suggest about the relationship between Louis XIII and Richelieu?
3　To what extent were the complaints of Source 3 justified?
4　Compare Sources 1 and 2 with the excerpts from Machiavelli on page 43. In what ways were Richelieu's ideas influenced by Machiavelli?

# B  Richelieu and the pursuit of war

The French state was at war, either with enemy states or internal rebels, during Richelieu's entire ministry. It is no surprise then that the huge cost Involved brought the war policy itself into question (Source 1) and obliged Richelieu to justify it. This he did with his customary assurance, turning the issue to his advantage.

## 1  The need for peace

It seems to me that it is principally owing to, and to the glory of, a good government to think in terms of alleviating the consequences of its decisions, and drawing up beneficial rulings for the good of the State, which can only be carried out in peacetime. Many people consider another war unnecessary . . . In order to survive, we have to impose new taxes and other burdens to an intolerable extent.

Source: Marillac to Richelieu, 15 February 1629 (from Bonney, 1988, p. 12).

## 2  The need for war

One must be capable of waging a long war, should <u>the good of the state</u> require it. In the judgment of men of the highest repute war is sometimes an unavoidable evil and, in some circumstances it is absolutely necessary and may even achieve some good.

States need war at certain times to purge themselves of their evil humours, to recover what belongs to them, to avenge an injury . . . to protect their allies from oppression, to halt the advance and pride of a conqueror, to forestall evils which apparently threaten and which one does not know how to evade any other way, or finally for various other reasons . . .

There is no nation in the world less inclined to war than our own . . .

If [the French had the military skill] to accompany their valour, the universe would not be big enough to accommodate all their conquests.

Source: Richelieu, 'Political testament', first published 1688 (in T. K. Rabb, *The Thirty Years' War*, 1964, 2nd edn, 1981, p. 135).

## 3  The damage done by rebellions

Rebellions are so common an occurrence in France that while we are considering <u>humiliating others</u> we may receive a worse blow from ourselves than we are able to give our enemies. The Huguenots . . . are accustomed to advance their cause at the expense of the State, and to seize their opportunity when they see us occupied against those who are our declared enemies.

Source: Richelieu to King Louis XIII, 1625 (from Bonney, 1988, pp. 4–5).

1  Explain the references underlined in Sources 2 and 3.

2  How convincing is Source 2's claim that there was 'no nation less inclined to war' than France? Refer to the source and to your own knowledge.

3  (a)  On what grounds did Marillac (Source 1) criticise Richelieu's foreign policy?

   (b)  Sources 1 and 3 propose different ideas about France's main problem. In what ways are they different?

4  In what ways do Sources 1 to 3 suggest that Richelieu not only did nothing to avoid war but actively sought it?

## Summary questions

1  (a)  Explain how Richelieu tried to achieve any *two* of his aims in domestic policy.

   (b)  With which one of these was he most successful?

2  (a)  How successful was Richelieu in any *two* of his foreign campaigns?

   (b)  What were the economic and political consequences of his foreign policy for France?

3  For discussion or full essay:
   Were the costs of Richelieu's achievements in terms of human suffering unacceptably high?

# 4 France: Mazarin

## Focus questions

◆ Why was Mazarin faced by rebellion?

◆ Why were Mazarin and monarchy in France able to survive?

◆ How far did the foreign policies of Richelieu and Mazarin extend the power of France?

## Significant dates

1640    Revolts in Catalonia and Portugal; French troops committed to help rebels.

1643    On Louis XIII's death Mazarin becomes first minister of France. French victory at Rocroi (Thirty Years' War).

1645    Judges who oppose unpopular new tax on Parisians are imprisoned.

1647    Revolts in Spanish Italy.

1648    *January*   Paris parliament refuses to approve special taxation to pay for continuing war with Spain. Beginning of first Fronde revolt.
*May*   Paris courts demand tax reductions and consultation.
Revolts in England (against unpopular king), the Ukraine (against Polish rule), in Moscow (against unpopular first minister), in Constantinople (against Sultan).
*September*   Royal household flees Paris.

1649    *January*   King Charles I of England executed.
*January to March*   Events in Paris escalate to direct military confrontation between parliament and Mazarin. Temporarily resolved by royal concessions.

1650    Mazarin arrests three leading nobles for treasonable conspiracy. This provokes the second or 'princely' Fronde.

1651    Mazarin releases Condé, Conti and Longueville. The princes return to Paris and Mazarin goes into exile in Cologne.

1652    *July*   Turenne defeats the rebel army of Condé, who flees to Spain.
*October*   The Paris parliament is excluded from any future role in government.

1653    Mazarin reappointed. The Bordeaux rebels surrender in August.

1658    Anglo-French defeat of Spain at the Battle of the Dunes. Marriage arranged between Spanish Maria Theresa and Louis XIV.

| 1659 | Mazarin achieves small gains of Spanish territory (Peace of the Pyrenees). |
|---|---|
| 1660 | Revolt in Marseilles, supported by Cardinal de Retz and a large part of the clergy (the 'religious' Fronde).<br>Charles Stuart leaves French exile; English monarchy restored. |
| 1661 | Death of Mazarin. The religious Fronde subsides. |

## Overview

The heavy taxation required to finance wars was a major cause of revolt in France, as elsewhere in Europe, in the 1640s. When Cardinal Mazarin took over the reins of power from Richelieu in 1643 he continued with the main thrust of his predecessor's policies. He was already unpopular as an Italian 'foreigner', and this strategy quickly made him hated. Revolution (the Fronde) broke out in 1648 and for a while it looked as if the French monarchy would go the way of the English. In September, civil war in Paris forced Mazarin and the royal household to leave the capital. Meanwhile, in England, rebels had taken over and declared England to be a commonwealth and free state. The tumultuous events in England caused alarm in the royal courts of continental Europe.

When, two years later, three great nobles pursued their own ambitions in the name of the rebel cause (the princely Fronde), Mazarin was again forced to flee. However, his exile was not for long, because Louis XIV claimed his majority in 1651 and the unpopular rebel princes were themselves forced into exile. Mazarin became once again first minister. With those who had called for reform defeated, he reverted to the pre-Fronde policies, now with the advantage of having the help of a young but popular and forceful king. The general distaste for any repeat of the chaos of the Fronde period also worked to his advantage. By the time of his death in 1661 France was externally in a stronger position but internally it remained weak.

## Why was Mazarin faced by rebellion?

### The European context: mid-century revolutions

In the 1640s and early 1650s there were major revolts not only in France (the Frondes), but also in England, the Spanish Empire (including Italy), Poland, Russia and the United Provinces. Each was unique but they had several similar factors: economic depression, anger about high taxation and unpopular, insensitive royal government. The last year of the Thirty Years' War, 1648, was a peak year for prices and one of near universal crisis in agriculture.

It is worthwhile giving some attention to the main causes of revolt at this point; the course of events in three quite different states – Spain, Russia and the United Provinces – shows that French history was not unique. In Spain the war-oriented policies of Olivares, an unpopular royal favourite, were bitterly resented. Even in the fairly prosperous United Provinces the achievement of peace in 1648 created as many problems as it solved. The estates of Holland refused to maintain the large army that had been created for the long war with Spain. The troubles that followed culminated in a constitutional revolt in 1651 against the House of Orange. A major revolt in Moscow in 1648 was inspired by increased taxation, royal neglect of the noble-led national assembly and the unpopularity of the royal favourite and first minister (Moruzov). Almost everywhere in Europe, state devotion to warfare, high taxation and 'divide and rule' policies for the nobility, combined with the devastating effects of economic depression, were creating classic conditions for revolution.

> Why were revolts so widespread in Europe in the mid-seventeenth century?

## The impact of the English revolution on events in France

Some of the more ardent and idealistic of the English revolutionary groups inspired those of like mind across the seas. Exiles, forced to flee revolution, spread alarm that the same might happen in their host nations. The execution of King Charles I and the establishment of a republic in England in 1648–49 was regarded in some quarters as an apocalyptic event, signalling the end of the world. States as far away as Venice voiced their deep disapproval of the revolution in England. After the Scottish rebellion of 1638, followed by similar events in Spain in 1640, Philip IV's envoy to London offered a military alliance against the 'conspiracy' of revolution in Spain and England. The British royal family now used their close connections with continental royalty for assistance. Through Charles I's marriage the Stuarts were connected to the French monarchy (see page 27). Charles I's son, Charles Stuart, the future Charles II of England, found refuge in France.

On the other side of the barricades, there were some direct contacts between the more extreme radicals in England and France. Radical English groups, principally the Levellers and the Diggers, drew inspiration from a literal reading of Jesus's preaching. They wanted to achieve greater democracy and a share-out of the land amongst the poor. In 1652 the Leveller Edward Sexby visited the radical Ormée group in Bordeaux, bringing with him a revolutionary manifesto, 'The agreement of the people'. After this visit the Ormée group adopted republicanism. The Christian religion, especially the moral teachings of Jesus, was the main inspiration of all the left-wing groups of this time. Jesus preached about the brotherhood of all men (meaning both sexes here), the sufferings of the poor and equality before God. Typically, a Catalan rebel leader titled himself 'captain-general of the Christian army'.

However, the English revolution had a more immediate political influence on events in France. The boldest moves of the first **Fronde** rebellion were made in January 1649, when Charles I was on trial for tyranny in London. On

> **Fronde** means sling or catapult in French. The word is used to describe the French revolts of these years.

8 January 1649 the Paris parliament declared Mazarin, the king's first minister, an enemy of the state. On 9 January it set up a fund to enable conscription of troops to advance its cause. Mazarin compared the Fronde's leaders to the leading revolutionaries in England. The greatest concessions to the Frondeurs' demands (under the Treaty of Rueil, March 1649) were made by a royal government frightened not just by internal developments but also by the execution of a monarch in England.

In what ways did the English revolution influence events in France?

### To what extent was Mazarin personally responsible for the outbreak of the Fronde?

Regular provincial peasant revolts were an established fact of life in France well before Richelieu and Mazarin's time and they continued to be so long after them. Parts of France were in a state of almost perpetual rebellion from the 1590s to the 1660s. There were, for example, revolts in the south-western provinces in 1621, 1637, 1652 and 1655. Normandy rose in revolt in 1595, 1615 and 1639; Provence rebelled in 1631 and 1660. France's mid-century crisis was prolonged. In a sense large parts of France were always ready for revolt and so the direct responsiblity of Mazarin for the burst of revolts in the middle of the century was limited.

The Fronde is sometimes described as a series of disconnected revolts, something less than a revolution. How far is this view supported by the contemporary pictures on page 55?

However, the Frondes were much more than provincial peasant revolts, though they did include this element. Above all, they amounted to a struggle between monarchy and nobility (first the lesser and then the greater nobility) for the government of the state. The two tough ministries of Richelieu and Mazarin met with continual resistance which culminated in the great revolts known as the first or 'parliamentary' Fronde of 1648–49 and the second or 'princely' Fronde of 1650–53. Sometimes they are described as civil wars. Some historians hesitate to describe what happened as a revolution as the state was not overturned, as happened in England.

The medium-term origins of the Fronde go back to Louis XIII's death in 1643, when Richelieu's protégé, the Italian-born Cardinal Jules Mazarin, became royal favourite and first minister. He was effectively joint ruler with Anne of Austria, to whom he may have been secretly married, during the minority of the infant Louis XIV. Mazarin persisted with Richelieu's policies in all essential respects. In many ways he was much like Richelieu. He was not only as clever, cunning and ambitious; he also had a more outgoing personality. He was, like Richelieu, an admirer of Machiavelli and it is typical of him that he had the reputation of a cheat at the gaming table, one of his favourite pastimes. On the other hand he lacked Richelieu's ability as a propagandist; he failed to persuade the public that his policies were the right ones.

There was continuity in foreign policy objectives from Richelieu to Mazarin. Though some historians make much of the fact that Mazarin sued

*Left:* An engraving showing barricades erected in Paris during the parliamentary Fronde of 1648. *Below:* Fighting around the Bastille in Paris during the Fronde.

for peace with Spain and Austria on a number of occasions, he put forward impossible conditions to the Habsburg powers, keeping France at war. There were military successes: at Rocroi in 1643 and Lens in 1648. French control of the Rhine was tightened by recapturing the strategically vital east-bank fortress of Philippsburg and there were victories in May 1648 against joint Austrian–Bavarian forces on the borders with Austria. Just as Spain had tried to ruin France in the civil wars of the sixteenth century, so France in its turn sought to break up Spain by committing troops to help the Portuguese and Catalonian rebels after 1640. At the peace settlement at the end of the Thirty Years' War in 1648, Mazarin succeeded in his demand that the small German states should now become independent of Austrian control in the Holy Roman Empire (see p. 134). Mazarin reaped the rewards for his own and his predecessor's toughness and resolution in foreign policy.

In spite of these foreign policy successes, Mazarin became a figure of hate for the many different groups of French people who joined the Fronde rebellions between 1648 and 1653. This was partly because he was so conspicuously successful in his career, so clearly self-seeking and so obviously a 'foreigner', proud to describe himself as such. Whereas Richelieu had

An engraving of Cardinal
Mazarin (1602–61) by
Nauteuil after Chauveau.
Mazarin was an adventurer,
fortune seeker, diplomat and
politician. Although he
became a cardinal he was
never ordained.

published a personal statement that he only had France and its people at heart
– a skilful piece of propaganda – Mazarin failed to 'sell' his foreign policy to
the people. Whereas only a few nobles had dared to criticise Richelieu, most
sections of the public attacked Mazarin, even though he was pursuing essentially the same foreign policy. Apart from Mazarin's public relations failure,
the continued taxation burden year after year was eventually the main reason
why the public turned sour on their leaders. The cost of the wars almost
doubled between 1642 and 1648, creating a government debt of more than
100 million livres. The government borrowed heavily, a task undertaken by
the unpopular finance minister, D'Emery. Judges who opposed the levying of
a special tax on buildings outside the city walls of Paris were imprisoned in
1645. Subsequently, one of the imprisoned judges, Barillon, died in prison, so
becoming a martyr. By 1648 Mazarin had lost the support not only of the civil
service in the capital and the provinces but also of financiers, the Parisian
poor and the Parisian middle class. With an economic depression causing
famine in the capital and elsewhere, the scene was set for revolution.

### The first Fronde, 1648–49: a brief civil war
The revolt was brought on by the enforcement through a 'lit de justice' (royal
edict) of special taxation to pay for the war with Spain. Issued from the royal
palace on 15 January 1648, this was not approved by the Paris parliament, the

highest court of the land. The proposed measures included the creation of 12 new government offices to raise money, a fine on feudal property acquired by non-nobles and new purchase taxes on food and wine sold in Paris. These taxes were particularly hated as the people of Paris were starving. An attempt to play off the Paris courts against each other backfired, with the courts deciding to meet together in the Chamber of St Louis on 13 May 1648. This kind of action had never been seen before.

The judges discussed their grievances and produced a number of radical demands:

- reduction of the **taille** tax by 25%;
- abolition of the powers of intendants;
- parliamentary consultation over the creation of new posts and taxes.

Anne of Austria, the queen mother, was against any concessions, declaring 'This is sheer republicanism!' – but Mazarin was more flexible and some concessions were made. The finance minister, D'Emery, was dismissed and some of the Paris parliament's authority over taxation was restored. However, buoyed up by a military victory at Lens in August, Mazarin decided to arrest two of the parliamentary rebel leaders, including **Pierre Broussel**. Immediately, barricades constructed of paving stones, barrels, carts and beams went up throughout Paris. An angry mob converged on the Notre Dame bridge. Bowing to the force of public anger, the government released the prisoners. For the time being the rebel cause was victorious and the **royal household** left Paris on 13 September. A month later most of the outstanding demands of the parliamentarians were met. However, at the start of 1649 the government went on the offensive again, ordering the prince of Condé to besiege Paris. On 8 January 1649 the Paris parliament responded by declaring Mazarin an enemy of the state and setting up a fund to pay for the levying of troops. Several disgruntled aristocrats and rather more of the lesser nobility now converged on Paris to join the rebel cause.

Trouble was not confined to Paris. It spread quickly to Aix and Rouen, the capitals of already discontented provinces. People there refused to pay taxes and at the end of January the governor of Provence was arrested. The parliament of Bordeaux prohibited the raising of any taxes which it had not approved and refused to obey the orders of intendants. It also mustered an army of 20,000 men.

In the event, the fighting in the capital did not amount to much for both sides were ready to negotiate. Mazarin and Molé, a leading minister, were frightened by the turn of events in England, by the growing strength of the opposition forces and by reports of Spanish support for the rebels. They were prepared to make short-term concessions. In the Treaty of Rueil signed on 11 March 1649 both sides agreed to an armistice. In exchange for a general

The **taille** was the main direct tax, similar to income tax and dating from the Middle Ages. It was not uniformly assessed, but everywhere the nobility were exempted. In most areas peasants contributed most.

Which of the rebels' grievances concern policies initiated by Richelieu rather than Mazarin?

**Pierre Broussel** (c. 1576–1654) was a fierce critic of the royal government in the Paris parliament. A popular figure, he gave some of his income to the poor.

Louis XIV was to move the **royal household** to Versailles, where he had a new palace built, mainly from fear of being in the city during the Fronde.

Which social classes were most involved in the first Fronde?

What concessions did Mazarin make to the parliamentary Fronde?

amnesty the most drastic of the parliamentary decrees were stopped. A similar compromise was agreed with the parliament at Aix, capital of Provence. In spite of this, civil war continued in both Bordeaux and Provence, with inconclusive results. In Bordeaux a radical party, the **Ormée**, emerged from the ranks of the lower middle class and artisans. These revolutionaries were dedicated to a more far-reaching social revolution than the limited political revolt of the 'parlementaires'. The parliamentary Fronde amounted to a push by some of the lesser nobility and town officials to achieve a greater political role. Temporarily successful, it eventually failed.

The **Ormée**, led by Christophe Dureteste, a lawyer who sided with the common people, seized power in the city of Bordeaux in June 1652. For a year the upper classes were deprived of their monopoly of power.

## Why were Mazarin and monarchy in France able to survive?
### The second Fronde, 1650–53: aristocrats take their chance

In January 1650 Mazarin had three great nobles, Conti, Langueville and the formerly loyal Condé, arrested for treasonable conspiracy. In response, the princess of Condé set up a rebel government in Bordeaux. By February 1651 the government had been compelled to release the rebel princes. For the next three years these nobles fought not only against the royal government but amongst themselves. As all this took place against the backdrop of the threat of Spanish invasion, it seemed as if France had returned to the chaos of the civil wars of the last century. In the short term Mazarin was again forced to flee as rebels demanded his expulsion. However, in the long term the second Fronde played into the hands of royal propagandists, who were able to argue that the stability of a strong royal government was preferable to the anarchy of prolonged civil wars.

It soon became clear that there was no unity between the Paris parliament and the princes and that Condé's ambitions were nothing less than to become king himself. By the end of 1651 **Turenne**, France's leading general, had been persuaded to support the royal government and to take the field against Condé. At this point Mazarin felt strong enough to return to France. Condé, in alliance with Spain, entered Paris and set up an alternative government. In July 1652 his forces were defeated by Turenne. The Paris parliament now declared Gaston, brother of Louis XIII, lieutenant general of the kingdom. However, the excesses of Condé's soldiers in Paris had by now discredited the rebel cause.

The Viscount de **Turenne** (1611–75) was a French soldier who fought with distinction in the Thirty Years' War for armies of the Protestant alliance, becoming supreme commander in 1641.

Mazarin was once more persuaded to keep away from France and leave the way open for the far more popular Louis XIV to claim full kingship now that he was old enough. Louis rallied support and entered Paris in triumph with great ceremony in October 1652. Condé fled and joined the service of the king of Spain. Gaston was exiled and the Paris parliament was forbidden to 'interfere' in politics. The Treaty of Rueil was torn up. Mazarin was invited to return

Why did the Fronde revolution collapse so quickly after 1652?

and in August 1653 Bordeaux, which had set up its own republic under the control of the Ormée, capitulated to royal forces.

From 1653 until his death in 1661 Mazarin once again became first minister and mentor of the still-teenage Louis XIV. The young king, whose bedroom had been invaded by the Paris mob during the second Fronde, grew up determined to exercise personal authority, unchallenged by nobles or parliaments.

The second Fronde saw a closing of ranks amongst most of the nobility in support of royal government and against the high aristocracy (the princes). Fear of anarchy, resulting from rebellion by the aristocracy on the one hand or from peasant social revolution on the other, turned most nobles away from their early enthusiasm for a revolution. They abandoned their temporary alliance with rebellious peasants who, they felt, might readily cut their throats and seize their land. They turned instead to the lesser evil of the royal government and Mazarin.

Why did the princely Fronde fail?

## Was the Fronde a rebellion against Mazarin or against monarchy itself?

The political cartoon of the time shown below, a so-called Mazarinade, shows Mazarin fleeing the second Fronde. Leading rebels made statements pledging

Cartoon attacking Mazarin's conduct of affairs during the Fronde.

What were the grievances expressed by the cartoonist against Mazarin?

Why was Mazarin even more hated than Richelieu?

'Sire, never have a first minister. Govern! Let the politician be a servant, never a master. Take the government into your own hands.' Mazarin's final advice to Louis XIV (Holmes, *Louis XIV*, 1983, p.14).

Why was the new king popular?

The **English royal exiles** were Charles Stuart, the uncrowned Charles II; and his brother James, duke of York and future James II.

What actions in relation to the Paris parliament were taken when Louis XIV assumed power?

respect for the royal person and for the monarchy. This fact has led many historians to conclude that the rebellion was against royal favourites rather than against the monarchy itself. However, cries of 'Republic' were said to have been heard in the streets of Paris and it is well to remember that, across the English Channel, Cromwell installed a republic while similarly declaring his loyalty to the crown. Mazarin was widely hated, but he was also a scape-goat. At this period in history the overwhelming majority of the nobility could not bring itself to a republican declaration that monarchy itself was at fault.

## How did Mazarin and Louis XIV respond after restoration?

Returning to Paris in October 1652 to resume royal residence, Louis had immediately reduced the powers of the Paris parliament, effectively suspending constitutional monarchy. This was to be the spirit of the restoration: tough and uncompromising. As for Mazarin, he was one of history's great political survivors. He had been public enemy number 1 to the Fronde rebels, who had repeatedly demanded his dismissal. In spite of that near disastrous turn of events and his own advice to the young Louis XIV that he should never have a first minister, he was to continue to rule until his death in 1661.

In the difficult days of the early 1650s Mazarin knew that Louis himself was the acceptable face of a royal government that was widely despised because of its association with himself and Richelieu. Here was a young, extrovert king who enjoyed playing to the crowd. Mazarin exploited the potential popularity of the young king. The boy performed his part well. Anne of Austria, the queen mother, gave up her powers as regent in favour of her son in 1658, a reflection both of her unpopularity and of Louis' self-confidence. Louis XIV was now king in more than name, though he chose to defer to Mazarin on most matters of government.

The final struggles of the 'princely' Fronde interrupted further schemes to restore royal power, but a year later the way was once again clear for a royal political offensive to cap military success against the rebels. On 21 October 1652 Louis returned to Paris accompanied by the **English royal exiles**. The following day he took his seat in the Paris parliament as a 'lit de justice' was announced, a procedure which allowed a king to assume complete judicial power. To the beat of drums, 100 Swiss guards occupied the chamber before the arrival of Louis and his entourage. The chancellor, Châteauneuf, an ex-Frondeur, read a declaration of royal amnesty, then the list of those who were excluded from it. Another proclamation forbade the parliament to negotiate with the higher nobility or to have any role in political affairs or the direction of finance. Further attempts by the capital's parliament to act independently prompted an even more stinging response. The teenage king was probably reading from a script prepared by Mazarin, but he brought to its delivery an impressive theatricality by dressing in boots and spurs and pointing to the parliamentarians as he rebuked them.

| | FIRST (PARLIAMENTARY) | SECOND (PRINCELY) |
|---|---|---|
| GROUPS MOST INVOLVED | 1 Upper middle-class.<br>2 Lesser nobility, represented in Paris parliament, Paris courts and provincial parliament.<br>3 Urban poor in Paris and provincial capitals. | 1 Three great nobles.<br>2 Paris parliament, but not consistently supportive. |
| BACKGROUND | 1 Two decades of rising taxation to finance wars.<br>2 Example of English revolution; parliamentary trial of Charles I.<br>3 1648: peak year for prices, and agricultural crisis.<br>4 Provincial peasant revolts frequent for 60 years; peasant poverty blamed on 'taille'.<br>5 Xenophobic hatred of Mazarin, his 'intendants' and the 'paulette'. | 1 Resentment of reduced role allowed to higher nobility since Richelieu's time.<br>2 Ambition of Condé to become king.<br>3 Peasant rebellion in south-west (1652). |
| MAIN DEMANDS | 1 Reduction in 'taille' tax.<br>2 Paris parliament to have bigger role in consultation over taxes and appointments.<br>3 Dismissal of Mazarin. | As left, especially no. 3, and with greater role for high nobility. |
| RESULTS | Temporary government retreat – Treaty of Rueil, 1649.<br><br>Royal government in exile. | Military defeat of Condé (1652) used as excuse to tear up Rueil treaty.<br><br>End of brief drive for constitutional monarchy. Role of Paris parliament reduced still further. |

The main features of the Frondes.

If Mazarin needed Louis, the teenage king needed Mazarin. Even if he frequently resented it, Louis always heeded his first minister's advice. In his memoirs, he described the cardinal as the minister who loved him and whom he loved. Louis had the option of dismissing a highly unpopular minister. Instead he recalled him to lead the government at the earliest possible opportunity. Mazarin had experience, one quality that the headstrong young man could not demonstrate. Mazarin made the training of Louis for kingship one of his main priorities. His several hours of daily tuition were taken very seriously. Batista Noni, the Venetian ambassador, observed (P. Erlanger, *Louis XIV*, 1965, p. 100):

> As soon as Louis has finished dressing he goes to see the Cardinal.
> These visits are made in a quite familiar manner. The Cardinal does not
> go to meet him and does not see him out. If he is busy, the King is

content to wait. Generally, the interview lasts for several hours ... Mazarin brings him up to date with everything, instructs him and moulds him.

However, the more immediate priority for Mazarin was the rebuilding of his massive personal fortune, most of which had been lost during the Fronde. Over the next eight years he built up immense wealth in the form of estates, bishoprics, cash and valuables. His relatives shared in the bounty. His possessions included pictures, jewels and mirrors. Animate luxuries included monkeys, clowns and actors. The cardinal loved gambling and was known to cheat at roulette. He left a fortune of 37 million livres, almost twice that of Richelieu and six times more than that of a typical wealthy nobleman.

Was Mazarin more self-seeking than Richelieu?

## A return to assertive foreign and domestic policies after 1653

Mazarin was determined to win the war with Spain. The Fronde had delayed this objective, both by diverting resources – offering opportunities for ambitious nobles to undermine France's war effort – and by further damaging the economy. If Spain had not also been affected by similar problems, the situation could have been far worse. As it happened, the Catalonian and Italian revolts gave Mazarin opportunities to divide and weaken his enemies.

Eventually there was a French victory in the Franco-Spanish war. The Peace of the Pyrenees in 1659 was a diplomatic victory, securing real gains for France. However, there were considerable costs and it is argued that the increase in French power was less spectacular than it appears to be at first sight. These issues are discussed in the conclusion to this chapter.

To finance the war, high taxation was imposed. There was no time to develop the economy and administration in depth because there was immediate pressure to find the money needed to support the war in 1653. There was no longer much of a call to produce alternative policies. Mazarin felt that the failure of the Fronde left the way clear for him to create a strong royal government. He knew that, in the minds of many, the alternative had failed and was identified with civil war, lawlessness and damage to the economic life of the countryside.

However, it would be a mistake to imagine that resistance ended with the last Fronde or the crushing of the Bordeaux Ormée in the summer of 1653. Sporadic insurrections by the peasants, towns and nobles continued. These were handled with the customary severity. Marseilles, centre of a revolt in 1660, was treated as conquered territory. Resistance broadened to include a section of the church, led by Cardinal de Retz of Paris. De Retz, who hated Mazarin and became his chief critic, couldn't be ignored because he was a popular figure. As an atheist, he was also a most remarkable churchman. De

Retz acted partly out of concern for the victims of high taxation. With the support of two-thirds of the Paris clergy, this 'religious' Fronde was much harder for the government to deal with than the earlier Frondes and ended only when Mazarin died.

Mazarin's only acknowledgement of the depth of hostility which had led to the Fronde was to be seen in the slowness and caution with which he revived Richelieu's system of government. Intendants were reintroduced, but diplomatically renamed 'masters of requests'. The financiers, who had been a major target of the rebels, were allowed to recommence their activities, once again making handsome profits at the taxpayers' expense. To run the whole system, Mazarin appointed three superintendents of finance. One of these, **Nicholas Fouquet**, made a princely fortune by corrupt practice. Along with the corruption, the centralisation and dictatorial style of the pre-Fronde system was revived. The role of the masters of requests included the suppression of opposition in the provinces. Richelieu's drive against great nobles holding provincial governorships was continued. The army that **Le Tellier** began to build up was, for the first time, a genuine royal army rather than a collection of private armies in aristocratic hands.

## The importance of Mazarin's domestic policies for the future of France

As a bridge between Richelieu and Louis XIV, Mazarin was very important. Louis XIV learnt from Mazarin, Mazarin from Richelieu. After almost two decades as first minister, Mazarin had accomplished nothing for industry and agriculture. The sale of offices, a means of both extending royal patronage and raising revenue, reached new heights in the second half of his time in power. Mazarin himself effectively creamed off some of the national income. By 1660 there were 60,000 office-holders. Those who went on to buy land, as many did, were particularly exacting as landowners, so deepening the economic problems caused by the fact that the peasantry were already so poor. The taxation system remained inefficient and riddled with corruption. The taxes were sufficient to sustain the war with Spain but insufficient to meet the crown's debts. The taille tax stunted agricultural development because the most successful peasant farmers ended up paying the highest burdens of tax. Louis XIV inherited from Mazarin a complete administrative system. It has been argued that, in part, he also took his political and social values from the cardinal. Cardinal de Retz, an arch critic, said that Mazarin kept a copy of Machiavelli by his bedside! Whether this was true or not, one of the typically Machiavellian ways of thinking that he taught Louis was that it was not the duty of kings to know anything of the emotions of the masses. Erlanger (1965, p.101) writes that 'Louis came under the spell of the luxury and the objets d'art with which the cardinal surrounded himself. He acquired a life-long

**Nicholas Fouquet** (1615–80) was superintendent of finance from 1653. He was arrested for embezzlement in 1661 and spent the rest of his life in prison.

Michel **Le Tellier** (1603–85) was war minister to Louis XIV from 1643. He improved methods of recruitment, supply and discipline. From middle-class origins, he reduced the military power of provincial governors, who were all nobles.

What actions did Mazarin take that suggest he had learned some lessons from the Fronde?

taste for display, elegance and fine manners.' This was an unfortunate result of Mazarin's influence.

Other historians have seen Mazarin's legacy as, on balance, a positive one. Mousnier (1970) and Hatton (1969) argue that royal absolutism was needed and welcomed by many people as preferable to the abuses of noble privilege and political power seen in the religious civil wars or the Fronde. Mazarin's system was justified because it continued in this direction. By 1661 a new alliance between the monarchy and the social elite had been forged. If there were losers amongst the old noble families, this was balanced by the creation of many new office-holders with a stake in the system.

## How far did the foreign policy of Richelieu and Mazarin extend the power of France?

In the peace settlements of 1648 and 1659, Mazarin achieved considerable gains for France (see p. 134 for the Peace of Westphalia, 1648). The most notable acquisitions in the Pyrenees Peace of 1659 were the regions of Roussillon to the south and Artois to the north, taken from Spain and the Spanish Netherlands respectively. France's frontiers were far more secure. The nightmare of Habsburg encirclement had ended. The Artois region included a number of key defensive positions. Mazarin's ambition to make the Low Countries a defensive barrier for Paris was partly achieved. France, not Spain, was now the dominant power in the western half of Europe. By the time Louis XIV assumed full power in 1661, the Bourbon monarchy could look forward to the future with more confidence than ever before. With more successes in war, Louis knew he might look forward to wider popular approval.

On the other hand, French gains in Alsace (1648) had been scattered and most of neighbouring frontier region of Lorraine remained part of the Holy Roman Empire. French retention of the vital fortress of Pinerolo in north-west Italy was made on the condition that France abandon all other territorial claims in Italy. Furthermore, the able minister Le Tellier had done no more than make a start on the mammoth task of eliminating corruption and introducing efficiency into the army. In the closing years of the war with Spain, France needed to enlist the help of England, and the English forces had been more effective than the French in achieving victory in 1658. Mazarin's plans to weaken Spanish authority in Italy failed and in 1659 he abandoned French claims to Catalonia. More fundamentally, historians ask whether the price of foreign policy successes was too high.

How far did the foreign policy of Richelieu and Mazarin extend the power of France?

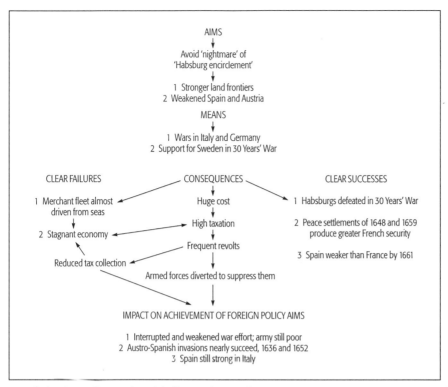

The diagram shows:

AIMS
↓
Avoid 'nightmare' of
'Habsburg encirclement'
↓
1  Stronger land frontiers
2  Weakened Spain and Austria

MEANS
↓
1  Wars in Italy and Germany
2  Support for Sweden in 30 Years' War

CLEAR FAILURES — CONSEQUENCES — CLEAR SUCCESSES
↓
Huge cost

1  Merchant fleet almost
driven from seas

1  Habsburgs defeated in 30 Years' War

High taxation

2  Stagnant economy

2  Peace settlements of 1648 and 1659
produce greater French security

Frequent revolts

3  Spain weaker than France by 1661

Reduced tax collection

Armed forces diverted to suppress them
↓
IMPACT ON ACHIEVEMENT OF FOREIGN POLICY AIMS

1  Interrupted and weakened war effort; army still poor
2  Austro-Spanish invasions nearly succeed, 1636 and 1652
3  Spain still strong in Italy

French foreign policy under Richelieu and Mazarin.

## Historical sources

# Points of view of different sides in the Fronde

The point of view of the nobility in the provinces is well documented (Sources 2 to 4). Their many, lengthy lists of grievances were wide ranging. Whether through custom or not, they profess loyalty to the king. Source 5 is a fascinating glimpse of the point of view of some of the common people.

### 1  The king rebukes the Paris parliament

Everybody knows what trouble your assemblies have stirred up in my state and what dangerous effects they have produced. I have been informed that you still intend to prolong them, on the pretext of debarring edicts which have already been read and published in my presence. I have come here expressly to forbid you to continue.

Source: The Dauphin Louis XIV, addressing the Paris parliament, 13 April 1655 (from P. Erlanger, *Louis XIV*, trans. S. Cox, 1970, p. 69).

## 2 The nobility complain about taxation

In as much as the nobility has been frequently vexed by an infinite number of commissions and taxes which have no other basis than decrees of the council sought and obtained by financiers . . . No edicts, declarations or commissions should be carried out before they have first been duly verified in his Parlements.

Source: Complaints of the nobility of the Angoumois to the Estates General, 22–24 February 1649 (from R. Bonney, *Society and government under Richelieu and Mazarin*, 1988, pp. 172–73).

## 3 The nobility complain on behalf of common people

23. A general complaint of the whole of France touching venality and the excessive price of judicial and financial offices, which is the cause of the great corruption found in those who exercise them . . . In the manner of cancer [the **paulette** tax] gnaws away at all the families of this kingdom . . . It is a monstrosity to see such a superfluity and excessive price of offices in the state.

77. . . . heed the pleas of the common people without whose labours none of us could subsist . . . They have been overburdened for the last forty years with so many levies of taxes.

Source: Grievances of the nobility of Champagne to His Majesty at the Estates in 1651, 31 July 1651 (from Bonney, 1988, pp. 182–83).

The **paulette** tax was an annual tax on office-holders. Introduced by Henry IV in 1604, it allowed them to make their posts hereditary in return.

## 4 The nobility complain about the 'foreign' favourite

20. . . . great wealth has suddenly been acquired by the bourgeoisie . . . it is now no longer possible to distinguish between nobility and commoners.

29. All foreigners should be excluded from the management of affairs of State in conformity with the decrees of the Parlement of Paris.

Source: Grievances of the nobility of Périgord to the Estates General at Tours, 8 September 1651 (from Bonney, 1988, pp. 184–85).

## 5 The common people speak for themselves

The restoration of the French state can only be accomplished by the people. The great nobles and magistrates are the accomplices and disciples of tyranny; if the people turn to other military leaders than those who are among them, in order to free themselves, they will prolong their hardship.

Source: The Ormist manifesto, *c.*1652 (from R. Wilkinson, *France and the cardinals, 1610–61*, 1995, pp. 109–10).

## Historical-source questions

1  Study Sources 2 to 5. List the grievances expressed by the provincial nobles and the common people.
   To what extent did they share similar grievances?

2  Account for the differences in the grievances of these groups.

3  What was the king's point of view (Source 1)? In what ways did events, particularly after 1650, back him up?

4  In what ways do the sources provide some pointers to the eventual failure of the Fronde?

## Summary questions

1  (a)  Explain how any *two* factors contributed to the outbreak of the first Fronde in 1648.

   (b)  Which one factor was the most important cause of the first Fronde?

2  For discussion or full essay:
   How far is it true to say that Mazarin left France in a stronger condition than he had found it?

# 5 Revolt and decline in Spain: Lerma and Olivares

## Focus questions

◆ What were the problems of governing Spain?

◆ How effective were Spain's kings and their ministers?

## *Significant dates*

**1598**   Death of Philip II. His son, Philip III, becomes king at a time when Castile is in the middle of a terrible plague.

**1600**   The Spanish Army of Flanders is defeated at Nieuwport by Dutch rebels.

**1604**   Lerma negotiates the Treaty of London, securing peace with England.

**1605**   Spanish successes against the Dutch rebels under the generalship of Spínola, but troop mutinies and lack of money halt further progress.

**1609**   Lerma negotiates the Truce of Antwerp with the United Provinces. Start of expulsion of the Moriscos to north Africa – continues to 1614.

**1612**   Royal decree states that orders from Lerma have as much authority as if they had come from the king.

**1618**   Lerma is dismissed; pro-Austrian 'activist' faction led by Zúñiga (uncle of Olivares) wins power. Money and troops are sent to the Austrian emperor to help him put down rebellion in Bohemia.

**1620**   Spanish forces under Spínola occupy Rhine territory of Frederick of the Palatinate. The Valtelline is taken, angering France.

**1621**   Philip IV ascends the throne, aged 16. Truce with the Dutch is not renewed and war is resumed. The Zúñiga–Olivares faction takes over.

**1622**   On the death of Zúñiga, Olivares becomes favourite.

**1624**   The Castilian cortes rejects most of Olivares' recommendations for reform. France invades the Valtelline.

**1625**   Spain at war with France and England. Victories in the Netherlands.

**1626**   Unpopular scheme for increased army recruitment across the empire. Dutch war carries on after Olivares insists on 'impossible' peace terms.

**1628**   Financial crisis; 50 per cent devaluation of currency. Dutch capture Spanish silver fleet off Cuba. Spanish intervention in Mantua.

**1630**   Loss of Pernambuco in Brazil (centre of sugar industry) to the Dutch.

**1631**   Mantuan war ends in Spanish failure.

| | |
|---|---|
| **1635** | Spain engaged in total war with France. Fresh taxes to pay for it. |
| **1640** | Revolts in Catalonia and Portugal following attempt to force more recruitment out of Catalonia; royal government overthrown. |
| **1642** | French military successes in border province of Roussillon. |
| **1643** | Olivares dismissed; he dies two years later. |

## Overview

As in France, the Spanish state was governed more by favourites than kings in the first half of the seventeenth century. These were Lerma (1598–1618) and Olivares (1622–43). Philip II had wanted to rule his empire as an absolute monarch, involved in all decisions. His son, Philip III, had no desire to rule in such a 'hands-on' way and delegated power to Lerma. Although Lerma's leadership was generally good for Spain, his quest for personal fortune may have contributed to his one major mistake, the expulsion of the productive Morisco community. Peace with the United Provinces, England and France (the *Pax Hispanica*), allowed Spain to recover from the hugely expensive war policy of Philip II. Diplomacy was given a chance to achieve what war had not: Spanish domination without extortionate expense and without the immediate risk of loss. However, the lack of initiative in domestic policies meant that a peacetime opportunity to tackle some of Spain's deep-seated problems was not taken.

The young Philip IV was a pleasure-loving king, content to leave the running of his empire to Olivares, an ambitious and very hard-working favourite. In foreign policy Olivares carried on where his uncle, Zúñiga, had left off. War was resumed with the United Provinces and over the next 20 years Spanish forces were sent to fight the French, the English and the Protestant rebels of Bohemia. This foreign policy was accompanied by a big push for domestic reform, the main aspects of which were centralising power and spreading the tax and military burdens across all the provinces of Spain and the empire. A broad-ranging reform package offended so many vested interests that most of the proposals were rejected. Anger over the reforms led to major revolts in Portugal and Catalonia in 1640. Portugal's revolt succeeded, and this valuable nation and empire passed out of Spanish control for good.

## What were the problems of governing Spain?

At the start of the seventeenth century Spain was the greatest power in the world. By marriage alliances, conquests and a measure of chance, the Spanish Habsburgs had inherited an extensive European empire and a world empire

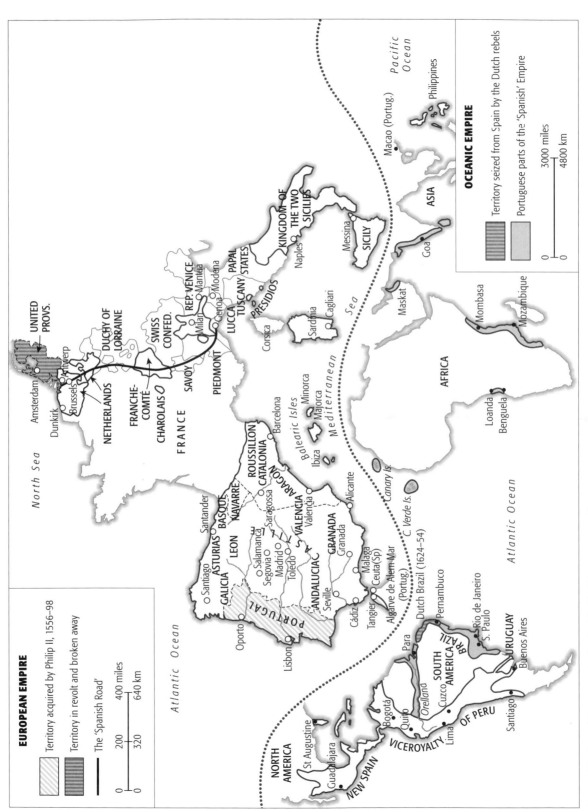

**EUROPEAN EMPIRE**

Territory acquired by Philip II, 1556–98

Territory in revolt and broken away

The 'Spanish Road'

0    200    400 miles
0    320    640 km

**OCEANIC EMPIRE**

Territory seized from Spain by the Dutch rebels

Portuguese parts of the 'Spanish' Empire

0    3000 miles
0    4800 km

*North Sea*

*Atlantic Ocean*

*Mediterranean Sea*

*Pacific Ocean*

*Atlantic Ocean*

UNITED PROVS.

Amsterdam
Dunkirk
Antwerp
Brussels
NETHERLANDS
DUCHY OF LORRAINE
FRANCHE-COMTÉ
CHAROLAIS
SWISS CONFED.
SAVOY
PIEDMONT
FRANCE

REP. VENICE
Milan
Mantua
Modena
Genoa
LUCCA
TUSCANY
PAPAL STATES
PRESIDIOS
KINGDOM OF THE TWO SICILIES
Naples
Messina
SICILY

Santander
GALICIA
Santiago
ASTURIAS
LEON
Salamanca
Segovia
Madrid
Toledo
CASTILE
BASQUE
NAVARRE
Saragossa
ARAGON
ROUSSILLON
CATALONIA
Barcelona
VALENCIA
Valencia
Alicante
Minorca
Majorca
Ibiza
*Balearic Isles*

PORTUGAL
Oporto
Lisbon
ANDALUCIA
Seville
Cádiz
GRANADA
Granada
Málaga
Tangier
Ceuta (Sp)
Algarve de Alem-Mar (Portug.)

Corsica
Sardinia
Cagliari

*Canary Is.*
*C. Verde Is.*

AFRICA
ASIA

Maskat
Goa
Macao (Portug.)
Philippines

Mombasa
Mozambique
Loanda
Benguela

NORTH AMERICA
St Augustine
Guadalajara
NEW SPAIN

Bogotá
Quito
Orellana
Cuzco
Lima
Santiago
VICEROYALTY OF PERU

Dutch Brazil (1624–54)
Pernambuco
Para
S. Paulo
Rio de Janeiro
BRAZIL
SOUTH AMERICA
URUGUAY
Buenos Aires

**Map 3: Spain and its empire in the first half of the seventeenth century.**

that spanned four continents. This empire had doubled in size with the acquisition of Portugal in 1581, for Portugal itself had built up an empire in South America, Africa and the East Indies. In spite of this, indeed partly because of this, Spain was confronted with several deep problems.

- Economically, Spain's own resources were under-developed and it was too dependent on bullion imports from the Americas for the financing of costly wars and a lavish court. Plague had a devastating effect on Castile between 1596 and 1602.
- Socially, the country was notorious for extremes of wealth and poverty and the laziness of its over-numerous nobles and clergy. There was no commercial middle class to speak of.
- Ethnically, a large and oppressed but very productive Islamic minority in the south had been driven into rebellion in the sixteenth century. If the logical final step of expulsion was taken, there would be serious economic damage.
- Politically, Spain's provinces were very independent minded, leaving Castile to shoulder most of the financial burden.
- Imperially, Spain had five major problems. The empire was huge, disjointed, diverse and rebellious. Like all empires, it was expensive to defend.

Spain's rulers had to find remedies or they might soon decline from superpower status. Each problem is worth some further attention, partly to reinforce the point that Spain had great strengths as well as weaknesses. Without those strengths it would not have risen to its exalted status and it would have declined much more rapidly than it did.

## The economy

Although there were deep problems at foundation level, Spain's economy was far from collapse at the end of the sixteenth century. Before 1600 there was economic prosperity. Spanish textile and metal manufacture had grown in the fifteenth and early sixteenth centuries, making Spain a leading producer in both industries. Spanish agriculture was providing enough to feed the population, though the situation varied considerably from region to region. Large areas of the Castilian interior were barren, just as they are today. However, by using irrigation south-east Spain produced not only wheat, oil, silk, wine, fruit and wool, but even sugar. Under Moorish stimulus, the region was also industrially vibrant, producing metal goods, leather, paper and steel. An even greater range of raw materials came from Central America. Barcelona, in the north-east, was a major ship-building and Mediterranean trading port.

Spain's undoing was partly that it had had it too good in the sixteenth century. With a low population in Iberia itself, it was self-sufficient in textiles and food, the basics for survival. By conquest and plunder in South and Central

America, the Spanish had come into the possession of so much gold and silver ('bullion') that they had succumbed to the temptation to pay for things with the help of imported bullion. When a country does this and its economy is not sufficiently dynamic to back up the expenditure, the result is high inflation. This was what happened in sixteenth-century Spain. If the bullion flow were to dry up or be cut, the country would be in severe economic difficulties, especially as it had failed to develop its industry and agriculture in the meantime.

Why were there economic problems in Spain?

## Society

Writing in 1600, soon after the onset of a terrible and prolonged plague, Martín **Cellorigo** complained of the extreme contrast of rich and poor, the laziness of the rich and the need for the kind of commercially minded middle class that was found elsewhere in Europe. Research has shown that his analysis was not accurate. Such a description could well have applied equally to most states of Europe at this time, but Spain was the worst in western Europe.

'Our condition is one in which we have rich who loll at ease, or poor who beg, and we lack people of the middling sort' (**Cellorigo**, *Memorial*, 1600).

Most of the aristocracy saw their ownership of the land simply as a sign of status. In the seventeenth century they enlarged the size of their estates to increase their prestige. Increasingly they were absentee landlords, preferring to be away finding favour at court. Below the aristocracy was an unusually large lesser nobility, the **hidalgos**. Since hidalgos did not pay taxes, anyone with any hope of finding a noble person in their ancestry claimed to be a hidalgo. Similarly swollen in number, partly because they too did not have to pay taxes, were the clergy, some 200,000 of them in 1660 (out of a population of 15 million). This left the peasantry to pay the taxes. Since they were fewer in number as a result of emigration and plague and were paying tithes to the church and rent to the landlord in addition to taxes to the state, they were in a desperate state. The few rich peasants exploited the many more poor ones. Landless peasants drifted to the town, where, in overcrowded shacks, they died in great numbers from infections.

About 10 per cent of the entire population of Spain claimed lesser noble or **hidalgo** status.

Spain, apart from Barcelona and the recently conquered ex-Moorish cities of Granada, was the least commercialised of European states. The small middle class was excluded from running town affairs by powerful local nobles. The church, though more firmly harnessed to the needs of the royal government than it had been a century before, was still hugely powerful and influential. Religious crusading had come before economic sense once before with the expulsion of the Jews in 1498; in 1598 the question was whether it would do so once again in the case of the productive Morisco community.

### Ethnic divisions

The Spanish Inquisition of the fifteenth and sixteenth centuries had been directed against all 'heresies'. By 1600 Spain was a rigidly Catholic state.

Spanish Jews and Protestants had already been ethnically cleansed: the Jews expelled and the Protestants forced to give up their faith. Spain's largest ethnic minority was the Moriscos, the descendants of the Moors who had conquered most of Iberia in the early Middle Ages. By 1600 they had been driven to the southern and eastern fringes of Spain. About a third of the population of Aragon and Valencia was Muslim and about half of them stayed put after the reconquest of Moorish Spain in the 1480s. Within a decade of Christian reconquest, Islam was outlawed and mosques converted into churches. Forced conversions followed. In popular speech the Moriscos were referred to as 'dogs'. Morisco customs and culture – their dances, food and dress – were ridiculed and prohibited. Those caught in acts of defiance were tortured and sentenced to be whipped or put into galley service. A Moorish rebellion (1568–71), combined with anxieties about the high rate of growth of the Morisco population, raised the fears of the majority community to fever pitch. By 1582 the Spanish government had already decided in principle on a policy of expulsion.

Spain's ethnic divisions did not stop there. There were Catalans to the east, Basques to the north, Portuguese and Galicians to the west. All spoke their own languages and viewed the royal government in Madrid with intense suspicion. Catalonia's closeness to France presented the French with the prospect of co-operation with Catalan rebels to break up Spain's fragile union.

## Political strengths and weaknesses

The unification of Spain – from the kingdoms of Castile and Aragon at the end of the fifteenth century and the later additions of Granada and Portugal – had been achieved fairly recently. Apart from ruthlessly enforced adherence to the Catholic faith by the Inquisition, there was little to hold these once proudly independent kingdoms together. They kept most of their own former privileges, parliaments and exemptions from taxes and military service. The potential for disintegration was always there. While appearing to be an all-powerful absolute monarch, in reality Philip II had maintained his authority only by permitting a large degree of independent control to the provinces of Spain and the colonies in Europe and America.

What factors made it difficult to govern Spain?

## The last years of Philip II: Spain on the eve of Lerma's coming to power

The empire was not only a source of plunder and of copious raw materials, but also an outlet for potentially rebellious, ambitious nobles. Spanish Italy, with a far greater population than Spain, was also a valuable source of manpower for the armed forces. If the empire had been whittled down to these colonies it might have proved an advantage for Spain. However, Spain's rulers were intent on keeping it all. When Philip II combined his instinct to preserve

Spain's high 'reputation' (a word often used by Spanish nobles and ministers) in the world with a determination to champion the cause of the Counter-Reformation, the result was massive **over-commitment**. Philip II saddled his successors with military and financial burdens, in particular with wars in the Netherlands, France, the borders of the Holy Roman Empire and England.

The Netherlands, economically the most valuable of Spain's colonies, had been divided by revolt for almost 40 years at the time of Philip II's death in 1598. The northern provinces of the Netherlands had broken off completely, beating off determined Spanish attempts to reassert control. Philip II's attempts to subdue Protestant England in the 1580s and 1590s had culminated in embarrassing defeats at sea. His attempts to create a Catholic client state in France had also failed. Increasingly powerful themselves, the English and the Dutch looked with envious eyes at the Spanish Empire and were ever ready to intercept its bullion ships, acquire its trade and seize its trading posts outside Europe.

## How effective were Spain's kings and their ministers?
### King Philip III

Philip III used to be seen as an incompetent king, but most historians now hold a different view. His father, **Philip II**, was a hard, cold man who thought that his son would make a weak ruler, which did not do much for the young man's confidence. When his flinty father died in 1598 and Philip III came to the throne at the age of 20, he asserted himself by dismissing most of his father's ministers. He turned against Philip II's whole style of government, trusting ministers and councils to rule responsibly, which on the whole they did. The council of state was once again given a leading role and the duke of Lerma was given the powers of a chief minister. This delegation of powers was a more modern approach to government than Philip II's. It was a recognition of the fact that that the empire was too vast and complex for one man's government. Instead of worrying over the day-to-day affairs of his kingdoms, Philip III enjoyed himself by hunting or going on pilgrimages to religious shrines. He stayed in touch with affairs by taking Lerma and the council of state with him.

Philip III had begun his reign by continuing the war against England and stepping up the campaign in the Netherlands. Following Lerma's dismissal in 1618 he determined to act as his own first minister. Unfortunately, he once again succumbed to the war-mongers amongst his advisers. He died unexpectedly in 1621 at the age of 42, leaving his 16-year-old son to succeed him.

## The duke of Lerma

Don Francisco Gómez de Sandoval y Rojas, the fifth marquis of Denia and the first duke of Lerma, born 1553, could be readily mistaken for a king in Rubens' imposing portrait. It was useful for him to be seen in such a light and Philip's endorsement of his supreme authority in 1612 probably reflects the need for both Philip and Lerma to shrug off the challenge of powerful, critical rivals.

The duke of Lerma, by Rubens (c. 1603), Prado Museum, Madrid. What message is the portrait intended to put across?

**Nepotism** is the showing of undue favour by appointing one's relatives to office.

Why did Philip III and Lerma work well together?

Like Richelieu, Lerma was dedicated to two things: himself and his state. He saw no contradiction between, on the one hand, leadership of the whole state on the king's behalf and, on the other, the amassing of a vast personal fortune and procurement of top jobs for his family and friends. By the end of his period in power he had created a fortune of 3 million ducats (about £1 million) and raised the standing of his family. Naturally, such open **nepotism** and fortune-seeking made him many enemies.

Lerma's style of leadership was rather like that of his patron, Philip III. He ruled from behind the scenes, attending very few of the meetings of the council of state. At the same time he made sure his advice was heard by the king, rarely being apart from Philip when he went on his frequent travels. Lerma did not like to get caught up in the minute details of day-to-day administration, leaving that to the councils of state, finance and war. When special commissions were required he used smaller groups of hand-picked men, the juntas.

Lerma was much criticised at the time, especially by admirers of his father and by powerful rivals, but his foreign policy is now mostly seen in a positive light by historians. Swimming against the tide of opinion amongst the king's advisers, Lerma negotiated peace with England (1604) and the United Provinces (1609). For over a decade – a long stretch in this war-obsessed period – this secured peace. Spain lost no more of its empire. Both conflicts had reached stalemate and to continue them would have involved even greater expenditure for the already overstretched Spanish treasury, with no certainty of victory. There were frequent mutinies in Spain's armies in the Netherlands. Peace gave Spain a breathing space – though, of course, the same can be said for Spain's enemies. Against this, some historians have argued that the successes of Spínola, commander of the army, against the Dutch in 1605–06 only needed to be followed through for the victory to be Spain's. Others have argued that the peace with the Dutch was gained at too high a price. A ruinous blockade of Antwerp, the chief city of the Spanish Netherlands, was allowed to continue, to the advantage of Amsterdam, chief port of the United Provinces. In similar vein, the Dutch were allowed to stay in conquered East Indian territory, their independence was acknowledged and the position of Dutch Catholics continued to be insecure.

In the period of peace following the truce with the United Provinces, Spanish diplomats succeeded in providing their state with a powerful and influential voice in the courts of western and southern Europe. It helped that Henry IV, France's strong and anti-Spanish king, had been assassinated in 1610. A Habsburg dynastic alliance with France in 1615 – Louis XIII married Anne of Austria while the future Philip IV married Elisabeth of France – increased Spanish influence in France. However, the French adventure was to be short lived as Louis XIII turned against the Spanish connection (see Chapter 3). For a while, Spain's supremacy was widely recognised. The English playwright Ben Jonson joked in *The alchemist* (1610):

> Your Spanish jennet is the best horse. Your Spanish
> Stoup is the best garb. Your Spanish beard
> Is the best cut. Your Spanish ruffs are the best
> Wear. Your Spanish Pavan the best dance . . .
> And as for your Spanish pike
> And Spanish blade, let your poor Captain speak.

Broadly successful in foreign policy, Lerma was less convincing in his domestic policies. The ending of wars saved a great deal of expenditure, but revenues still fell short of spending. In that he did not attempt a major tax overhaul, spreading the burden more fairly across Spain's constituent provinces, he shirked the necessary task taken on by Olivares. Worse still, his decision to expel the Moriscos in 1609 was a serious economic mistake, whatever the benefits sometimes claimed for this as a means of unifying the Christian majority of Spain. Against their will, 300,000 out of Spain's 320,000 Moriscos were transported to north Africa on Italian galleys. Families of mixed marriages were forcibly split by the **expulsion**. Those that were allowed to stay were told to pass on their skills in farming and irrigation. The idea was to replace the remainder with Castilians, but this did not happen. By 1700 only a thousand had resettled in the once thriving towns of southern Spain that the Moriscos had left. Spain had lost a source of manpower, tax revenue, rents and the most productive part of its economically active population.

In a speech for one of his characters, Cervantes wrote that the **expulsion** was 'expelling poisonous fruit from Spain'. A Morisco saw it quite differently: 'wherever we are we weep for Spain, for we were born there and it is our native land', (Kilsby, *Spain – rise and decline*, 1986, pp. 90, 91).

Why did Lerma agree to the expulsion? Pressure had been building for it for 40 years but short-term considerations were more important. In 1609 Lerma was looking for a popular policy to balance his unpopular peace with the Dutch. Expulsion was favoured by the church and the masses in Castile, though not wanted by the parliament of Castile or the kingdom of Aragon, who knew how much southern Spain depended on the Moriscos. Furthermore, Lerma and his patrons stood to gain from the expulsion as they would take over the lands left by the Moriscos; Lerma owned estates in the region they inhabited.

Why did Lerma fall from power?

Lerma had made enemies because of his nepotism and his foreign policy. After about 1615 there were signs that he was losing his influence on policy-making to the activists led by Zúñiga, who wanted Spain to give a full commitment to joint Habsburg interests in Europe. Philip retired Lerma in 1618, at the age of 65. He remained on good terms with him, elevating his son, the duke of Uceda, to the status of favourite, but chose to rule alone at last.

*Philip IV of Spain*
(1605–65), by Velásquez, Prado Museum, Madrid. Philip was also a lover of poetry, carnivals, paintings, architecture, plays and mysticism. He took mistresses and fathered illegitimate children.

Baltasar de **Zúñiga** (d. 1622), a career diplomat, was pro-Austrian and a believer in assertive Spanish foreign policy. He was very influential on Philip IV in the king's last years and on his nephew Olivares.

Why did a change of monarch often mean a change in the dominant faction as well?

### King Philip IV

The young Philip IV not only lacked confidence but was also lazy and uninterested in state responsibilities, in spite of the strictures of Olivares that he must not evade his share of the burden, under pain of grave and mortal sin. However, later in life Philip IV became more conscientious following a serious illness in 1627, which he saw as God's judgement on his laziness. As a young man he revelled in a life of pleasure at court, a court famous for its luxury, decadence and vicious intrigues. As a middle-aged man he turned to the more sedate pleasures of translating history books.

### The triumph of the Zúñiga faction and its new champion, Olivares

A change of monarch always presented rival aristocratic factions with the chance to seize the power behind the throne. Philip III's premature death presented just such an opportunity to the Olivares faction (this consisted of Zúñiga, Guzmán, Haro and Olivares – all of whom were related). **Zúñiga** was the leader and Olivares was the keen young champion ready to step into his uncle's shoes. By pushing successfully for a change in direction to a more active foreign policy over the last few years of Philip III's reign, Zúñiga and his supporters were already in a strong position to take over. When Philip III died, the career of Lerma and his faction effectively died with him. Lerma himself was an old man. He had made himself a cardinal to obtain immunity from the takeover bid that he had been anticipating. Lerma kept his head but had some of his fortune taken away. His son was not so lucky. Zúñiga had him sent to prison, where he died. By 1622 Zúñiga and Olivares were ruling together; had he lived perhaps historians would write of the Zúñiga period rather than the Olivares period. Fortunately for Olivares, his uncle died in October 1622, leaving the way clear for the younger man.

A hard-working minister was just what the young Philip IV needed when it came to the difficult task of running the empire. At 34, Gaspar de Guzmán (Olivares) was almost exactly twice Philip's age. He came from one of the leading aristocratic families. He had been born and brought up in Italy where his father had been Spanish viceroy in Sicily and Naples. Olivares was very intelligent and worked hard, but he had one big fault. Once he was convinced that he was right, nothing would shift him from his chosen course of action. He would pursue the most ambitous and unrealistic of schemes, refusing to adjust them in the face of criticism. He had no capacity for compromise.

Already holding several honorary titles, in 1625 Olivares became a duke and was from then onwards known as the count-duke. These titles yielded him a tremendous income. He steadily increased his power and wealth throughout the 1620s and 1630s, in spite of repeated policy setbacks and some outright failures. It is sometimes claimed that he was entirely honest and above self-interest, but the evidence points in the opposite direction with regard to the last point. Like Lerma before him, and like Richelieu and Mazarin in France, he used his powerful position to promote his family and friends to leading positions in the royal household and government.

## Policies

Olivares' chief concern was to maintain Spain's reputation as the greatest of powers. Wars were no longer to be avoided, as they had been under Lerma. However, to underpin such a policy, there was a need to grapple with fundamental problems in the finance and government of the country. He created a junta for reformation in 1622, his first move being to try to stop vices, abuses and bribes. His objectives were commendable but far too extensive and bold to be achievable in every respect. He wanted to reduce the absurdly high number of office-holders, cut court expenditure, close brothels, reduce emigration, simplify the tax system, create a national banking system and broaden responsibility for defence beyond Castile.

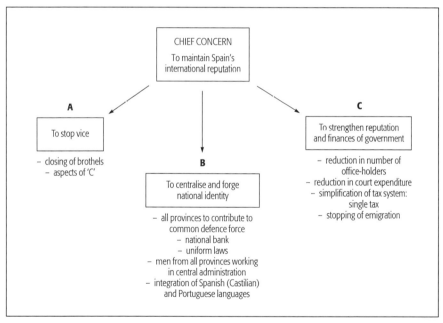

**Aims of the domestic policy of Olivares.**

In addition to having too many plans, Olivares made a number of tactical mistakes. He attempted to introduce most of his reform programme at one go, offending too many powerful people. When the laws were finally put before the Castilian **Cortes** for approval, it refused to back most of them. In 1624 the new single tax was abandoned and a tax on food (the 'millones') reintroduced. These were major setbacks for Olivares; the result was that it was not possible

There were separate **Cortes**, or parliaments, in Castile, Aragon and Catalonia. The Cortes of Castile, in Madrid, later became the national parliament of Spain.

**Mantua** was an independent dukedom of strategic importance because of its location near Spanish-owned Milan. In 1628 Richelieu and Olivares backed rival candidates to the succession of the vacant dukedom. The Mantua campaign cost 10 million ducats (over £3 million), at a time when Spain was already at war with the United Provinces.

**Imperialists** are supporters of aggressive expansion of empire.

Why did the outlying provinces of Spain rebel against Olivares?

to balance budgets through the tax system. In the face of failure to reform tax, cut down the spending of the court and raise money from the Catalans, he continued to pursue an expensive war policy. Olivares' armed intervention in **Mantua** in 1628 led to a costly and unsuccessful two-year war. It also provided an excuse to Richelieu to start a longer-term campaign against Spanish control of Italy. The result was that by the early 1640s Spain was in deep crisis. The state was bankrupted in 1647 and 1652. Olivares might reasonably be blamed for this. His attempt to bring in long-overdue reforms was brave. Having failed to achieve those objectives, he would have been wise to modify his aims in foreign policy by scaling them down.

With the prospect of total failure staring him in the face, Olivares began to push more strongly than ever for centralisation, which he saw as the key to all his policies. He had reason. Spain would be stronger if all the parts contributed more to the whole enterprise. The rich province of Catalonia in particular needed to be brought under the tighter control of Madrid. Olivares believed this had to be done, whatever the opposition. However, to the Catalans and Portuguese Olivares was simply a dangerous Castilian **imperialist**. He was regarded as being as much of a foreigner and an enemy as the English have been to the Irish or to the Welsh for long periods of their history. Olivares proceeded with his centralising plans in the face of formidable opposition from the Portuguese and the Catalans – who, up to this point in their history, had been permitted to pursue a largely independent line under the Spanish monarchy. He insisted on the uniformity of law for the whole of Spain and employed men from the former kingdoms in his administration. He tried to create a common defence force and even tried to integrate the Spanish and Portuguese languages. Olivares was not known for his flexibility in the face of criticism, and the results were personally disastrous and almost fatal for Spain. His measures sparked off rebellions in the Basque provinces, Portugal and Catalonia. Long after the damage was done, in 1643, Olivares was sacked and retired to his estates, a bitter man.

### Olivares and Richelieu – a comparison

France and Spain were large countries at a comparable level of development. Richelieu and Olivares were trying to do similar things – centralise, increase the powers of royal government, reduce those of the provincial nobility, and increase income from taxation.

In some respects Olivares was faced with a harder job than Richelieu. The Iberian peninsula, what we might call Spain proper, was itself a huge and diverse country. The kinds of problems of control arising from distance, already noted for France, were greater here. Across the empire they were even worse; it took at least a fortnight for a letter from Madrid to reach Milan or

Brussels. Spain was even more recently united than France and therefore there were different laws, customs barriers and languages prevailed in different regions. Provincial nobles and provincial parliaments (the cortes) were used to holding sway. They were not ready to give up their powers or to start paying taxes for the sake of a remote royal government. For his part, Olivares was just as uncompromising as the opposition; Richelieu had the sense to compromise when it suited him, though he never lost sight of his objectives. Olivares boiled with anger at what he saw as the selfish obstinacy of the provinces. He tried hard but, lacking Richelieu's guile and skill with propaganda, he found his policies collapsed. Yet Richelieu, even with his greater managerial skills, also failed to carry the people with him. Neither of the chief ministers made any significant progress in developing their economies. In short, it can be argued that in both countries there were not simply failures to carry out wise policies in the face of unreasonable and selfish opposition, but policies that were ill-chosen in the first place. Only a few years after Richelieu's death the Fronde revolts gave voice to pent-up anger about unpopular policies. Spain's equivalent to the Fronde, the several major revolts of the 1640s, nearly brought about the complete disintegration of the Spanish Empire and the mother country itself.

> Why did the reforms planned by Olivares fail?

## Historical sources

## Frustration of the policies of Olivares

Sources 1 to 4 mark the different stages in Olivares' career in his own words. Source 5, the observation of an outsider, provides us with a clue to the reasons why he failed. What else was involved?

### 1 Olivares advises the king to extend his powers

The most important piece of business in your Monarchy is for Your Majesty to make yourself King of Spain. By this I mean, Sir, that [you] should not be content with being king of Portugal, Aragon and Valencia and Count of Barcelona, but should work and secretly scheme to reduce these kingdoms of which Spain is composed to the style and laws of Castile, with no differentiation in the form of frontiers, customs posts, the power to convoke the Cortes of wherever, and the unrestrained appointment of ministers of different nations.

Source: Olivares to King Philip IV, his 'Great Memorial', 25 December 1624
(in G. Darby, *Spain in the seventeenth century*, 1994. pp. 100–01).

*Revolt and decline in Spain: Lerma and Olivares* **81**

## 2 Olivares blackens the name of a rival

Your Majesty has lost land and <u>reputation</u> in all parts because of the presumption . . . of Spínola's policies. Everywhere he has been willing to sacrifice honour for peace.

Source: Olivares to King Philip IV, 1630 (Darby, 1994, p. 103).

## 3 Olivares attacks provincial obstinacy

By now I am nearly at my wit's end, but I say, and I shall be saying at my deathbed, that if the constitutions do not allow this, then the devil take the constitutions.

Source: Olivares, October 1639 (in J. H. Elliott, *Imperial Spain*, 1963, p. 375).

## 4 Olivares attacks the Catalans

. . . forgive my language . . . but no king in the world has a province like Catalonia. It has a king and lord, but it renders him no services, even when its own safety is at stake. This king and lord can do nothing that he wants in it, nor even things that need to be done. If he invades it, the king has to defend it without the help from the inhabitants.

Source: Olivares, 29 February 1640, letter to the viceroy of Catalonia (Darby, 1994, p. 105).

## 5 Insight into a flawed personality

Olivares loves novelties, allowing his lively mind to . . . hit upon impossible designs as easy of achievement. For this reason he is desolated by misfortune: the difficulties proposed to him at the beginning he brushes aside.

Source: The Venetian ambassador (J. Kilsby, *Spain: rise and decline*, 1986, p. 92).

## Historical-source questions

1   Study Sources 1 and 2. Explain the passages underlined.
2   With reference to the content and tone of Sources 1 to 4, explain how they show Olivares' increasing frustration with his attempts to carry through his reform programme.
3   Use the sources and your own knowledge to explain the difficulties that frustrated the achievement of Olivares' reform programme.

## Summary question

1 (a) Explain the domestic and foreign policies of *either* Lerma *or* Olivares.

(b) How far did the different personalities of Lerma and Olivares contribute to their different levels of success?

# 6 The extent of decline in Spain

## Focus questions

◆ What were the problems of governing Spain in its period of deepest crisis (*c.*1640–60)?

◆ Why were there economic problems?

◆ How far did Spain remain a major power?

## *Significant dates*

| | |
|---|---|
| 1560s | Revolts in the Spanish Netherlands and recently conquered Granada. The Dutch rebels are successful and fight on. |
| 1580 | With the acquisition of Portugal and its overseas empire, Spain reaches its peak in size and power. |
| 1640 | Outbreak of revolts in Portugal and Catalonia. |
| 1643 | Dismissal of Olivares; Philip IV resolves to rule without a favourite. Spanish army of Flanders defeated by the French at the Battle of Rocroi. |
| 1645 | French successes in the campaign in Flanders; Dunkirk taken. |
| 1646 | Spain concedes Dutch independence and recognises Dutch colonial conquests from Portugal. |
| 1648 | Bankruptcy declared. Revolts in Sicily, Naples and Granada. Conspiracy in Aragon. Catastrophic harvests. Plague in Andalucia. The Peace of Westphalia confirms Spanish loss of northern Netherlands (United Provinces). |
| 1652 | Second bankruptcy declared. |
| 1652 | Spain captures Casale in Italy and Dunkirk in Flanders and, over the next two years, Ypres and Mardyck (1653), Rocroi (1654) and all of Catalonia. |
| 1656 | Against the advice of his ministers, Philip IV rejects a peace deal with France. Plague in Naples weakens the war effort by ruining its economy. Two silver fleets are captured by the English. |
| 1658 | Spain defeated by French and English forces at Battle of the Dunes. |
| 1659 | Peace of the Pyrenees confirms French gains from Spain. |

## Overview

In 1776 a historian called Edward Gibbon wrote a famous book called *The decline and fall of the Roman Empire*. The reasons why very powerful states decline and sometimes dramatically fall fascinate historians.

The Catalonian revolt and Mazarin's all-out war effort between 1643 and 1647 put a tremendous strain on Spain. It could not match French military expenditure. High taxation and poor harvests brought further revolts in Spanish Italy and Granada in 1647. Combined with bankruptcy, these brought the government to a crisis point. However, the revolts failed and the Fronde revolts in France between 1648 and 1653 gave Spain a chance to recover. The price of renewed success on the battlefront was an even higher financial burden and a deeper economic crisis. With the Frondes out of the way, the campaign went France's way again in the late 1650s and the eventual peace settlement (1659) favoured France.

Spain's kings, ministers and social elite failed to rise to the challenge of investing in economic growth for the time when the bullion would run out. Neither Spain nor its empire's excellent resources were developed, either agriculturally or industrially. Expenditure exceeded revenue and too much of the tax and manpower burden fell on Spanish Italy (see Map 3, page 70). Actual tax revenues fell far short of what they should have been. Terrible plagues, deepening poverty and emigration meant that Spain and Spanish Italy were less and less able to sustain the burden. Defence of the empire on the seas and within Europe took up even more of the already over-stretched military budget. With the loss of the northern Netherlands and the Portuguese Empire Spain lost valuable territories. To different degrees, Spain's weaknesses were common to almost every state in Europe, and it therefore remained a great power in the late seventeenth century.

## What were the problems of governing Spain in its period of deepest crisis (c. 1640–60)?

### From one revolt to another: the crisis period of the 1640s

Revolts in Catalonia and Portugal in 1640 were directed against Castilian domination of the Spanish state. They were a reaction to the hated centralisation and high taxation policies of Olivares. In 1639 a less stubborn man than Olivares might have done a U-turn. In that year complaints reached him from all over the empire that taxation had reached saturation point. Instead, he targeted Catalonia to supply him with the extra military support it had denied a few years earlier. The Catalan cortes refused to increase their level of military support, insisting that their historical rights were being infringed. Antony

Sherley from England observed that 'Portugal is opposed to government by Castile and in everything remains an old enemy' (R. A. Stradling, *Europe and the decline of Spain*, 1981, p. 26). Though there were strong elements of social revolution, these were small-nation revolts; the peasant army that seized Barcelona attacked public buildings and killed the Spanish viceroy. In as much as the reason for the centralisation scheme was to increase tax revenues and the state's military capacity, the uprisings shared the same underlying causes as the Fronde revolts in France. The pronounced regionalism of Spain and poor leadership on the part of Olivares were Spanish-specific factors, but a deeper issue far from unique to Spain was arguably even more significant: the addiction of European royal governments to warfare.

The people's revolt in Catalonia was suppressed within six months, leadership having been taken away from the peasants by the nobility – who had second thoughts when they saw it turning into a revolution of the poor against the rich. Catalonia then became a pawn in the power struggle between France and Spain, with the Catalan elite offering Catalonia to the Bourbons of France in exchange for military support against the rebels and the Spanish monarchy. The French gladly pledged that support in exchange for French sovereignty. A war between the French and Spanish was fought in Catalonia over the next 12 years. Spain was ultimately victorious, the French having made themselves exacting and unpopular overlords. So many resources were poured into the recapture of Catalonia that the Spanish crown did not have enough left to push hard enough against Portugal. The Portuguese fought a bitter and prolonged war with great determination. As a result Portugal remained independent.

Revolts seven years later in Sicily, Naples and Granada were inspired by a different set of factors, not without some overlap with the earlier ones. Rather than being small nation break-away bids, these dramatic popular insurrections were caused by bad harvests (widespread across Europe in 1647), high taxes and local resentment of noble privilege. In Sicily the social elite was having none of this disruption and rallied to the Spanish viceroy. They went on to help in the suppression of a even more serious revolt in nearby Naples. The Neapolitans had had to suffer the largest increase in taxation of their recent history, the burden falling most heavily on the poor. Grievances over taxation schemes on staple foodstuffs like fruit, poor harvests and increasing prices led to a rising of peasants and the urban poor in July 1647. It is important to note that their first target was not their Spanish overlords but their own upper classes, for they had begun to suspect that the landowners, bankers, tax-collectors and grain merchants were working together to create new taxes and raise prices. They declared Naples a republic. However, the nobles soon regained control and, as in Catalonia, offered their province to

What were the causes of the revolts in Spain?

Why were there insurrections in some provinces?

What does the failure of the revolts in Catalonia and Spanish Italy tell us about the strengths of the Spanish state, even during its decline?

France. The subsequent French military campaign was botched and the revolt disintegrated, with townsmen, peasants and nobility quarelling amongst themselves.

### Partial recovery in the 1650s

Spain was saved from further disintegration and collapse in this period only because the French people were reacting in a similar way to similar unpopular policies in their own country. The Fronde revolts weakened French military campaigns and took the heat off Spain for a while. This did not last for long. The eager Louis XIV and Mazarin could not wait to get back to war after the failure of the second Fronde in 1653. When they did so, the tide of battle turned once more in France's favour.

Poor leadership was a significant factor in the failure to achieve more than a slight recovery by the end of the 1650s. King Philip IV decided that the example of Olivares showed that favourites were not to be trusted with government. He frequently overruled the advice of his able first minister, **Haro**, generally with disastrous results. Approaching a financial crisis in 1647, Philip rejected Haro's scheme to use some of the income earned by the state on loans to the crown in favour of a declaration of bankruptcy (debt conversion). Payment was denied on short-term loans worth 10 million ducats, causing severe difficulties for the bankers who had kept Spain solvent for two decades. Even more foolishly, Philip – against the advice of all his ministers – refused to make a peace deal with France in 1656, when Spain had a marginal advantage over its enemy. Holding out for another three years proved to be an expensive mistake, financially and strategically. The debt grew enormous.

# Why were there economic problems?

### Economic and social problems

Economic strength was vital if Spain was to remain a superpower. With more money and manpower Spain might have won more of its many wars. As it was, Spain's leaders had to make hard choices. The state's limited resources were prioritised for the war of reconquest against Catalonia and the increasingly defensive war against France. Unfortunately, this meant that too few troops remained for the war against the Portuguese and Dutch rebels.

Economic weakness was the result of several factors. First, there were problems associated with maximising tax revenues. Even without having superior natural resources, a more developed economy or a larger population than the Spanish Empire, France was able to raise twice as much tax revenue. This was achieved through the relentless pressure of royal officials such as the unpopular intendants. The French government also made no concessions

---

Don Luis de **Haro** (1598–1661), first minister 1643–61. A nephew of Olivares, he was quite different in temperament, being a realist in foreign policy and in his relations with the powerful nobles.

How did events outside Spain come to the rescue of the Spanish?

In what ways did Philip IV misjudge matters in the 1650s?

to provinces unwilling to pay up. Neither Lerma nor Olivares instituted anything like the intendant system. Olivares failed in his bid to extract more from rich Catalonia and Philip IV rejected Haro's inventive tax proposal of 1647. Finally, as in France, much of the tax revenue never reached the government, thanks to corruption and inefficiency. Officials at every level creamed it off; as much as a third may have vanished in this way. The result of Olivares' bid to share the tax burden evenly across the empire was that Castile and, above all, Naples grew increasingly bitter as they shouldered an excessive burden of tax.

The second major source of royal revenue was **gold and silver bullion**. This was not, as is sometimes imagined, the largest source of income. It was used as freely as it had been obtained to support a lavish royal court and an extravagant lifestyle for the nobility, as well as to finance the numerous military campaigns. The results were inflation, indulgence of noble laziness and the most extravagant court in Europe. The gold and silver currency minted disappeared quickly. In the early seventeenth century much of the bullion was legally re-exported, while increasing amounts were seized by English and Dutch pirates. By 1650, 98 per cent of Spain's coinage was copper; the Dutch, the bankers and the sea-bed had most of the silver and gold. In the middle of the 1650s the Dutch sank two Spanish silver fleets, further depleting Spain's bullion stock.

Spain's overall wealth in natural resources has already been noted. The challenge was to make the most of it. Agriculture needed to be developed so that Spain might feed its people properly, giving them the strength to resist killer epidemics and an incentive not to emigrate. Sadly, it was not improved. Farming methods remained primitive. The landholding aristocrats invested nothing in better farming methods, valuing land only for the status and the rents it provided. Both arable and pasture farming suffered in the seventeenth century. Declining population meant shortages of labour and a higher tax bill for those who remained in the villages. Many were spending half their income paying taxes. This left them too poor either to feed themselves or to buy any manufactured goods, so weakening Spain's already struggling industries. The expulsion of the Moriscos from Valencia ruined agriculture there; after that Spain no longer produced enough grain to feed its people. Industry needed to be developed to reverse Spain's massive trade deficit. If it could have manufactured more ships, weapons and finished textiles it would have had to buy fewer from its rivals like the Dutch, who were supplying most of Spain's ships by the middle of the seventeenth century. By exporting the greater portion of its raw materials for manufacture elsewhere, it was being drawn into the same pattern of under-development that blights many Third World countries today. Reluctance of nobles and merchants to invest money in industry was

**Gold and silver bullion** was brought over from the Spanish mines in Central and South America. By the middle of the seventeenth century the mines were past maximum productivity and the metals were mostly in the form of a dwindling supply of coinage.

What were the results of the bullion imports?

The role of bad luck in history should be acknowledged for balance. Spain experienced poor climatic conditions in the 'mini Ice Age' (see p. 5). Output slumped in Castile during decades of floods and droughts (1589–1614). Harsh winters in southern Italy in 1611 and 1622 reduced the sheep stock by 80 per cent.

the problem; buying titles and land and lending money were easier options. Heavy taxes on manufactured goods and customs duties on the movement of goods between all of Spain's regions made development even less likely.

It is important to recognise that for a large and thinly populated state like Spain, sufficient human resources were as essential as good natural ones. In 1598 it barely had enough human resources. Castile needed the populous colonies of Spanish Italy and the more productive provinces of Catalonia, Andalucia and Granada more than these places needed Castile. They made a substantial contribution to the manpower needs of Spain's armies, the tax revenue for its wars and manufactured goods such as armaments. The industrial and agricultural productivity of the skilled peoples of these regions was high compared to that of Castile. Through **plague**, voluntary emigration due to poverty and the forced emigration of hundreds of thousands of Moriscos, the population of Spain and its empire went down in the first half of the seventeenth century. Castile's population declined from over 6 million in 1600 to less than 5 million in 1650. The population of Naples declined from 3 million to 2 million over the century and Milan dropped by a third to 800,000 in the plague year of 1630. It was no wonder that there were too few Castilians to replace the evicted Moriscos.

A **plague** epidemic between 1596 and 1602 affected most of Castile and led to the death of 10 per cent of the population. There was a second great plague between 1647 and 1652 which killed another half million people.

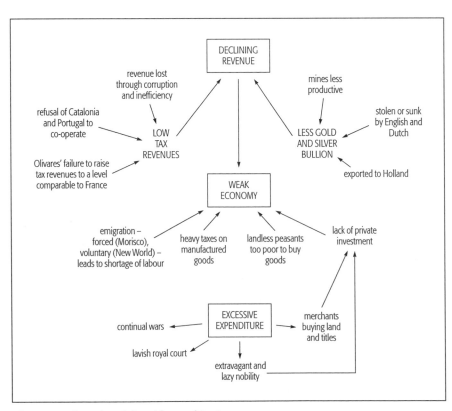

**The economic and social problems of Spain.**

Above all, Spain was in economic difficulties because of its leaders' refusal to make the state live within its means. Castile's huge trade deficit was financed by the indulgent practice of borrowing and re-exporting silver bullion. Philip IV made an effort to cut court expenditure (still 5 per cent of the national income) but more than cancelled this out by embarking on fresh wars. The result was that by the 1650s expenditure was regularly in excess of revenue and Spain went into the red. The state borrowed and spent.

What were the reasons for Spain's economic weakness?

## The empire

The possession of an empire has always been a source both of strengths and of problems for great powers, from the ancient Romans to the British Empire. The Spanish Empire was no exception. Gradually, over the first half of the seventeenth century, Spain's empire ceased to be an advantage and instead became a liability, a millstone round the government's neck.

The lure of precious metals made Spain's oceanic empire particularly envied by other powers. The English and Dutch, with strong navies, had the means to do more than simply watch. Their piratical engagements made increasing dents in Spanish bullion imports. The Dutch were also well aware of the potential value of the sugar, spices, coffee and **dye-woods** that came from Spain's American colonies. By the middle of the seventeenth century, thanks to their capture of Pernambuco in 1630, the Dutch had taken over half of Spain's profitable Brazilian sugar trade. Defence of the oceanic empire was an increasing expense in the first half of the seventeenth century; the Atlantic fleet cost about half of the value of the bullion imports.

**Dye-woods** are woods yielding dyes used in the textile industry.

Philip II had ruled the colonies by relying for the most part on government by the native social elites and on the whole this had worked well. By contrast, Olivares' drive for centralising power was not limited to the Iberian provinces. He wanted to control the colonies more closely and to extract more revenue from them. Politically this was a mistake because it angered local rulers. From Brazil to Brussels the local leaders felt that they knew best how to run their homelands. On the other hand, Olivares experienced some economic success. He succeeded in extracting more revenue from Naples, Sicily and the American colonies.

Quite simply, Philip II had created an empire that was too big. In the desperate years of the late 1640s and early 1650s Spain found itself fighting the French, the English and the Dutch to hold on to Flanders, Catalonia, Franche-Comté, Naples, the Americas and the East Indies. With hindsight we can say that it would have been better for Spain to cut its losses and concentrate on saving the most valuable territories – perhaps the Netherlands, Catalonia, Brazil, Milan and Naples. Mexico, Peru, Chile, Franche-Comté, the Philippines and Portugal itself might have been jettisoned. However, we must remember that Olivares and Philip IV did not have a crystal ball to know which campaigns they would lose. A policy of concentrating on saving the most valuable territories – a tactical retreat – might well have looked like weakness, an invitation to rivals like France and Britain to seize the rest of their overseas colonies. Furthermore, economically rational choices were not obvious since much less comparative economic information was available at that time. Besides, honour and reputation were everything – and a large part of the problem.

## Revolts

Revolts were amongst the problems of empire. Some interpretations of Spain's decline do not give them enough prominence. In a sense, as both the consequence of weaknesses and the cause of further collapse, they were at the heart of the decline of Spain. That decline began with the revolts of the Netherlands and Granada in the 1560s. Spain went through another deep crisis with those of Portugal and Catalonia almost a century later and reached its lowest point a century and a half after that with the break-away of the South American colonies. Though political miscalculation and economic crisis brought them on, the revolts themselves took on their own momentum. They stimulated each other and, because they involved long wars, they deepened economic problems, making further revolts more likely.

The revolt of the Netherlands involved Spain in a war on its far northern frontier for the best part of a century. Because of its proximity to England and France and because of Philip II's championing of the Counter-Reformation, it brought both these powers into the conflict several times. Though the rebellion did not succeed in the southern provinces of the Netherlands, the blockade of Antwerp ruined the prosperity of this formerly prosperous part of Spain's empire. The Portuguese revolt involved Spain in a war on another front for 30 years. The Catalonian revolt involved a war on Spain's northeastern front for 12 years and gave France the perfect excuse for expansion into the weakest link in the immense natural frontier of the Pyrenean mountains. The Naples revolt of 1647 necessitated another military commitment when France became involved. In short, most of the wars in which Spain was engaged in the first 60 years of the seventeenth century were defensive responses to revolt. The Thirty Years' War was the exception, and some historians have argued that even this was defensive. With the defeats against the United Provinces and Portugal, Spain lost a good deal more than its prized reputation. Holland itself and the Portuguese Empire were of great economic value.

In what ways was Spain weakened by the revolts?

## Military

At the turn of the seventeenth century Spain was regarded, with reasonable justification, as the greatest military power in the world. This reputation rested largely on the successes of illustrious commanders in the sixteenth century. Defeat by the Dutch at Nieuwport in 1600 was the first serious indication that other powers could more than match its military might. This defeat was no fluke, but the product of more sophisticated tactics suited to a state that had fewer men to put on the field of battle – the first stage of the 'military revolution' associated with the Dutch **Maurice of Nassau** and the Swedish king Gustavus Adolphus (see pages 131–33). In response, Spanish commanders developed a less cumbersome version of their **Spanish square** tactic, which had served them well for a long period. Nevertheless, it was to be the Dutch and the Swedes who took warfare onto a higher level, not the Spanish. France and England caught on more quickly with the required organisational changes.

Against this it must be said that Spanish weaponry remained amongst the best in Europe and the Spanish square still proved effective in many battles, especially if the enemy was lacking in numbers. Low morale, a result of arrears in pay, was at least as important a reason as old-fashioned tactics for the occasional defeats against the Dutch in the early 1600s. Diversions to other fronts and problems in recruitment were major disadvantages for Spanish forces in the 1650s.

## Poor leadership

One of the more difficult issues for historians is to decide how much poor leadership was to blame for what happened. Chance and bad luck played their part. The more capable of the two seventeenth-century royal Philips, Philip III, died young and with him went the commonsense foreign policy of Lerma. In the middle of the 1650s Philip IV had every reason to think that France would degenerate into yet another civil war. It did not. In the same decade, just when Philip needed the treasury to be strong, Naples was struck by plague and the Dutch sank two of his silver fleets. Rebels, provincial cortes and rival powers had their own agendas and none of those involved any respite for Spain.

However, Spain's leaders were not simply unlucky. Philip III and Philip IV were not as dynamic as either Louis XIII or Louis XIV of France. Olivares was no Richelieu. Spain needed outstanding leaders and it did not have them. None of Spain's kings, from Charles I (1516–56) and Philip II (1556–98) to Philips III and IV, properly addressed the financial problems. Philip II over-committed Spain to wars on too many fronts against too powerful enemies, emphasising religious cold war – a provocation to his enemies (see Chapter 8).

**Maurice of Nassau** (1567–1625) was a leading statesman in the United Provinces and an outstanding military tactician.

The classic **Spanish square** was a large rectangle of pikemen, 2,000 to 3,000 strong.

Why did Spain's military might decline over the first half of the seventeenth century?

Philip III did not have the courage to persist with Lerma's wiser foreign policy; the intervention in the Thirty Years' War at Zúñiga's urging, though successful in the short term, ultimately proved disastrous. The loss of the Moriscos was a government decision, not mischance – this time Lerma's mistake. Philip III was extravagant with his court. Both he and his son were, when all is said and done, fundamentally lazy. Philip IV often displayed incompetence when he took decisions against good advice, as he did with increasing frequency. Even issues that appear at first sight to be purely a matter of bad luck turn out to be less so on a closer inspection. The effects of plague were worse on a poor and enfeebled population. In Spain they were devastating; in contemporary England, never so serious. Poverty was preventable. The economy could have been developed; the Dutch and English managed to do that.

Warnings and advice were on offer. By the start of the seventeenth century many scholars were writing about Spain's difficulties. Martín Cellorigo's *Memorial* of 1600 was an excellent observation on the social chasm underlying Spain's economic under-development. His recommendation to build a commercial middle class, though hard to achieve by government direction alone, went entirely unheeded. The church and nobility – the elite that led Spain in a wider sense – did nothing to help. In spite of having all the resources it needed, Spain never developed the carrying trade or the textile, ship-building and sugar-refining industries that were every day making the United Provinces and England more capable of pushing Spain further down the pecking order of great powers.

> In what ways did Spain's kings and leading ministers contribute to its decline?

## How far did Spain remain a major power?

### Was Spain a world-beater as a great power?

At its peak, Spain appeared to be all-conquering. The fears of the French, the English and the Dutch – of Spanish or of Habsburg world domination in the period *c.*1570–1630 – were genuine. In spite of this, the consensus of most historians today is that Spain was only the strongest of a number of fundamentally weak powers, and that only marginally and for a brief period.

On the purely military side, defeat at Nieuwport in 1600 showed that Spain was not all-conquering, even at the height of its expansion. What the French feared was Austro-Spanish Habsburg encirclement, not Spain alone. In reality Spain's commitment to Austria's cause in the Thirty Years' War was limited and fixed on its own interests in the Netherlands and northern Italy. Since the death of the combined Spanish and Austrian emperor Charles I in 1558, the real menace of total Habsburg domination had disappeared; Philips II, III and IV were monarchs of Spain alone. As for the Spanish Empire, after Spain's takeover of Portugal in 1580 it was in reality a Spanish–Portuguese empire.

Philip II had agreed that only the Portuguese were to hold office in their kingdoms and colonies. Portuguese colonies were half in, half out of Spain's empire, with the Portuguese attempting to retain exclusive trading rights. Spanish control of its empire in Italy and the Mediterranean islands was fairly loose from the beginning, with the **Aragonese** having control of these colonies. The only cement that united the empire was the Roman Catholic faith and that was imposed rather than chosen in many places. Besides, on a world scale Spain's empire was almost matched for size by those of the Ottomans and the Russians and in population terms it was smaller than the Mogul Empire of India.

Beneath the surface Spain was economically weak and vulnerable when over-stretched. It was like almost all the states of Europe in having a sluggish economy. In Chapters 3 and 4 we have seen how France too was vulnerable to collapse when its fragile economy and poverty-stricken people were over-burdened with taxation.

The marriage of Ferdinand of **Aragon** and Isabella of Castile in 1469 brought the two kingdoms together to form Spain. Though Aragon was the more dynamic, Castile dominated because of its much greater size.

Was Spain ever Europe and the world's most powerful state?

## Was Spain still a major power in 1661?

By 1661 Spain was almost matched as a power by France, Russia, the Ottoman Empire and the United Provinces, with Austria and England not far behind. Territorially, shorn of the Portuguese Empire, it covered about the same area as the Ottoman Empire and the Russian Empire. Economically it was on a par with France, but falling behind the United Provinces and England. Militarily, it was inferior to France on land and to England and the United Provinces at sea. Culturally – always a difficult area to compare – more figures of note in different fields of learning and the arts were to come from France, England and the United Provinces in the second half of the century than from Spain.

If by 1661 Spain's recent claim to be the leading power in the world was hard to sustain, it was far from finished as a great power. Its European and Oceanic Empires were still very extensive. It was in purely military terms that its decline was apparent, due to its incapacity to finance armies of sufficient size. Its Milan army, for example, had been reduced from 40,000 to 10,000 by the 1660s.

What evidence is there that Spain remained a major power in *c*.1661?

## A slow decline or a sudden collapse?

Spain was never supremely powerful at its peak, nor was it amongst the weakest of powers by 1661. This suggests that its decline was fairly gradual. The argument that has been made is that decline began in the 1560s with the revolts in the Netherlands and Granada, did not end until the nineteenth century and was the result of weakening factors over a very long period.

However, there were sudden collapses. The most obvious of these was in 1640, when Portugal and Catalonia broke away. This was a sudden 'political'

Did Spain slowly
decline from the
1560s, collapse in the
1640s, or was there
some combination of
the two?

collapse following a long period of mainly economic decline. Though usually less dramatic than political events, economic collapse could be rapid. Spain's economic fortunes dived sharply after 1600 and once again in 1647.

## Was Spain a special case in its rise and decline?

Other formerly great powers were also in decline in the seventeenth century. Poland was slipping in the same period as Spain, as were the Ottoman Empire and Sweden by the end of the century. Space does not allow any detailed consideration of these, but a look at the main features of their decline throws light on our special study of Spain.

What is striking is that, like Spain, they reached their peak shortly before starting a visible decline. Thanks to marriage alliances, Poland in 1598 included a much larger area than it does today. It was technically speaking Poland–Lithuania, just as Spain was Castile–Aragon. In 1610 the Polish Vasas (the royal family) conquered most of European Russia and it looked for a time as if a new superstate would be created, stretching from central Europe to China. This project did not succeed and 30 years later it was Russia that was acquiring territory from Poland. Thanks to earlier diplomatic and military advance, Sweden in 1598 included a much larger area than it does today, taking in Finland as well as modern Sweden. Sweden's expansion was steadier than Poland's, but by 1661 it was just as remarkable. It fought regular wars against all its neighbours to make these advances, using modern and well-trained forces. By peace treaties in 1648 and 1660 it acquired parts of Denmark and many territories to the south and east of the Baltic Sea. It had also made many enemies. Half a century later it had lost most of the colonies it had gained to a revived Russia and Brandenburg. The Ottoman Empire was enlarged steadily by conquest, mainly from Venice and the Austrian Habsburgs, reaching a peak in the 1680s; 30 years later it was in rapid retreat from a revived Austria. Expansion came quickly in every case, including Spain's, because of military strength, dynastic marriage alliances and the weakness of opponents. Once those opponents revived, the expansive states shrank. In every case the expansive power grew to dimensions that it could not sustain, being itself economically and socially backward. It is clear that the similarities between large states in the seventeenth century were more significant than their differences. None was able to achieve European or world domination for more than half a century.

Which other great
powers of the period
had similar
weaknesses to Spain?

# Spain's problems

Spain's economic and social problems were deep and prolonged. Cellorigo's critical *Memorial* was one of many from the time. The sources here cover economic and social problems; there were, of course, other major areas of concern.

## 1 Castile shouldering too much of the financial burden

Everything is met out of the resources of Castile and out of what comes from the Indies, and literally nothing is contributed by Aragon, Valencia, Catalonia, Portugal and Navarre. As a result, Castile's revenues are pledged to the hilt, and it finds itself in such a state that one cannot see how it can possibly go on paying such vast sums.

Source: Complaint of the Council of Finance, 2 December 1618 (in J. H. Elliott, *The revolt of the Catalans*, 1963, p. 190).

## 2 Income and expenditure of Spain, 1621–40

**Income, 1621–40 (per cent)**
From cortes of Castile 38.0
From cortes of crown of Aragon 1.1
From Spanish church 15.6
Bullion from New World (Americas), 1621–39, 9.5
Discounts on the sale of juros (titles) 9.0
Re-coinages 7.5
Gifts 5.5
Sale of office, vassals, etc. 3.5
Salt tax 2.9
*Media anata* (tax on government salary) 1.3
Seizure of private bullion 1.2
Other 4.9
Total: 237.3 million ducats

**Expenditure, 1621–40**
Loans and bankers (i.e. debts) 70.4
Mediterranean fleet 5.3
Atlantic fleet 4.5
Forts and frontiers 3.7
Army in Spain 3.2
Royal household 5.0
Administration 2.5
Other 5.4
Total: 249.8 million ducats

Source: Adapted from H. Kamen, *Spain 1469–1714*, 2nd edn, 1991, p. 218.

### 3 Rich or poor, with nothing in between

Our republic has come to be an extreme contrast of rich and poor . . . Our condition is one in which we have rich who loll at ease, or poor who beg, and we lack people of the middling sort, whom neither wealth nor poverty prevent from pursuing the rightful kind of business . . .

Source: Martín Gonzalez de Cellorigo, *Memorial*, 1600 (cited in G. Darby, *Spain in the seventeenth century*, 1994, p. 99).

## Historical-source questions

1   To what extent does Source 1 explain the financial difficulties of Spain in the first half of the seventeenth century?
2   How far is Source 1 supported by Source 2?
3   How useful is Source 3 to the historian studying the decline of Spain in the period 1598–1661?
4   Use the sources and your own knowledge to account for the decline of Spain by the middle of the seventeenth century.

## Summary questions

1   (a)  What did any *two* of the problems facing Spain contribute to its decline, c. 1640–61?

    (b)  Explain which problem was the most important cause of Spain's decline.

2   For discussion:

    What actions might have kept Spain in its pre-eminent position amongst the great powers?

# 7 The economic and social foundation of the United Provinces

## Focus questions

◆ How did the Dutch take advantage of the decline of the Mediterranean economy?

◆ What were the secrets of Holland's success?

◆ What was the impact of war on the Dutch economy?

## Significant dates

**1590** Dutch ships enter Mediterranean waters, carrying Baltic grain for Spain; Spain becomes dependent on this supply.

**1599** First Dutch ship circumnavigates the globe. A Rotterdam captain returns from Indonesia with a cargo of spices.

**1602** Dutch East India Company created; England starts rival company.

**1608** Grotius produces legal basis for Dutch rights to free trade in all parts of the world. Amsterdam stock market established.

**1609** Truce in war with Spain allows Dutch economy to do even better. Exchange bank established in Amsterdam.

**1612** 'Tulipomania' sweeps Holland; more than 100 varieties available.

**1616** Holland achieves dominance in export of British coal.

**1621** Dutch West India Company established.

**1624** A Spanish armada is established to patrol the English Channel. Over the next 16 years it sinks thousands of Dutch ships.

**1637** West India Company seizes control of north Brazil from Portugal.

**1650** Haarlem reaches peak of textile production; Leiden 14 years later.

**1651** English parliament passes the Navigation Laws, restricting Dutch access to trade in English goods.

**1652** Dutch found colony of Cape of Good Hope (South Africa).

**1652** Start of Anglo-Dutch War (fought at sea); ends in Dutch defeat.

**1660** Navigation Laws tightened in England; other rivals follow suit.

## Overview

In 1598 the United Provinces was still, on paper, one small part of the Spanish Empire. In practice it was already independent and a growing power. The challenges for this emerging state were as follows:

- Economically, its own resources were small. The new state would have to look elsewhere to increase its prosperity.
- Socially, there was a clash of interests between a large and influential merchant class living in the towns of Holland and the landed aristocracy of the country areas.
- Religiously, could moderate and extreme Calvinists live together? Could a wide range of faiths – from Catholics to Jews – co-exist in one state?
- Politically, could a collection of independent-thinking provinces pull together enough to win a war against Spain, a more powerful state than the United Provinces in 1598?
- Diplomatically, the rebel provinces had to obtain legal recognition from other powers. This would involve a continuation of the war until Spain gave up the struggle. Should the rebel provinces try to take the south of the Netherlands, which Spain still held?

If the rulers of the United Provinces could solve these problems they stood a chance of survival – but even then only if Spain were to weaken or to continue to be distracted by other wars. In 1598 few Dutchmen could foresee a situation where they would be on a par with Spain within 60 years and, in some respects, be more powerful. Against the odds, the **United Provinces** had already stood up to Spain for 30 years. Natural defences – bogs, lakes and river barriers – had helped. Even more important were the distractions provided by France and England for Philip II's armies. Chance alone does not entirely account for the rebels' success. In 1600 they were able to defeat the Spanish at Nieuwport using more advanced tactics developed by Maurice of Nassau.

The Dutch used a largely mercenary army. They could only afford such a luxury because their economy was strong. As Map 4 shows, they were meeting the challenge to raise prosperity by exploiting the resources of the rest of Europe and the world. The structure of Dutch society, with a large and influential middle class and an upper class based on business, helped their economy. Tensions remained – between merchants who made the money that kept the state afloat and aristocrats who led the campaigns that kept it from invasion. Conflicts between the moderate and the extreme Calvinists continued. The external threat remained; Spain had still not given up the struggle to regain control. Nevertheless, when Spain negotiated a 12-year truce with the United Provinces in 1609, with terms that were favourable to Amsterdam's further growth, there was reason for growing optimism.

The northern provinces of the Netherlands had been in revolt against Spain since 1568. In 1581 the **United Provinces** declared independence. Spain fought on to re-possess them.

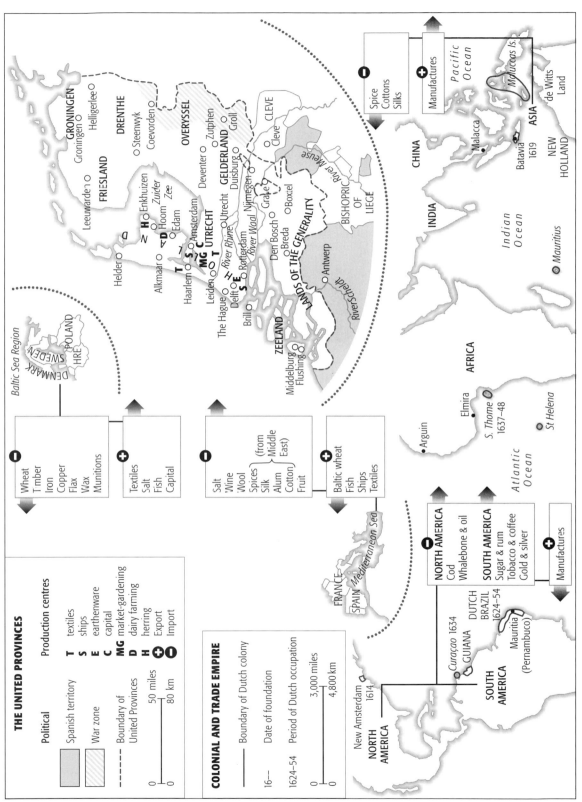

**THE UNITED PROVINCES**

| Political | | Production centres | |
|---|---|---|---|
| | Spanish territory | **T** | textiles |
| | War zone | **S** | ships |
| | | **E** | earthenware |
| - - - - | Boundary of United Provinces | **C** | capital |
| | | **MG** | market-gardening |
| | | **D** | dairy farming |
| | | **H** | herring |
| 0      50 miles | | ⊕ | Export |
| 0    80 km | | ⊖ | Import |

**COLONIAL AND TRADE EMPIRE**

| | |
|---|---|
| ——— | Boundary of Dutch colony |
| 16— | Date of foundation |
| 1624–54 | Period of Dutch occupation |

0      3,000 miles
0    4,800 km

*Baltic Sea Region*

SWEDEN
DENMARK
POLAND
HRE

⊖ Wheat
Timber
Iron
Copper
Flax
Wax
Munitions

⊕ Textiles
Salt
Fish
Capital

⊖ Salt
Wine
Wool
Spices } (from Middle East)
Silk
Alum
Cotton
Fruit

⊕ Baltic wheat
Fish
Ships
Textiles

GRONINGEN
Groningen ○
Helligerlee ○
FRIESLAND
Leeuwarden ○
DRENTHE
Steenwyk ○
Coevorden ○
OVERYSSEL
Deventer ○
Zutphen ○
Groll ○
GELDERLAND
Duisburg ○
CLEVE
Cleve ○
*River Meuse*
Helder ○
Enkhuizen ○
*Zuider Zee*
Hoorn ○ **D**
Edam ○
Alkmaar ○
**N**
**H** Amsterdam
**MG** **C** UTRECHT
Utrecht ○
**S** **T**
Haarlem ○ **T**
Leiden ○ *River Rhine*
Nijmegen ○
The Hague ○ Delft ○ **E**
**S** Rotterdam ○
Grave ○
*River Waal*
Brill ○
Den Bosch ○
Breda ○
Boxtel ○
BISHOPRIC OF LIEGE
LANDS OF THE GENERALITY
Antwerp ○
*River Scheldt*
ZEELAND
Middelburg ○
Flushing ○

*Mediterranean Sea*
FRANCE
SPAIN

⊖ Spice
Cottons
Silks

⊕ Manufactures

*Pacific Ocean*

CHINA
INDIA
ASIA
Malacca ●
Batavia ● 1619
NEW HOLLAND
*Moluccas Is.*
de Witts Land

*Indian Ocean*

*Mauritius* ◎

AFRICA
Arguin ●
Elmira ●
*S. Thomé* ◎ 1637–48
*St Helena* ◎

*Atlantic Ocean*

⊖ NORTH AMERICA
Cod
Whalebone & oil
SOUTH AMERICA
Sugar & rum
Tobacco & coffee
Gold & silver

⊕ Manufactures

New Amsterdam □ 1614
NORTH AMERICA

SOUTH AMERICA
Curaçao 1634 ◎
GUIANA
DUTCH BRAZIL 1624–54
Mauritia (Pernambuco)

**Map 4:** The United Provinces and its trade empire in the first half of the seventeenth century.

The Dutch developed an economy that was largely based on international trade. Patterns of trade across Europe and the wider world were changing. With daring boldness the Dutch were successful in securing the lion's share of the growth routes. Since the sixteenth century the major routes of international trade had been moving away from the Mediterranean towards the Atlantic Ocean, the North Sea and the Baltic Sea. Holland became the hub, outdoing France, Britain and Spain.

The people of the United Provinces had to overcome a lack of natural resources in their own territory. This put them under pressure to succeed. They had to work hard to reclaim and farm the limited land they possessed. The continuance of war in the eastern provinces put pressure on Holland to make the money needed by the state. A policy of religious toleration allowed the Dutch to make the most of the skills of textile workers from the southern Netherlands and refugee Jews from Spain and Portugal. Dutch society was highly urbanised. Its middle and industrial working classes were larger than in other parts of Europe and the great merchants had a real influence on the policies of the state. Successful financial institutions supported the economy.

## How did the Dutch take advantage of the decline of the Mediterranean economy?

### Trade across Europe

In the absence of railways, good roads and good navigable rivers, the movement of goods by sea was the main means of international trade before the Industrial Revolution. The Dutch came out on top in competition with the English and the Swedish to secure the sea-borne carrying trade in the sixteenth century and the first half of the seventeenth century. Dutch merchants, using Dutch ships, functioned as middlemen, moving the goods of other states across Europe and the world (see Map 4 on page 99). The Dutch commercial fleet numbered about 2,500 in 1636, with a further 2,000 large fishing boats. The carrying trade was very profitable. The French, the Spanish, the Swedes and the English could have supplied their own ships, but because they lacked merchant capital and initiative they let the Dutch almost monopolise the trade. For many years English coal was traded by Dutch merchants in Dutch ships.

Why did the Dutch succeed in dominating most of the valuable sea-borne carrying trade in Europe?

Dutch merchants concentrated on the trade in bulk foodstuffs rather than luxuries such as spices and silks, which had been the mainstay of the trading empires of Venice, Antwerp and Genoa in the late medieval period. The main trade which they dominated was that running from the Baltic to Spain. The Baltic region was one of Europe's major suppliers of grain and all the materials required for ship-building (masts, tar, wax, pitch, hemp, flax and iron).

From the end of the century onwards Spain and Spanish Italy were short of grain to feed their populations. The Dutch supplied them with grain from the south Baltic region and in the process obtained for themselves the raw materials they lacked for ship-building and the salt they needed for preserving their huge catches of herring. Cargoes of grain from north Germany and Lithuania, iron and copper from Sweden and timber from Norway were traded for salt, wine and fruit from Spain, Portugal and France. In purely territorial terms, the Baltic Sea had become a 'Swedish lake' by 1660, but in economic terms it practically belonged to the Dutch. Until the middle of the seventeenth century half the ships passing between Sweden and Denmark to the Baltic ports were Dutch. For this operation the Dutch used a new type of merchant ship, the **fluit** or 'flyboat'.

As important to Dutch success as the flute was their specialised fishing boat, the herring **buss**. From the middle of the sixteenth century fishing and trade in fish had been the second most important aspect of their economy. A good deal of the catch fed the growing population at home, but much was exported to southern Europe and to the Baltic – whose own herring industry had declined in the sixteenth century when the herring shoals migrated from there to the North Sea. The annual herring catch was worth £2 million to the United Provinces in the early seventeenth century, equivalent to the value of Britain's yearly cloth exports at the time.

As war destroyed old markets in north-central Europe, the Dutch sought out new markets in the Mediterranean. In particular, Leiden concentrated on producing the new lighter cloth that was becoming popular in southern Europe. A growing urban population throughout Europe created a demand for brighter, lighter and cheaper types of cloth, both for clothing and furnishings. In the middle of the sixteenth century only the southern Netherlands possessed the technological know-how to produce the new textiles. By the end of it both the technology and the lead that went with it had passed to the United Provinces. English spun and woven cloths were dyed and dressed in Holland and exported to southern Europe, leading to English resentment and eventual English revenge in the second half of the seventeenth century.

## American, Asian and African trade

In the later centuries of the medieval period (*c.*1000–1500) the Mediterranean and the Baltic Seas were Europe's two hubs of trade. The former was dominated by Venetian and Genoese merchants and the latter by the north German cities. There was no regular cross-European trade on a large scale. By 1600 the European economy was more closely interlinked and the countries bordering the Atlantic had all established contact with the Americas, Asia and Africa. As a result the centre of gravity of trade moved steadily farther to the west of

The **fluit** was in effect a sea-going barge. Cheap to build and operate, it was ideal for bulk cargoes.

The Dutch developed a fleet of 2,000 herring **busses**, famous for their good design and efficient operation. They were capable of pulling large nets and fish could be cured on deck.

> What factors made the Dutch fish trade successful?

The Dutchman Hugo Grotius (1583–1645), author of *The laws of war and peace*, 1625, first defined international **law**, conveniently arguing that the tropical seas were open for access to the most enterprising of European states.

Formed in 1602, the larger of the two companies, the **Dutch East India Company** took over the prosperous spice trade.

Europe. Southern England, north-west France, northern Spain and the Netherlands were all well placed for the trades to the Baltic, the Mediterranean and the Atlantic. In the first half of the seventeenth century it was the Dutch who succeeded in dominating all areas. They asserted themselves against existing rivals like the Portuguese and potential rivals like the English with amazing self-confidence. In addition to enterprise in business, all their skills in science (for the mathematics of navigation) and **law** (to establish their right to move into the existing colonies of rivals) were brought to bear.

In terms of tonnage the cargoes carried by the **Dutch East India Company** and the West India Company were small in comparison to the total tonnage passing through the ports of Holland. They never amounted to more than 10 per cent of the income from all trade. However, in terms of value they were greater and they helped to give the edge over rivals to the Dutch economy. Dutch merchants made profits from the import and re-export of precious metals and spices, some of which were simply captured from Spanish ships. Manufacturing and food-finishing industries grew up as a result of the imports of sugar and tobacco, creating a significant multiplier effect on the Dutch economy. New industries boosted local economies by providing jobs in local services.

Map 4 gives only an indication of how far afield Dutch merchants reached. Their enterprise was truly global. The East India Company forced the Portuguese out of Indonesia and took over the valuable spice trade. By the 1660s they were moving into India. The West India Company, for a time at least, forced the Portuguese out of northern Brazil and took over the sugar trade. Dutch merchants were the first to trade with Japan (carrying gold and silver from there) and Taiwan and were amongst the first Europeans to sight western Australia. A small whaling industry in the most northerly province of the Netherlands was linked to the activities of whaling ships off Greenland, Newfoundland and Norway. Dutch merchants ventured north of the Arctic Circle to the far north of Russia via the White Sea.

Actual territorial colonisation was slight and short lived, most notably in the case of Dutch Brazil. However, many trading posts and small spice island chains – such as the Moluccas in Indonesia – were retained and proved valuable, without presenting the heavy defence and administrative commitment of large colonies. Nearer to home the port of Göteborg in Sweden was founded by Dutch merchants and laid out by Dutch engineers, a Dutch town in all but name. Commercial colonies were established in Moscow and Riga, monopolising the export of tar, caviar, hemp, oil, salmon and wool. A little more territorial colonisation would have been worthwhile, as we can see in retrospect. Dutch New Amsterdam became English New York, demonstrating what opportunities were lost. The main obstacle to the Dutch achieving colonies

Give some examples of Dutch trading enterprises.

Why didn't the Dutch create a large territorial overseas empire?

was their small population (about 1.4 million in 1600); they did not have enough people to settle overseas.

While they lacked the population, they certainly did not lack the money or the specialist skills to colonise other parts of the world. Capital (money), what economists call an 'invisible export', was to be one of their major exports to Sweden. The Dutch De Geer family became the major manufacturing and iron- and copper-mining firm in seventeenth-century Sweden. Heavy industry was introduced to Russia in 1632 by Andrey Vinius, who set up iron foundries near Tula. At various times between 1618 and 1650 Dutch finance helped the Danes and Swedes to create their fleets and fight their wars. In Poland Dutchmen organised the mint. Dutch bankers lent to Venice and financed mercury and copper mining in Austria and Hungary. Dutch engineers were called in to carry out major drainage schemes in France and England; they had developed skills for this to a high level through the reclamation of northern Holland – most of which lay below sea level.

> What specialist skills did the Dutch have that they used in other countries than their own?

## What were the secrets of Holland's success?

### A new Venice and an early Manchester

Holland became the Venice of the early modern period. **Venice** was also a state that was small in territory and resources. By 1660 it was in the humiliating position of borrowing from Dutch banks – banks modelled on its own – to finance its debt. With its numerous canals Amsterdam even resembled the Italian city physically.

Manchester is another great city with a very extensive – though largely hidden – canal network. If seventeenth-century Amsterdam took after Venice (some financial institutions were direct copies), it also looked forward to industrial Manchester. Holland industrialised to an extent not seen again in Europe until Britain's Industrial Revolution more than a century later. This was not a matter of setting up factories or making major technological advances. Homes or large workshops were used, but on a much greater scale then before. Dutch industries were based on imported raw materials or half-finished manufactures. Most of what was produced was exported and profit yields were high. The most important industrial centres were the textile towns of Leiden and Haarlem. Leiden became the largest manufacturing centre for new draperies in Europe. Haarlem bleached and finished coarse linens from Germany. Amsterdam dyed and finished semi-finished cloth from England. Sugar-refining, tobacco-cutting and the manufacture of earthenware goods also developed into substantial industries. Malting, distilling, brewing, silk-throwing (making silk thread), glass-making, armament manufacture, printing and paper-making also grew, many of these industries using skills brought

> By the mid-1600s some Dutch observers were afraid that their state was declining in the same way as **Venice**. In Venice, former merchant families had turned from trading to land-owning.

**Peter the Great**
(1672–1725) was tsar of
Russia. He introduced
many reforms in
government and
technology, based on
western European
developments.

How did the Dutch
maximise the value of
their native and
imported resources?

What evidence is there
of Dutch religious
toleration?

How did religious
toleration help the
Dutch economy?

Contrast this with Venice,
where 5,000 **Jews** (by the
mid-1600s) were confined
to an island outside the
city. The word 'ghetto' is a
Venetian dialect word.

by immigrants from the south. Ship-building became a major industry. The port of Zaandam, a little to the north of Amsterdam, became Europe's largest centre for ship-building. There was growth in the associated industries of timber, rope and sail-making. Zaandam was also Europe's largest centre for the timber trade. Later in the century **Peter the Great** of Russia, himself an amateur ship-builder, was to make the Zaandam shipyard his main point of call in western Europe. Agriculture too was transformed. Dairy farming and market gardening developed strongly, especially the cultivation of flowers. Visitors to Holland today, travelling from the Hook of Holland to Rotterdam or Amsterdam, will be struck by the huge areas devoted to growing under glass and the colourful bulb fields – these intensively commercial enterprises date from the early seventeenth century.

## Religious toleration and an urbanised society

Spanish religious persecution drove thousands of Protestant refugees from Antwerp and the great textile centres of Flanders to Holland. By 1622 about a third of Amsterdam's 100,000 population consisted of Protestant immigrants and their children. Many of them were skilled in the latest techniques of textile production, giving another advantage to the Dutch economy. The rebel provinces did not discriminate strongly between followers of the different Protestant faiths and did not persecute those belonging to non-Christian ones. Officially, Catholics did not and could not hold public office, but sometimes they did. Laws against the exercise of their faith were loosely enforced, especially in the second quarter of the seventeenth century, and they were generally accepted as part of the community. The way the **Jews** were treated was unique in Europe outside the Ottoman Empire. In Amsterdam they lived in a proper quarter rather than a ghetto and worshipped openly in a splendid new synagogue. This degree of toleration set Holland apart from most other states in Europe at a time when the Counter-Reformation was at its peak.

## A comparison of Dutch and French society

Society in the United Provinces was radically different from society in the great Catholic states, mainly because of the economy of Holland. The contrast is clear in the diagram showing the occupational structure of France and the United Provinces. The typical Dutch person lived in a town or city, the typical French person in a small village. By the middle of the seventeenth century 56 per cent of Holland's population were townspeople and well over half the population of the entire United Provinces were urbanised. One-sixth of the population lived in Amsterdam. Though France was also densely populated by seventeenth-century standards, 90 per cent of the French population was scattered in villages; only 1 in 40 lived in Paris. Lyons and Rouen were simply

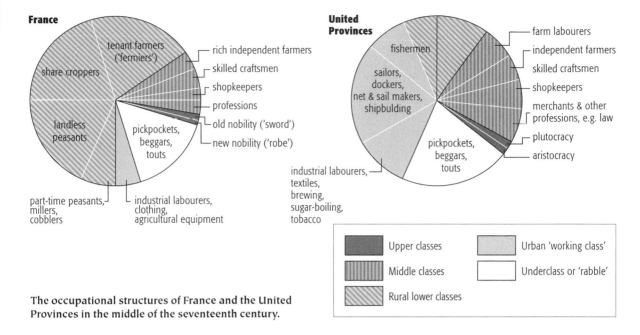

**France**

- tenant farmers ('fermiers')
- share croppers
- landless peasants
- rich independent farmers
- skilled craftsmen
- shopkeepers
- professions
- old nobility ('sword')
- new nobility ('robe')
- pickpockets, beggars, touts
- part-time peasants, millers, cobblers
- industrial labourers, clothing, agricultural equipment

**United Provinces**

- fishermen
- sailors, dockers, net & sail makers, shipbulding
- farm labourers
- independent farmers
- skilled craftsmen
- shopkeepers
- merchants & other professions, e.g. law
- plutocracy
- aristocracy
- pickpockets, beggars, touts
- industrial labourers, textiles, brewing, sugar-boiling, tobacco

Upper classes | Urban 'working class'
Middle classes | Underclass or 'rabble'
Rural lower classes

The occupational structures of France and the United Provinces in the middle of the seventeenth century.

large towns; Bordeaux, La Rochelle and Marseilles were sizeable ports – a small number of big towns for such a large country.

In the United Provinces, no less than in France or Spain, the typical successful merchant dreamed of buying a title to land. Aitzema, writing in 1652, complained that Dutch trade was suffering because the regents (town leaders) were deriving too much of their income from fixed assets like land rather than the commercial enterprise that had made them rich in the first place (see Historical sources). However, the lack of land space prevented this from getting out of hand. Many Dutch merchants ploughed their profits back into further commercial expansion. They had the incentive of enjoying real power in the towns and cities in which they lived. In France and Spain the landed aristocracy even controlled the commercial life of the towns, usually in a restrictive way, discouraging free movement of goods. Goods moved more freely within Holland than anywhere else in Europe.

## Financial institutions

The new commercial and financial institutions of seventeenth-century Holland were not original. Most of them followed Venetian patterns. However, the Venetian models were improved upon. After the 1609 truce an exchange **bank** was created at Amsterdam to meet the need of traders for a convenient way of settling accounts. The merchant paid into his account and took what he needed, without actually borrowing. A loan bank and a bourse were established, the latter for dealings in stocks, shares and speculations. The bourse was the special province of the growing community of Spanish and Portuguese Jews.

> How did social and political structures boost business enterprise in the United Provinces?

This was an 'exchange and deposit' **bank**. Bullion and coins stayed in the bank's vault. Payments were made by paper. It lent money only to the government at 4 per cent or less, the lowest rate of interest in Europe.

> What was the role of Amsterdam in the Dutch economy?

By the 1660s Holland's extraordinary success was attracting the attention of commentators in England, partly because Dutch interest rates were the lowest in Europe. Richelieu was an envious French onlooker (see Historical sources, p. 108); he lacked both the policies and the wider support from nobles and merchants needed to bring Dutch-style economic success to France. Until the last decade of the century most French observers, not as alert as Richelieu to Dutch superiority in the economic field, simply attacked and mocked.

## What was the impact of war on the Dutch economy?

### War as harmful to the Dutch economy

It would be wrong to imagine that the Dutch economic miracle was without some serious setbacks, for the United Provinces was a key player in the great conflicts of the period. In the 1620s and 1630s a combination of Spanish action against Dutch ships and raised taxation damaged the economy. In the 1620s taxation levels had to be raised by almost 50 per cent and this led to serious disturbances in Dutch cities and towns. The Spanish economic blockade began with the exclusion of Dutch vessels from Spanish ports. In 1624 Spain set up the Northern Board of Admiralty (the Almirantazgo) to enquire into the origins of cargoes and to issue licences for transit. A Spanish armada was constructed to patrol the English Channel and North Sea. Privateer (pirate) raids from Dunkirk were encouraged. The Almirantazgo worked with great effect. Two thousand Dutch ships were captured and a thousand sunk between 1629 and 1638. The Dutch textile industry went into a deep slump. Only the Dutch–English–French defeat of the Spanish at the Battle of the Dunes (1658) saved the day for the United Provinces.

In the longer term Dutch economic supremacy was not set to last. England was to overtake the United Provinces in the second half of the seventeenth century. Dutch near-monopoly of the textile-finishing and coal trade, using English and Irish wool and Newcastle coal, caused much resentment in England. No longer an ally in spite of a tradition of English Protestant support for the rebel provinces in the sixteenth century, the English parliament passed the Navigation Laws in 1651. These were designed to cut down Dutch intrusion into what the English thought should properly be their trade. They led to war at sea between the two states in the early 1650s and again in the mid-1660s and early 1670s. The first of these wars went very badly for the Dutch and they were defeated.

Why did England cease to be an ally of the Dutch from the mid-seventeenth century?

### War as helpful to the Dutch economy

In the first period of the Dutch war of independence, war was generally of benefit to the rebel side because – thanks to Dutch blockade of the river that serviced Antwerp – it diverted trade and resources to Amsterdam. The pendulum swung the other way in the 1620s and 1630s. The advantage was again with the Dutch in the 1640s. In this decade, while most of Europe sank into a deep economic depression and was racked by revolt, the Dutch economy again moved forward. Spain and France were absorbed in their own crises, and Spanish defeat at the Battle of the Dunes allowed Holland to reassert its economic power. Spanish trade was monopolised by Dutch merchants once again. Throughout the first half of the seventeenth century, even in the troubled 1620s, Holland's ample food supply from the herring catch, Baltic grain and its own dairy produce from newly reclaimed land in the north of the state allowed it to feed its own population. Consequently there were none of the famines and major popular revolts that followed in the tracks of hunger and war as in France and Spain.

> To what extent did the United Provinces benefit from war in the period 1598–1661?

## Historical sources

## The Dutch economy as the envy of the world

This is a sample of the usually envious and hostile and only occasionally admiring observations of French and English commentators. Only Richelieu begins to apply powers of analysis to the 'mystery' of Dutch success. Aitzema, the only Dutch source, is more critical than the foreign observers.

### 1 English envy of Dutch enterprise

This trade of the East Sea is one of the greatest mysteries in trade, they venting there what they bring out of the east, south and west; and again, supplying other countries with commodities of that sea . . . and although their Spanish and East Indy trade be richer yet, the destroying this trade is also the destroying of those other.

Source: Robert Albion, Forests and Sea Power, 1658 (quoted in J. Lisk, *Sample examination answers: 'A' level European history, 1648–1789*, 1994).

### 2 A cynical observation on Amsterdam

Hence Amsterdam – Turk, Christian, Pagan, Jew,
Staple of sects and mint of schism grew:
That bank of conscience where not one so strange
Opinion but finds credit and exchange.

Source: A. Marvell, 'Character of Holland', 1653 (quoted in C. Wilson, *Dutch Republic*, 1968, p. 27).

### 3 Debate on the reasons for Dutch success

In the 1670s two English writers debated the causes of Dutch prosperity . . . Mandeville, a physician, was Dutch by birth and training . . . Sir William Temple, in his *Observations on the United Provinces* (1673) argued that 'thrift and parsimony' was the basis of Dutch prosperity. Mandeville, in his *Fable of the bees, or private vices, public benefits* quarrelled with Temple's view of the importance of thrift and savings. He argued that luxury was the basis of Dutch success.

Source: Wilson, 1968, p. 34.

### 4 Richelieu's analysis of Dutch success

The wealth of the Dutch, who, to tell the truth, are only a handful of folk crammed into a corner of the earth where there are only water and fields, is an example and proof of the advantages of trade which cannot be denied . . . Although that nation gets from its land only butter and cheese, yet it supplies nearly all the nations of Europe with the greater part of their necessities.

Source: Richelieu, 'Political testament', first published 1688 (in T. K. Rabb, *The Thirty Years' War*, 2nd edn, 1981).

### 5 A Dutch observer's anxiety about social trends

[Our trade is suffering because] the regents are not merchants, but draw their income from houses, lands and investments.

Source: Aitzema,1652 (quoted in Wilson, 1968, p. 44).

## Historical-source questions

1   What is Marvell's opinion of Amsterdam?
2   What are the similarities and differences between the views of Temple and Mandeville (Source 3) and Aitzema on the basis of Dutch prosperity?
3   Why must the reliability of Sources 1 and 2 be questioned?
4   Use the sources and your own knowledge to explain why the Dutch economy was so successful.

## Summary question

1   (a)  Explain how any *two* factors helped the economy of the United Provinces.

    (b)  Which of these factors was most important?

# 8 Causes of the Thirty Years' War

## Significant dates

**1580s** Reinvigorated Catholic Church takes on Protestant minorities in France and parts of the Austrian Empire.

**1591** Christian I of Saxony forms the Torgau alliance of Protestant princes in 'Germany' (Lutheran and Calvinist). Divisions between the Protestant principalities re-emerge after his death later that year.

**1609** New Protestant Union is formed in 'Germany' as anxieties rise about the religion of the successor to the duchies of Jülich–Cleves. In response Maximilian of Bavaria forms the Catholic League.

**1612** Emperor Matthias of Austria withdraws concessions to Protestants in Bohemia, provoking a growing rebellion.

**1614** Catholic–Protestant war is narrowly averted after brief skirmishes between the forces of Spain and the United Provinces over Jülich–Cleves.

**1618** Protestant revolt in Bohemia ignites the Thirty Years' War.

## Overview

Between 1618 and 1648 there was an enormous war in Europe. Generally known as the Thirty Years' War, it was fought out mostly within the Holy Roman Empire between the Habsburgs and a broad coalition of powers opposing them. The war was immensely destructive. This chapter examines the causes of this conflict.

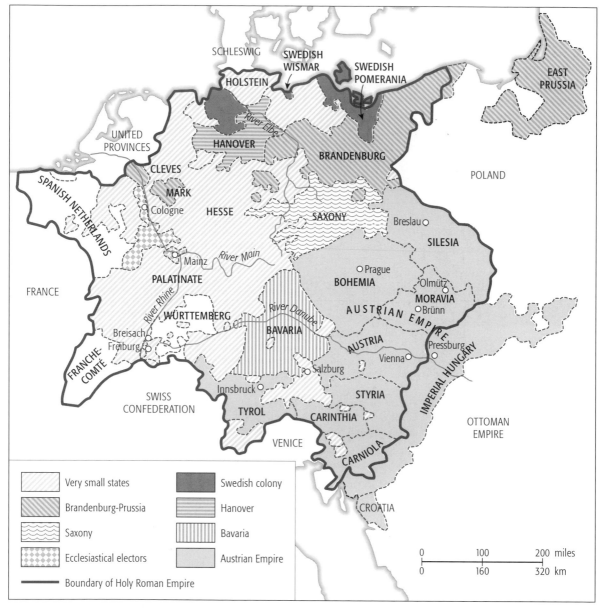

**Map 5: The Holy Roman Empire and the Austrian Habsburg Empire (after 1648).**

The large and powerful state of Germany was later to be created out of most of what was the Holy Roman Empire. In the seventeenth century the region was prey to the ambitions of several of the surrounding great powers. A conglomeration of small principalities, independent cities and independent church lands, the Holy Roman Empire had been a more viable entity in the Middle Ages, when much of Europe was similarly divided. Even in 1600 it was a very old institution, having been set up by the Emperor Charlemagne in 800 to sustain Christian influence and authority north of the Mediterranean. It was supposed to be a new Christian version of the old Roman Empire and accordingly its formal title was 'The Holy Roman Empire of the German Nation'. By the early seventeenth century the justification for its continuation was open to question.

- Religiously, it was now divided between Catholic, Lutheran and Calvinist principalities, most of which were hostile to each other.
- Politically, the authority of the Holy Roman emperor, who was usually the archduke of Austria, was widely resented. At the same time this central authority at least provided some kind of defensive bond against takeover by stronger neighbouring states or bullying by the larger states within the empire. With an elected emperor and an imperial assembly it still had some of the trappings of a unified state.
- Strategically, the region was vital to Spain's rulers, as long as Spain had a colony in the Netherlands. Being at the centre of Europe, the Holy Roman Empire was at a crossroads for overland trade and communications. Unfortunately there were no major natural barriers to its north, north-west and east, making it vulnerable to attack.
- Economically, prosperity was very patchy and much of the region was now in decline. Nearly all landlocked, the German states were starting to lose out to the maritime powers.

Between 1618 and 1648 the Holy Roman Empire was engulfed in the greatest conflict of the period, the Thirty Years' War. The war arose because the first three kinds of problems for the region – religious, political and strategic – converged.

## What were the effects of the Catholic revival in France, Spain, Austria and Bavaria?

### Religion as a driving force in the state

In the late sixteenth and early seventeenth centuries Europeans were caught up in a 'cold war', a religious one. Each side claimed to be the victim, their leaders and propagandists insisting that the other side was plotting their destruction. There was a fierce war of words. It is important to remember that this was not simply a propaganda war. Protestants wanted to belong to Protestant Europe, Catholics to Catholic states. To be in a religious minority in the early seventeenth century was to be exposed and vulnerable to persecution. There were appreciable differences in the organisation and values of society between Protestant and Catholic-dominated states. The seventeenth-century traveller noticed real changes when moving from Catholic to Protestant parts of Europe, due in part to religion.

With its stress on obedience and hierarchy, Catholicism appealed to rulers seeking a means of securing their authority over kingdoms that were ethnically or physically divided. In the early seventeenth century the Spanish and Austrian Habsburgs used the vigour of the reformed Roman Catholic Church to secure and then expand their authority. The difference between the United Provinces and the Spanish Netherlands illustrates the gap between the two sides in the religious cold war. The Czech historian **Polisensky** argued in *The Thirty Years' War* (1971) that the values of the United Provinces were wholly opposite to those of Catholic Spain; Dutch values were republican, democratic and commercial. The government of the archdukes in the Spanish south between 1596 and 1621 removed the power of provincial estates and the merchants in the towns. Local rights were destroyed. A study of cultural life provides an illustration of the importance of the difference between the two regions. In Holland, middle-class demand made it possible for painters of intimate domestic subjects to succeed, while in Spain and Catholic Europe most art was the result of religious and royal commissions (see picture case study, *Art and society in Italy and Holland*, pages 121–24).

In spite of real differences, **Polisensky** overstated his case. The United Provinces was republican by default more than choice – Queen Elizabeth I of England refused to take up the Dutch rebels' bid for her sovereignty. Local government was in the hands of the rich, not the Calvinist congregations.

## The success of the Counter-Reformation in Spain and France

In the sixteenth century, power passed not only from popes to Protestant monarchs but also from popes to Catholic monarchs. From the point of view of the preservation of European peace this was a dangerous development as it further splintered Christendom.

By the early seventeenth century an assertive, European-wide papal foreign policy was a thing of the past. This was in part because all popes after the Dutchman Adrian VI (1522–23) were Italian. It did not help either that, like Adrian, they were almost always short lived in the post, having attained it only after a lifetime of pious ladder-climbing. A side-effect of the clampdown on corruption, which had been one aspect of Catholic reform, was a drastic reduction in papal income. Thanks to this the papacy was unable to support its territorial claims with military force. Though the papacy still arbitrated between Catholic powers at war, its declining authority was all too clear, for France and Spain ignored papal interventions.

Authority was passing from the papacy to monarchs. Kings and queens preferred to control the form and the speed of Counter-Reformation in their own lands for their own purposes. Philip II of Spain argued that his authority came directly from God and he resented any papal interference. With scant regard for what today would be called human rights, he encouraged his Spanish-run Catholic **Inquisition** to complete the work of ridding Spain and its empire of 'heretics'.

The main targets of the Spanish **Inquisition** were Jews, Moors and Protestants.

When the Counter-Reformation came to France, it was also on the terms of the local monarchs rather than those of the papacy. Although Henry IV was assassinated by a Catholic fanatic, Catholic extremists had less to complain about than the French Protestants as the country was steadily moving back to Catholicism. By the end of Henry IV's reign there were only 800 Huguenot (Calvinist) congregations, compared with over 2,000 in 1562. A combination of brute force and a steady improvement in the image of those in holy orders made further inroads into the Protestant minority during the reign of Louis XIII (1610–43). Louis XIII and Cardinal Richelieu could have no real objection to the suppression of the revolt of the Bohemian Protestants in the 1620s, because they were pursuing a similar strategy in France.

In summary, the passing of authority from popes to kings helped the Counter-Reformation to victories in Spain and France. Harnessed to the needs of the government, the Catholic faith was no longer independent, no longer to be seen as an interfering busybody. Instead, it was an invaluable tool for establishing unity under the royal banner. Religious minorities were considered not only to be dangerously misguided but also disloyal.

'Though great rivals and often enemies, the leaders of France and Spain had much in common when it came to internal policies.' Explain this comment.

Why were monarchs rather than popes taking the lead in the Catholic Counter-Reformation?

## Why did religious conflict escalate in the German-speaking lands?

By the start of the seventeenth century Protestants were dangerously divided. All attempts to bring Lutherans and Calvinists together into a defensive front against the Catholics were short lived. Part of the problem was that the Reformation had started in 'Germany' with Luther, so passions for or against Lutheranism were keenly felt in 'Germany'. Political agreements favoured the Lutherans. The Peace of Augsburg of 1555 had accepted the existence of Lutheran but not of Calvinist states, denying Calvinist rulers the right to decide the faith of their subjects. The Lutheran faith became the safe option for any ambitious Protestant ruler. It allowed him to take over some former Catholic church property and to distance himself from meddlesome imperial authority without the risk of a head-on clash with Catholic Austria. Calvinism was more suited to the sovereign of intense religious conviction. To take up Calvinism was to go into open rebellion against the international order.

Luther and Lutheranism struck roots in the north-east of 'Germany', Calvin and Calvinism in Geneva and the south of the Holy Roman Empire. Why were Protestants so divided in 'Germany'?

For a brief period at the end of the 1580s it looked as if German Protestants might be able to work together. However, the split resurfaced in the early 1590s when Saxony once again took up the Lutheran cause and the Palatinate, under the leadership of **Frederick IV** (1584–1616), adopted Calvinism. The University of Heidelberg in the Palatinate became a centre for German Calvinists.

German Protestants, whether Lutheran or Calvinist, were afraid of what was happening in neighbouring Bavaria and Austria. In Bavaria the revival of Catholicism had started in the 1560s with the assistance of the Jesuits. Bavaria's rulers did not even consider the possibility of religious co-existence.

**Frederick IV** was the son of William the Silent, who had led the struggle of the Netherlands for independence.

Maximilian I led the Catholic League. Though usually allied with and overshadowed by Austria, he steered an independent course for periods of the Thirty Years' War.

Under William V (1579–97) and **Maximilian I** (1597–1651) Bavarians were offered the stark choice of Catholicism or exile. Attendance at church, the taking of the sacraments and the use of the confessional were all made compulsory.

The Protestant faiths had achieved a higher proportion of converts in the Austrian Empire than anywhere else in Europe. By about 1600 two-thirds of the population of Bohemia was Protestant and only one in ten was Catholic. In Bohemia a largely Catholic nobility was now a minority among their own subjects. This was a recipe for civil war. Fear that tolerance of Protestants would open the door to an Austrian version of the revolt of the Netherlands spurred the Austrian ruling class to abandon religious toleration. Each Austrian emperor moved further towards an extreme position. In the 1580s Austrian Protestant ministers were expelled and Catholics appointed to local government posts. A Jesuit university was founded at Graz. The Habsburg family associated itself with the saints, the sacred symbols of the distant past and the cult of the Virgin Mary. In the late 1590s Protestants were forced out of the countryside in Upper Austria. Everywhere, except in Bohemia, earlier concessions to Protestants were withdrawn. In 1590 Archduke Ferdinand stepped up the campaign, telling Protestants to emigrate. Protestants wondered if a future Austrian emperor, perhaps the aggressive Archduke Ferdinand when he succeeded Matthias, would use his powers as emperor of the Holy Roman Empire to attack the Protestant principalities.

Why did religious conflict escalate in the German-speaking parts of Europe?

## How was the Holy Roman Empire caught up in the ambitions of the Bourbons and Habsburgs?

### A war of religion?

As the immediate cause of the opening conflicts and as a long-term source of tension between states, religion was undoubtedly important. It was a major cause of the Thirty Years' War and it is important to study the relentless build-up of the religious cold war in the four decades before the war started. However, no modern historian would argue that this was the last great war fought solely for religious reasons. Almost all historians of the twentieth century have agreed that, to a greater or lesser extent, religion mattered less than more hard-headed political considerations. This conclusion is largely based on the record of the powers during the war itself (see Chapter 9). However, it will be apparent that even before the war started Catholic Spain did not always work alongside Catholic France, and that both were frequently at odds with the papacy. Neither did Protestant states always work alongside other Protestant states – in fact, more often than not they were at odds with each other.

Why do most historians now think that religion was less important than the ambitions and needs of the powers involved?

## A war for great power dominance?

Some historians have argued that the Thirty Years' War was entirely the result of the ambition of two great powers to dominate Europe, and that religion had hardly anything to do with it. This conclusion is largely based on the record of the powers during the war itself. However, this interpretation can also be taken too far. It is doubtful whether any of the great powers had ambitions and strategic goals that amounted to a clear long-term plan to dominate Europe or whether they planned a major war in the Holy Roman Empire.

Nonetheless, there certainly were great power ambitions and defensive strategies that were highly likely to involve intervention in any major conflict in the Holy Roman Empire. Perhaps most ambitious of all were the rulers of France – the Bourbon kings – and Cardinal Richelieu. Using the attempts of Spain to dominate France in the sixteenth century as justification in his propaganda, Richelieu pursued an alternating policy of diplomacy and war to break what he called 'Habsburg encirclement'. Both Spain and Austria were seen as enemies, both possessed territories which he wanted France to acquire: Alsace, Lorraine, Franche-Comté, Artois and Flanders. Richelieu bided his time before fully committing France to the Thirty Years' War. The Habsburg victory against Sweden at Nördlingen in 1634 promised a full French engagement. Of all the powers involved in the war, the argument that there were long-term ambitions for expansion into 'Germany' is strongest in the case of France. Just before his assassination in 1610 Henry IV had been about to initiate a war with Spain in the Rhineland over the small yet strategically vital duchies of Jülich and Cleves. However, some historians have argued that Richelieu entered the Thirty Years' War in 1635 purely out of necessity.

A revival of the old **joint Habsburg Empire** was never seriously contemplated by the rulers of the two branches of the Habsburg dynasty, even if Zúñiga and the activist faction in Spain dreamed of such a thing. Spain's own problems were far too great for either Philip III or Philip IV to contemplate anything so ambitious. On balance, Spanish objectives were more defensive. The overriding aims were to keep the empire intact and to maintain Spain's high international reputation. Above all, this meant hanging on to the Netherlands and defeating the Dutch rebels. That in turn meant keeping open the 'Spanish Road', the ribbon of Spanish territories along the River Rhine that linked the Mediterranean and North Sea. Although Spain intervened in the Thirty Years' War forcefully and early under the influence of the hawkish Zúñiga, this was no long-term Spanish plan. Many years before, under the leadership of Lerma, Spain had withdrawn from its wars against the Netherlands and England. If Lerma had stayed favourite after 1618 the chances are that Spain would not have become so heavily and so quickly committed to this new war.

The former **joint Habsburg Empire** existed between 1519 and 1556, the result of a marriage alliance. Emperor Charles V divided it between his brother and son, creating the Austrian and Spanish branches.

In what ways was the war the result of a struggle for dominance between the Habsburg powers and Bourbon France?

## Why did the Thirty Years' War break out in 1618?

### 1609: a cold war crisis over Jülich–Cleves almost turns to war

By 1609 the Protestant princes of 'Germany' felt sufficiently anxious about the intentions of Catholic Austria and Bavaria to attempt another Protestant Union. When, in response, Maximilian I of Bavaria formed the Catholic League, events started to take a dangerous turn. Later that year a crisis blew up over the strategically important principality of Jülich–Cleves on the border with the United Provinces. There was a possibility of a Protestant succeeding to what had been a Catholic state. The Catholic powers would have none of this. When the Calvinist Prince Christian of Anhalt appealed for French assistance, only the hesitation of Saxony and the assassination of Henry IV saved the dispute from turning into all-out war. Eventually the dispute was resolved by military pressure from Dutch troops. Jülich–Cleves was divided between the Protestant and the Catholic claimants. All-out war was avoided, but the Jülich–Cleves crisis sharpened diplomatic divisions in Europe, with the creation of a new Protestant Union and an entirely new Catholic League in 1609.

### 1618: cold war turns to 'hot war' over Bohemia

The accession of Emperor Matthias in 1612 intensified the persecution. Matthias aroused resistance in Bohemia by attacking a 'letter of majesty' granted as recently as 1609 by his father, the Emperor Rudolph II, that had given freedom of worship to the nobles and towns of Bohemia. From now on Protestants were no longer to be allowed to build churches. Their religious publications were censored and they were excluded from public office. Finally, Matthias withdrew their right to assemble and present grievances. This was the spark that ignited a Protestant-led rebellion in Bohemia, which itself started the Thirty Years' War. In the year 1618, as cold war gave way to real war, each side felt they had reason to make a firm stand in Germany. From a Catholic point of view, the northern Netherlands, England, most of Scandinavia and much of the Holy Roman Empire had already been lost to the 'heretics'. Bohemia must not be next; like the Netherlands it was strategically and economically far too important to lose to the enemy camp. Protestants saw a mirror image of the situation. From their point of view, Protestant states had every reason to feel insecure. Protestant minorities had already been squeezed out in Spain, Poland and Bavaria. France was not far behind. Austria's new emperor was Ferdinand (elected 1619), a man who as archduke had proved to be the most unrelenting of counter-reformers. Having dealt with Protestants in Austria itself, he was turning on Bohemia's Protestants just when they had started to feel that their position was more secure.

In 1614 Cleves went to the elector of Brandenburg (Protestant) and Jülich to Wolfgang of Neuburg (Catholic). Why was Jülich–Cleves so desired by each side in the religious cold war?

Both Rudolph II and Matthias had been educated at the court of Philip II of Spain, where they had witnessed the difficulties caused by the revolt of the Netherlands. Why did Austria's rulers move from reluctant religious toleration to a position of uncompromising intolerance?

Rebel resentments were political and religious. On the first score, Emperor Matthias and his government had deserted Prague and made Vienna the chief centre of government, a loss of honour and patronage for the Czechs. Eleven lieutenants (or regents) – seven Catholic and four Protestant – were appointed to rule Bohemia. Initiated by Michna and the Catholic regents, heavy-handed repression of the religious freedom of Protestants followed. Michna said he would restore Catholicism. A deputation of protesting Protestants was arrested and imprisoned, churches were attacked and meetings of the Protestant Diet (parliament) were forbidden. Propagandist books from each side fanned the flames. In the face of threats from Michna, their chief target, to wipe out Bohemian Protestantism altogether, Protestants felt driven to use force to defend themselves. At an illegal Protestant assembly on 21 May 1618 three leading Calvinist nobles – Thurn, Ruppa and Colonna de Fels – planned a spectacular token protest to begin a revolt, a **defenestration** – throwing people through windows. As the protesters left for the fateful summit meeting on 23 May Protestant crowds cheered on the rebel leaders.

Hostilities began on 23 May 1618 with the ejection of three leading Habsburg officials – Martinitz, Slavata and Fabricius – through the windows of a tower in the old palace at Prague, Hradčany castle. This was the 'defenestration of Prague'. Falling a considerable distance, but landing either in the moat or a basement full of paper and rubbish (**sources** vary), all three survived, only one sustaining serious injuries. Two years later 26 of the rebel leaders were hanged, their rebellion having failed.

However, before the defeat of the Bohemian revolt it escalated into an international war. Within months it involved the Calvinist principalities of Germany as the rebels quickly mustered support outside Bohemia. Against the advice of most of his counsellors the young, ambitious and hot-headed Frederick V of the Palatinate, son of Frederick IV, seized the crown of Bohemia on behalf of the rebels. The first major foreign interventions came very quickly. Within a year Spain and Bavaria were involved in the war.

Earlier in this chapter (pages 111–14) and in Chapter 2 are explanations of why the international atmosphere was so inflammatory when matters of religion were concerned, particularly in Germany. Page 115 and Chapter 5 have looked at the readiness of Spain to commit itself to the aid of the Austrians under the guidance of Zúñiga and Olivares. Other parties to the conflict – mercenaries and their commanders, more distant great powers and German princes from the far reaches of the Holy Roman Empire – were equally eager to fight given the smallest of pretexts. The remainder of this chapter examines their motives.

**Defenestration** had been used as a token of protest before in Bohemian history, during the Hussite rebellion of the early fifteenth century.

Some Catholic **sources** said the falling men had been supported by angels.

### The fears and ambitions of the other great powers and the German princes

France and the Habsburg powers were not the only major players in the conflict. The United Provinces, Sweden, Denmark and the larger German principalities were far from being innocent bystanders or victims in the war. Denmark and Sweden played a big part. For the United Provinces the Thirty Years' War was simply an extension of its long **war with Spain**. The rebel state financed the Protestant German principalities in the conflict, fearful that a Habsburg triumph in Germany would make it easier for the Spanish to increase pressure on them. The Rhineland was of some importance to the economy of the United Provinces. Economic considerations lay behind the ambition of the leaders of Sweden and Denmark to control the Baltic ports, including the river outlets from north Germany. Both were actively expanding. Sweden conquered Estonia in 1617, just a year before the Thirty Years' War began. Sweden's ambitious king, Gustavus Adolphus, was pursuing narrow national objectives in wars with Poland, Denmark and Prussia. Swedish successes in the south Baltic region were coming dangerously close to 'Germany' itself.

After a twelve-year truce, the United Provinces and Spain resumed **war** in 1621 and carried on until 1646.

Focus on the portrait as propaganda. This engraving had a propagandist message. What was it?

**Gustavus Adolphus, king of Sweden and hero of the Protestant side in the Thirty Years' War, lands at Peenemünde in June 1630, launching Sweden's intervention. From a contemporary broadsheet, 1631.**

Into this heady mixture must go the ambitions of the German principalities. The larger ones like Brandenburg and Saxony were already electorates with a higher status and more power than their neighbours. Some of their leaders were ambitious to increase their size and consolidate dispersed pockets of territory into something more manageable. This was especially true of Brandenburg, the largest of the north German principalities. When war broke

What were the aims of the German principalities?

out their territories suffered greatly from the constant trampling of armies moving on to campaigns further south. However, this does not mean that their leaders had nothing to gain from the conflict. By carefully shifting from side to side as fortunes varied, the leaders of Brandenburg in particular were to succeed in their goals of expansion and consolidation.

## A war for the convenience of mercenaries and war-loving princes?

There were special causes of the Thirty Years' War, but it is well to remember that war was an ever-present feature in the normal relationships of seventeenth-century states. Only a few years of peace punctuated a century of war in Europe. It is for this reason that some historians have seen this war as only a symptom of a deeper crisis. Too many princes loved war for its own sake and tens of thousands of mercenary soldiers were assured of a regular job fighting wars on their behalf.

All the powers involved in the Thirty Years' War, with the exception of Sweden, relied on mercenaries for the greater part of their armies. The mercenary soldier fought for whoever was his paymaster. War was in his interest. Some of the mercenary commanders, notably Wallenstein (see page 126) and **Mansfeld**, were powerful figures in their own right. Mercenary forces played a greater part in this European war than in any conflict on a comparable scale before or since. The Historical sources that follow show how the mercenary commanders and one of the German princes could not wait for conflict to commence. The heavy mercenary involvement may also have prolonged the war. Gustavus Adolphus liked to train and employ his own nationals, but there were not enough of them for the largest of his campaigns. Without employing mercenaries he would not have been able to sustain his distant campaigns in southern Germany, 1,000 miles from Sweden. The mercenary system allowed human resource and other costs to be spread throughout Europe as these men came from all corners of the continent – from Poland, Italy, Ireland, Scotland, England and Germany.

The unscrupulous Count Ernst von **Mansfeld** (1580–1626) was employed by the Bohemian rebels and the Dutch.

## Historical sources

## Princes, mercenaries and the taste for war

Mercenaries relied on war to make a living. Sources 2 and 3 leave little doubt that this was their own cynical view. Christian of Brunswick also had a 'taste for war'. He was not unusual amongst his fellow-princes in voicing this sentiment. Unlike Wallenstein (Source 4), he combined that conventional princely love of fighting with devotion to his religion, the Calvinist faith.

## 1 A prince with a taste for war

I must confess that I have a taste for war, that I have it because I was born so, and shall have it indeed to my end.

Source: Prince Christian of Brunswick, letter to his mother (cited in C. V. Wedgwood, *The Thirty Years' War*, 1938, this edn 1962, p. 149).

## 2 A mercenary faces unemployment

The Bohemian Revolt had been manna in the wilderness to Mansfeld, who had found himself in 1618 faced with the prospect of disbanding his men.

Source: Wedgwood, 1962, p. 88.

## 3 The problem of finding 'just causes'

Count **Tilly** (1559–1632) was a Flemish general employed by Maximilian I of Bavaria. He was a fanatical Catholic.

I brought up the proposal that we go to war against the Turks. [**Tilly**] jumped at the idea . . . [He] told me that there would be nothing more difficult in such an undertaking than finding a just cause for declaring war.

Source: Wallenstein, letter of April 1629 (cited in T. K. Rabb, *The Thirty Years' War*, 1964, 2nd edn 1981, pp. 107–08).

## 4 Wallenstein's ambitions

[Wallenstein] lived in the midst of his grand designs, in which the public interest was mixed up with his private aims. It was all clothed in a self-confidence that blinded even Wallenstein himself . . . His ambition [was] to break free of all subordination and to assume an independent position among the leaders of the world . . . If it became impossible to achieve this with the approval of the Emperor then it would happen anyway with himself and the House of Austria on opposite sides.

Source: L. V. Ranke, *Geschichte Wallensteins*, 1872 (transl. and ed., Rabb, 1981, pp. 112, 113).

## Historical-source questions

1   What are the similarities between Sources 1, 2 and 3?
2   What are the differences between Sources 1, 2 and 3?
3   To what extent does Source 3 support line 1 of Source 4?
4   'War was as much pleasure as business for the kings and princes, no less than it was for the mercenary generals.' Do you agree? Use the sources and your own knowledge in your answer.

# Art and society in Italy and Holland

Dutch art reached a high point in the seventeenth century. This was the period of Rembrandt and Vermeer and several other artists of the highest reputation. As artists were drawn to France in the early twentieth century, so were they drawn to the Dutch Republic in the seventeenth.

Dutch art developed in a different way from art in the rest of the continent, though it is important to remember that what is being talked about here is the leading Dutch style. The art favoured by patrons across most of Europe was Baroque: elaborate, colourful, swirling, decorative, illustrating classical themes, depicting luxurious settings and people of high birth. Kings, Catholic Church leaders, courtiers and aristocrats all commissioned works in the Baroque style. Mainstream Dutch art differed from this in every respect. Realistic, generally sombre in tone and restrained in colour, it favoured simple domestic scenes and realistic portraiture of the merchant class. Dutch churches were now bare but, for the first time anywhere, the general public was buying pictures on the open market from picture dealers and auction houses. Visitors to Holland were amazed to find that even farmers and crafts-men had paintings in their homes. Baroque art, often to be found in Dutch Catholic churches and the palaces of aristocrats and monarchs, stood for everything most middle-class Dutch patrons and buyers despised. They saw it as propaganda for the Catholic Counter-Reformation.

## 1 Baroque art

*Aurora* (1613–14), a fresco in the Casino Pallavicini-Rospigliosi, Rome, by Guido Reni (1575–1642). 'The Sun's Chariot rides on the clouds, drawn by a quadriga, accompanied by a procession of the Hours and preceded by Aurora, who is carrying flowers.'

## 2 Baroque art

*Madonna of Loretto*, Agostino church, Rome, 1604–05, by Caravaggio.

## 3 Dutch realism

*Four officers of the Amsterdam Coopers' and Wine-rackers' Guild*, 1657, by Gerbrand van den Eeckhout (1621–74).

## 4 Dutch realism

*A woman and her maid in a courtyard*, c.1660–61, by Pieter de Hooch (1629–84).

## 5 Dutch realism

*Female surgeon*, engraving after Adriaen Brouwer (1605/6–38).

## Picture case-study questions

1 Compare Sources 1 and 2 with Sources 3 to 5.
  (a) How are they different in subject and style?
  (b) How would you account for the differences?

2 Why were paintings such as Sources 3 and 4 popular purchases for display in the homes of Dutch merchants?

3 Compare Sources 3 to 5 with Leeuwenhoek's microscope illustration on page 166. What are the connections? Look at the other paintings in this book and see if you can find any other interesting pairings, either by contrast or similarity.

4 Why did art develop in such distinctively different ways in Holland and Italy? (Use the sources and your own knowledge; the answer does not require detailed knowledge of art and art movements.)

## Summary question

1 (a) Explain any *two* factors that increased the likelihood of a major European war in the Holy Roman Empire in the early seventeenth century.

  (b) Explain which one factor was the most important long-term cause of the Thirty Years' War.

# 9

# The war and its consequences

**Focus questions**

◆ What were the effects of foreign intervention?

◆ Why could the Habsburgs not maintain their early successes?

◆ What was the outcome of the Thirty Years' War?

## Significant dates

**1618–20** Protestant revolt in Bohemia attracts support from the Palatinate, the most ardent Calvinist German princes and Transylvania, but is defeated by Habsburg Austria, Spain, Poland and Maximilian's Catholic League.

**1621–24** The Palatinate Wars. Habsburg forces take on Frederick V in the Palatinate. A Spanish push into the Valtelline Pass in the Alps provokes a localised French intervention.

**1625–29** Denmark enters the war on the anti-Habsburg side. Withdraws four years later after unsuccessful intervention. Big Habsburg victories in northern Germany.

**1630** Sweden enters the war on the anti-Habsburg side, with French financial support. Over the next four years its intervention tips the balance against the Habsburgs.

**1635** France enters the war on the anti-Habsburg side. Over the next seven years France takes over Sweden's role.

**1642–45** Revolts and other wars divert the energies of France, Spain and Sweden. Unpredictable victories by each side over next three years.

**1645–48** String of French–Swedish victories against Bavaria, Austria's main ally. Peace agreed after Prague is reached by anti-Habsburg forces; this is the Peace of Westphalia.

## Overview

Except as a good memory-jogger, the term 'Thirty Years' War' has few merits. Most historians would be unhappy if the Second World War were to be renamed 'The Six Years' War' or the Napoleonic Wars retitled 'The Nineteen

Years' War'. More effective titles convey either something of the geographical scope of a war (e.g. 'Russo-Japanese War'), a crucial cause (e.g. 'Napoleonic Wars') or their sequence (e.g. 'Second Anglo-Dutch War'). In defence of the name 'The Thirty Years' War', perhaps the very absence of a causal clue or number gives some indication of the nature of this particular bunching of wars. There was no one clear cause, no clear sequential place – just a long period of almost continuous warfare. Referring to what we now call the Thirty Years' War, contemporaries generally spoke about the 'wars'. The Dutch do not speak of a Thirty Years' War but of an 80 years' war of independence between 1568 and 1648. For the French the war is memorable for the 24-year combat with Spain between 1635 and 1659.

## What were the effects of foreign intervention?

### A summary of the effects

By the end of 1618 foreign interventions had turned a civil war in the Bohemian region of the Austrian Empire into a major war in 'Germany' and Bohemia. By the end of 1619 this was no longer simply a German affair, for Spain was involved. Polish forces were also fighting for the Habsburgs by the end of the same year. The composition of forces on the rebel side had already expanded beyond Germanic Europe, with the intervention of the Transylvanian leader **Bethlen Gábor**. After 1625 further full-scale foreign interventions turned the conflict into a war involving north, central, southern and eastern Europe. By 1635 all Europe's major powers and dozens more minor states were involved.

Foreign interventions prolonged the war. Many intervening powers had little concern for the issues involved in the original dispute, Austria's persecution of Protestants and the Bohemians' revolt. Rather they were reacting to the perceived danger of Habsburg expansion into northern Europe. Others joined one side or the other or even changed sides to take advantage of the opportunities offered by the tide of battle at different times in the war. This was true of Saxony and **Brandenburg**.

Foreign intervention decisively influenced the course of the war. In 1619 the Transylvanian intervention encouraged Frederick V to take the bold move of accepting the crown of Bohemia on behalf of the rebels. At the end of 1619 the ardent Catholic King Sigismund III of Poland organised raids into Upper Hungary and Transylvania that forced Bethlen Gábor's Transylvanian forces to withdraw from Vienna. In the early 1620s the might of Spain helped the Habsburgs to victory over the rebels. In 1620 rebel forces were heavily defeated in the Battle of the White Mountain, near Prague. A year later they were routed in the Palatinate. The rebel forces were badly co-ordinated and

Transylvania covered what is now western Romania and eastern Hungary. Its self-proclaimed Calvinist king, **Bethlen Gábor** (1620–29), recognised Ottoman overlordship but in practice ruled independently. His was a thriving state with a strong army.

In the 1620s **Brandenburg** sided with Austria. In 1631 it joined the anti-Habsburg side, when it was winning. In 1635 it switched to a neutral position after a big Habsburg victory in 1634.

Why did the rebellion escalate into a multi-power war? Use the list of key dates to plot the escalation.

Mansfeld's army was unpopular due to its plunder of civilian populations. Only the financial aid of the United Provinces allowed Frederick V and the Protestant Union to hold on in the Palatinate. Spectacular Habsburg victories in northern Germany in the late 1620s saw off a Danish intervention on the Protestant side. By the end of 1629 the Habsburgs seemed to be in a winning position.

In the 1630s the might of Sweden and France turned the balance of forces slightly to the advantage of the anti-Habsburg side. Military innovations made by the Swedish king, Gustavus Adolphus, contributed to its success; these are considered later in this chapter.

## The composition of each side

There were many combatant states. The combatants may be divided into two camps, the Habsburg and the anti-Habsburg. However, it is important to remember that the situation was unstable. When it suited them, some of the German principalities – such as Brandenburg – changed sides or went through periods of neutrality. In such cases the state has been identified with the side it most frequently supported.

### The Habsburg camp

Involved from the start and throughout were the Austrian Habsburgs. Ferdinand II, emperor between 1619 and 1637, was an ardent Catholic and the main war leader on the Habsburg side. He had provoked revolt in Bohemia in 1618 by his harsh rule and on the defeat of the Bohemian rebels he pursued a policy of revenge. Ferdinand III (emperor between 1637 and 1657) was more moderate than his father, but felt duty-bound to continue the war to ensure that the family dynasty came out of the conflict well.

Bavaria was Austria's main ally. Maximilian of Bavaria (1597–1651), had received a Jesuit education and shared the Habsburg zeal for the Counter-Reformation. Later in the war, although Bavaria stayed on the Habsburg side, he was prepared to compromise so that a diplomatic solution could be reached. In spite of these later waverings, he is placed at the heart of the Habsburg camp because of the crucial role he played in the defeat of the Calvinist rebels and their allies in the early stages. His Catholic League army, which was composed chiefly of the forces of Bavaria and the German Catholic princes, was essential to the Habsburg side at several points in the conflict.

The principal generals on this side were the mercenary Wallenstein and the Flemish general Tilly, employed by Maximilian. He was commonly known as the 'monk in armour' and his loyalty was never in question. This could never be said of **Wallenstein**, who would have liked to have become a ruler in his own right. Nevertheless, at vital times, both through his financial

Albrecht von Wallenstein (1583–1634), the greatest mercenary general of his age, was the son of a Protestant landowner and orphaned as a child. He was a violent youth who converted to Catholicism and married a wealthy widow. He developed his estates in a grand manner and dressed in a weird mixture of European fashions. In 1634 he was assassinated by English and Irish mercenaries.

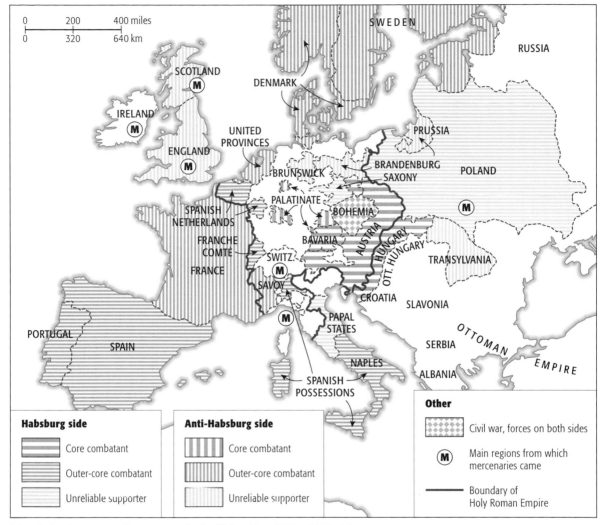

**Map 6: Combatants and supporters in the Thirty Years' War, 1618–48.**

Map legend:

**Habsburg side**
- Core combatant
- Outer-core combatant
- Unreliable supporter

**Anti-Habsburg side**
- Core combatant
- Outer-core combatant
- Unreliable supporter

**Other**
- Civil war, forces on both sides
- (M) Main regions from which mercenaries came
- Boundary of Holy Roman Empire

Scale: 0 – 200 – 400 miles / 0 – 320 – 640 km

contributions and his creation and leadership of great armies, Wallenstein was a great asset to the Habsburg cause. When later he became too ambitious and difficult to handle, Ferdinand sacked him and had him assassinated.

Between the Spanish and Austrian Habsburgs there was a degree of family loyalty, but it was not as strong as enemy propagandists suggested. Spanish support against the rebels in 1619 was important to early Habsburg success. In spite of this, Spain's commitment to the Austrian cause in Bohemia was less than total, their continued involvement in the war being largely centred around their desire to continue the fight against the rebel provinces of the northern Netherlands. Spain's energies were mostly directed against the Dutch. Later, in the 1640s, their priority was to prevent the disintegration of Spain itself. Ferdinand II was astute enough to realise this and he rewarded

Spain with a valuable prize for its early support, the province of Alsace. This was a useful stepping stone on the 'Spanish Road' from the Netherlands to the Mediterranean (see Map 3, page 70). However, this move backfired because it angered the French. Richelieu committed France fully to the war in 1635, forcing Spain to become more deeply involved than it wished.

John George of Saxony (reigned 1611–56), the infamously drunken prince of a Lutheran principality, helped Ferdinand II in the suppression of the Bohemian revolt. He followed this up by sending his forces to fight against Frederick V. He was rewarded with neighbouring territory, the Lusatias. After that he was a far from reliable ally. In the early 1630s he switched sides to the victorious Swedes. When the tide moved back in favour of the Habsburg side in 1635, he hastened to make peace with Ferdinand II. He then stayed with the Habsburg side until it became obvious that they could not win the war.

Poland under Sigismund III (reigned 1587–1632), a zealous Catholic, offered support to the Austrian Habsburgs in the crucial first year of the conflict. Sigismund permitted the Austrians to recruit in Poland.

### The anti-Habsburg camp

One of the weaknesses of this side was that no one great power was at the helm of their forces throughout the war. Particularly in the early years, it consisted of small second-rank powers. The fighting centred on Bohemia and southern Germany, and rebel forces were supplied by Frederick V of the Palatinate, Christian of Anhalt, Christian of Brunswick and Mansfeld. That they survived at all was largely thanks to the financial backing of the United Provinces and the assistance of the Transylvanian forces.

Frederick V's Palatinate territories were small and scattered. They were easy to surround. Christian of Anhalt and Christian of Brunswick were, like Frederick, dedicated Calvinists. However, their territories were even smaller than his. The Protestant League's general, Mansfeld, had the ability to raise armies quickly, but his victories were rare and his loyalty never extended beyond the expiry of his current contract. Even so, it was his forces that were at the heart of the anti-Habsburg camp before 1625.

As a Calvinist, Bethlen Gábor, prince of Transylvania, was expected to offer his support to fellow-Calvinists in nearby Bohemia. He gladly did so, especially as this helped to stave off internal unrest. His intervention in 1619 was significant as it encouraged the Bohemian rebels to elect Frederick V of the Palatinate as their king, widening the conflict. In the later stages of the war he was to justify his reputation for unreliability. As monarch of a sizeable Protestant power and uncle to Frederick V, James I of England was expected to offer support to the Palatinate. In the event, help was given on a modest scale because James was unwilling to commit England to a conflict from which it

What were the weaknesses of the anti-Habsburg side in the early stages of the war?

was unlikely to gain anything and which had started badly for his nephew. He frequently urged Frederick to back down. Even less reliable in the anti-Habsburg camp, in spite of their Calvinism, were the electors of Brandenburg. Frederick William, the 'Great Elector' of Brandenburg (1640–88), was above all anxious to survive the onslaughts of marauding armies upon his widely scattered and vulnerable territories. As an elector he was formally obliged to support the 'Emperor of the German Nation', his sovereign, in spite of the title-holder's Catholicism.

In 1625 England subsidised Denmark's entry into the war. When he committed his forces to the conflict on the anti-Habsburg side in 1625, **Christian IV** of Denmark hoped for prestige and territory. As duke of Holstein as well as king of Denmark he was technically a German prince and so could claim an interest. He argued that his interests as king of Denmark were also threatened because his kingdom held pockets of land on the north German coast. Although his motives were partly defensive, his ambition was soon obvious when his troops occupied additional pockets of territory in his opening campaign of 1625. Christian aspired to be the leading statesman of Europe, ahead of his Swedish rival Gustavus Adolphus. However, he over-estimated his country's strength. Heavy defeats in 1626 made it clear that Denmark was no longer a great power.

**Gustavus Adolphus**, king of Sweden between 1611 and his death in battle in 1632, likewise talked only of defence. He presented himself as the protector of the Protestant north against the Catholic world. The degree to which he was really ambitious for himself and for Sweden is much debated. It is clear that, like Christian of Denmark, he enjoyed war. In the short term Sweden's intervention was more successful than expected, thanks partly to French subsidy and partly to Gustavus's military genius. In 1634 – after a serious reversal of fortunes and faced with the task of salvaging the fruits of earlier successes – Sweden's able chancellor, **Axel Oxenstierna**, kept Sweden in the war but at a lower level of involvement.

France's limited intervention against Spain because of its occupation of the **Valtelline Pass** in 1620 marked a hardening of French attitudes to the Habsburgs. Richelieu's coming to power in 1624 brought an alliance between France, Sweden and Denmark in the same year. Full-scale French intervention followed hard on Sweden's defeats of 1634. On the surface the motives of Louis and Richelieu were again defensive. They argued that the Habsburgs were now a real threat to the whole of Europe and only a great power like France could stop them. If this were so, it is hard to account for France's failure to intervene at the start of the war in 1618. There seems little doubt that some territorial ambitions were involved. Savoy followed France into the fray in 1635.

**Christian IV**, king of Denmark 1588–1648, had ambitions to expand further south, into Schleswig and Holstein. Though Denmark's empire was mostly in Scandinavia, German was the language of the court and the government.

**Gustavus Adolphus**: 'The fight will be for parents, for wife and child, for house and home, for fatherland and Faith' (speech of 1629, cited in T. K. Rabb, *Thirty Years' War*, 1964, 2nd edn, 1981, p.87).

Count **Oxenstierna** was Chancellor of Sweden 1612–54 and successfully directed Swedish foreign policy for most of the Thirty Years' War.

The **Valtelline** was a vital Alpine pass on the route of Spanish troops to the Netherlands. It was a good distance from France and separated by huge mountain ranges.

The 'Dutch were consistent supporters of the anti-Habsburg side, though infrequently involved in battle. At several points they helped finance anti-Habsburg partners, and their parallel war with Spain diverted powerful Spanish forces from 'Germany' itself.

What were the motives behind the interventions of Denmark, Sweden, France and the United Provinces?

## Why could the Habsburgs not maintain their early successes?

### Fear of a Habsburg conquest of Europe

At the start of the conflict, most sovereigns across Europe, including Lutheran German princes, felt that the moral high ground was held by the Austrian emperor, Ferdinand II. In their view the Calvinists had organised a violent revolt. They felt that Frederick V, who took the crown of Bohemia for the rebels, was inspired by youthful passion and personal ambition. Besides, in the early stages the Habsburg victories were not felt to threaten the balance of power in Europe, though anxieties began to increase as early as 1621 with their successes in the Palatinate.

Fears of Habsburg expansion well beyond the borders of the Austrian Empire played a major part in the development of the war after 1621 and a decisive part after 1630. Anxieties about loss of territory were combined with fear of the annihilation of Protestantism across Europe. Ferdinand's policies of revenge in Bohemia in the 1620s – an Austrian inquisition to match the Spanish one – stored up further resentments and helped to keep the war going. Even Maximilian began to believe that his Habsburg neighbours were becoming too powerful. For this reason he conducted his own negotiations with France and in 1631 Bavaria joined France in a defensive alliance. The Bourbons of France had no intention of intervening with any large-scale force in the first 12 years of the war and Louis XIII's sympathies had originally been with the Austrian Habsburgs. The rewarding of Spain with Alsace and Wallenstein's promotion to the fabulous-sounding title of 'General of the Oceanic and Baltic Seas' in 1628 seemed to confirm Scandinavian and French fears that the Habsburgs aimed to extend their empire to northern Europe. In spite of being bitter rivals and regular adversaries in wars, the Danes and Swedes came together to relieve the Habsburg siege of the important Baltic port of Stralsund in 1628 – a rare instance of Scandinavian co-operation in this period. Even the papacy refused to continue to back the Habsburgs, fearful of taking sides between Catholic France and the Catholic Habsburgs. Pope Urban VIII, an admirer of France and Louis XIII, pushed for a compromise. After 1629 Ferdinand alienated another former ally, John George of Saxony, by issuing the **Edict of Restitution** requiring return of all church lands taken over by Protestants since 1552. This alarmed all the Lutheran princes of Germany

The **Edict of Restitution** demanded the 'return' of 2 archbishoprics, 12 bishoprics and 50 abbeys. Immediately, Wallenstein started to enforce it.

Why did the Austrian Habsburgs lose the support of 'natural allies' as well as Lutheran leaders after 1628?

and northern Europe as it seemed to mark a new aggressive spirit in the Counter-Reformation.

After 1630 the interventions of Sweden and France tipped the balance of forces against the Habsburg side. In 1631 the Swedes and Saxons defeated Tilly's army at Breitenfeld. The Saxons captured Prague and Gustavus headed for the Rhineland. The next year the Swedish invaded Bavaria and Swedish-led forces defeated Habsburg armies at Lützen, where Gustavus was killed. Anti-Habsburg success was not consolidated; they were themselves defeated at Nördlingen in 1634. However, the Swedish intervention had turned the tide at a crucial point in the war and the French now took up the baton from them. If Gustavus had not intervened in 1630 the likelihood is that the war would have ended more quickly, with Ferdinand II victorious in the German lands. Gustavus Adolphus introduced better weaponry and superior tactics, backed up with armies of sufficient size to match those of Tilly and Wallenstein. For these reasons his impact on the course of the war lasted beyond his death in the Battle of Lützen in 1632. In retaliation for his run of defeats between 1630 and 1632 and his scheme to set himself up as an independent sovereign free of his Habsburg paymasters, Wallenstein was dismissed as imperial commander in 1631 and assassinated in 1634. Ironically, or perhaps fittingly, his assassins were mercenaries. On balance, his death was probably to the advantage of the anti-Habsburg side, for although Wallenstein was an eccentric and dangerous figure he was also a very capable mercenary commander.

In the 1640s, the last quarter of the war, the distractions of revolts and other wars of an equal or higher priority weakened the effectiveness of many offensives. France and Spain were particularly anxious about internal difficulties in the 1640s, while Sweden was distracted by wars with Denmark. If, on balance, the anti-Habsburg coalition had the advantage in the last years of the war, the 'defeated' side was far from thrashed.

Why did the war last so long?

## Gustavus Adolphus and the 'military revolution'

At a time when warfare was a regular instrument of state policy it would have been remarkable if there had not been major improvements in tactics, weaponry and organisation. Many of these were the work of the Swedish king, Gustavus Adolphus. They helped the Swedes turn the tide and, because they were more efficient, they also increased the military death toll in the Thirty Years' War. For these reasons and because of their wider significance it is worth spending some time looking at the detail of warfare in this period.

The influence of the changes in tactics was to stretch to the present century. Their origins lie with the 'Dutch school' of Maurice of Nassau (see page 91), which trained Swedish officers. In the sixteenth century each side had deployed three or four 'Spanish squares', solid rectangles of pikemen surrounded by a girdle of men bearing firearms. This was a style of warfare best suited to defence. The square, a 2,000–3,000-strong force of 6-metre pikes, created a huge bristling hedgehog that was effective against cavalry charges. In the early seventeenth century Maurice and the Dutch school devised formations that maximised firepower. These were elongated blocks of musketeers interspersed with pike formations to protect them against charging cavalry. Instead of the great Spanish square, Dutch armies were arranged in two or three lines and units consisted of only 550 men. Cavalry units were also thinned. The result was an increased capacity to manoeuvre quickly and to harass the enemy. However, thorough training, a high level of discipline and sufficient manpower were essential for success and some battles in the Thirty Years' War were won by commanders sticking to improved Spanish square tactics against poor commanders using the new Dutch tactics.

Realising that to be effective the new tactics would require an adequate supply of men, Gustavus built up an army based on national conscription. From the 1620s service was to last for 20 years. The Swedish state took on responsibility for supply and logistics. National conscript armies of this kind proved to be cheaper, better disciplined and more loyal. Other states followed suit later in the century.

Improvements in armour and weaponry were also required to maximise the effectiveness of Dutch school tactics. Gustavus gave these close attention. He made his men wear light armour even though armour was becoming unfashionable. Infantry were equipped with a new iron-clad short pike. A lighter musket was issued as the standard weapon of the infantryman. The cartridge, a fixed charge with powder carefully measured and ball attached, was introduced. Gustavus's greatest advances were in **artillery** design. Cannons were made lighter and smaller so that they could be mobile. Artillerymen were given more prominence in the armed forces.

The smaller **artillery** piece could be pulled by a single horse and had a high rate of fire.

Gustavus's innovations in tactics reached their highest level of sophistication after 1627. The objectives were to combine maximum hitting power, mobility and defensive strength. To this end his lines were only six deep instead of ten, as they had been in Maurice's army, so that they could hear the order of command. Cavalry was thinned to three deep. Pikemen and cavalrymen were supported by more firepower and given a new offensive role. Musketeers and artillery gunners fired simultaneously to blow a hole in the enemy ranks. These tactics were almost as effective when followed by other generals. However, later in the war generals employed by the Habsburgs adopted many of the new tactics themselves, evening out the balance on the battlefield one more.

It must be remembered that Gustavus was only able to intervene so forcefully thanks to heavy subsidy from France. After 1635 and again after 1639

Richelieu stepped up the level of French involvement. The French role was twofold: sapping the energies of Spanish forces and keeping the Swedish commitment afloat beyond the point when, left on its own, Sweden would have had to withdraw.

## What was the outcome of the Thirty Years' War?

From the day the peace settlement was signed, debate has surrounded the consequences of the war. In spite of what had essentially been a Habsburg defeat, Protestants in the Austrian Empire were denied religious freedom by the terms of the settlement. On the other hand the United Provinces was now formally recognised as an independent state. Heads of state who had fought on both sides of the conflict made territorial gains. Sweden and France did especially well. Seemingly, there was hardly a losing party other than the Calvinist rebels on whose behalf the original states on the anti-Habsburg side had intervened. However, there is clear evidence that the people of central Europe were also losers by the war, though the extent of the war's economic impact has been much debated.

### The balance sheet

The greater powers involved were in no hurry to negotiate peace. During the seven years of peace negotiations the Habsburg side delayed in the hope that the Swedish–Danish war would improve their military position. The opposing side also delayed until their campaigns were more successful. Such cynical tactics heaped more ruination upon the war's greatest losers, the people living in areas of repeated campaigning.

Issues of individual religious rights were largely swept aside by the peace-makers. Calvinism was admitted as an official religion so long as the ruler chose it. If a subject did not agree with his ruler, his only option was to emigrate. Calvinists lost the freedom to practise their faith in Bohemia, Moravia and Silesia because the terms of the peace allowed the Habsburgs to withhold religious toleration in their territories. Church lands were returned to the owners of 1624, not to the position at the start of the war, so giving the religious advantage from the conflict to the Catholics.

> How effective was the settlement in dealing with the religious issues over which some had fought the war?

### Impact on the balance of power

The balance of power was altered by the Peace of Westphalia, but not as dramatically as one might imagine when one side defeats another in a major war. Almost all the heads of state, even those on the losing side, had something to celebrate. This was hardly surprising as the representatives agreed terms on behalf of their sovereigns, not of their people. Six of the eight principal combatants made territorial gains, while even the Austrian Habsburgs lost very little land. The Austrians retained the crown of Bohemia, to be hereditary in the Habsburg line. They also recovered Upper Austria. Thus, Austria remained the predominant power in east-central Europe. Bavaria, Saxony and Brandenburg all made significant territorial gains, in spite of being on opposing sides. Brandenburg received the bishoprics of Minden, Halberstadt and Cammin and the right of succession to the archbishopric of Madgeburg. Maximilian of Bavaria obtained the Upper Palatinate and the right to keep his status as an elector.

Austria may have remained dominant in east-central Europe, but any future plans for thrusts into western and northern Europe were now to be firmly blocked off. The greatest gains were made by Sweden and France. France, in combination with Sweden and the United Provinces, had stood up to the Habsburg powers and emerged victorious. Western Pomerania and lands west of the mouth of the Elbe were given to Sweden. This was rather less than the Swedes had hoped for, but still substantial. In addition Sweden was to be paid reparations (compensation) of 5 million Reichstaler and to be given representation in the Imperial Diet, so giving Sweden a stake in German affairs. France gained most of Alsace and the three disputed bishoprics of Metz, Verdun and Toul in Lorraine, gains of strategic importance, allowing it to outflank Spanish Franche-Comté. The Breisach and Pinerolo fortresses were also given to France. Though the terms of France's acquisitions in Alsace were to be the matter of legal dispute for a long time ahead, the French themselves did not doubt their right to full territorial control and they acted accordingly. Arguably, the peace settlement achieved a better balance of power between Habsburg Austria and France, though the warmongering of France's King Louis XIV over almost fifty years (1667–1713) might suggest it went too far in the French direction.

The princes of the Holy Roman Empire gained virtual independence, a blow to the prestige and power of the emperor and a diplomatic victory for France. The Dutch Republic and the Confederation of Switzerland were recognised as fully independent states. The long struggle of the Dutch to be free from Habsburg control was finally successful, with all its implications perhaps for the future development of an economically vibrant society in that corner of Europe. After 1648 it becomes a little more correct and meaningful to talk about the 'countries' or 'nations' of central Europe, for the settlement emphasised the national character of the Austrian Habsburg lands, as well as encouraging sovereigns of smaller principalities within the Holy Roman Empire to act in a more independent way. Princes and electors within the Holy Roman Empire were granted the right to draw up treaties with powers outside the empire, so long as these were not directed against the emperor.

This meant, for example, that Spain's sovereignty over the southern Netherlands was now recognised as outside the control of the Holy Roman emperor. When in 1659 Spain drew up a peace treaty with France, this was done quite independently of the emperor. Though the Holy Roman Empire remained, the emperor's authority was greatly reduced. It became more and more of a fossil as the rest of Europe gradually organised into nation-states. The emperor's control over German politics was practically ended, as the way was opened for small German states to develop as independent powers, instead of dependent feudal fiefdoms.

The Peace of Westphalia was the most important adjustment to the European state system until the Settlement of Utrecht (1713) and it was still considered relevant until the French revolutionary wars of the 1790s. However, its importance must not be exaggerated. It did not put an end to the conflict between France and Spain, which continued to 1659. Nor did it affect the northern and eastern states of Europe, other than Sweden.

How did the outcome of the war affect the balance of power?

In what ways did the settlement look to the past and in what respects did it look to the future?

## Social and economic consequences: a disastrous war?

### The debate between historians

Most contemporary observers viewed the war as disastrous, arguing that it was a catastrophe for Germany. This view was popularised in the nineteenth century and rarely challenged until the late twentieth century. In the 1960s a different view emerged – arguing that the war was not a disaster and Germany had already been in decline before it began.

Some contemporary chroniclers, diarists, letter-writers and artists – like the more sensationalist journalists today – were inclined to exaggerate and to

A scene from Jacques Callot's etching *The appalling miseries of war* (1633) shows a mass execution of looters. Callot, a Frenchman, was probably working from Franck and Wouwermans, earlier Dutch artists.

How useful are these pictures for the historian studying the impact of the war?

dramatise. Others were too personally affected to be objective. All too easily the image of a particular scene in the war becomes a general image of the horrors of war. Pictures such as those of Callot are startling and unforgettable in their grisly depiction of seventeenth-century warfare, but it is doubtful if they show any particular verifiable incident. From less exciting but more reliable sources such as local tax and census figures there is evidence that many parts of Germany were in economic decline before the outbreak of the war, others actually prospered during it and Germany made rapid progress afterwards. The effects of the war varied greatly throughout the Holy Roman Empire, and the war may simply have accelerated an existing trend towards economic and population decline in Germany.

## A look at the figures

Estimates of population change for the Holy Roman Empire as a whole have ranged from a loss of 6½ million, approximately a third, to a net gain of 1 million. Revised estimates, taking account of population displacement (many people moved rather than be killed) and miscounting, put the decline in population in the Holy Roman Empire during the war at between 15 per cent and 20 per cent, rather less than earlier estimates, but still amounting to over 3 million people. This was a catastrophic event; compare, for example, losses for soldiers and civilians in the Second World War to the order of 6 per cent. Regionally, losses of between 66 per cent and 80 per cent were experienced in the Palatinate, Pomerania and parts of Bohemia, Brandenburg, Silesia and Bavaria. Magdeburg lost 25,000 of its 30,000 inhabitants and some historians estimate that the population of Augsburg, the largest German city in 1620, was reduced to less than half by 1650. In spite of these huge losses it is probable that by the start of the eighteenth century Germany had made a complete demographic (population) recovery.

There was an unusually high proportion of deaths in battle, especially after 1630 and the introduction of deadlier methods of warfare. The high number of military deaths from disease and famine was nothing out of the ordinary for this period. At a conservative estimate, military losses in action were over 300,000, or just over a half per cent of the combined population of the main catchment areas for mercenaries. Thus, in spite of the high proportion of military losses, the civilian figures were worse.

Most historians consider that the Holy Roman Empire was in economic decline before 1618. Most of the cities had suffered from over-taxation in the first half of the sixteenth century by Emperor Charles V. Strong competition from Sweden, England, France and the Netherlands proved too much for German merchants throughout the sixteenth century. However, the war generally accelerated decline. Formerly great cities like Magdeburg were devastated. Rural as well as urban areas were ruined by the high tax demands of military commanders and ambitious electors, particularly in Brandenburg. The fighting itself and the forced billeting (housing) of troops with civilians ruined trade by fouling up the overland routes. Although outlying trade routes were boosted, many of these were held by the Swedes and the Dutch.

Agriculture was already in severe difficulties because of a collapse in prices. Again, the fighting made a bad situation worse, bringing destruction and insupportable losses to the labour force. In some areas there were more mouths to feed and homes to find because of the influx of refugees. On the other hand, there were good side-effects even in the most devastated areas. In these areas there were fewer mouths to feed and in south-west Germany serfdom (virtual slavery) declined because the peasants used their reduction in numbers to good advantage to press for better rights.

What were the social and economic effects of the war in Germany?

## Historical sources

## A The contribution of Gustavan military advances to the failure of the Habsburgs to maintain early successes

At least one historian has argued that the 'military revolution' of Gustavus was of no great importance to the outcome of the war (G. Parker, *The Thirty Years' War*, 1984). His argument is that two of the most decisive battles of the war were won using traditional 'Spanish square' tactics (White Mountain, 1620, and Nördlingen, 1634). This is a minority view and not one shared by the historians represented here. However, significant as they were, it is important to keep the military advances in proportion.

### 1 Swedish musketeer and three-pounder regimental piece

Source: R. E. and T. N. Dupuy, *Harper encyclopedia of military history*, 1993, pp. 524, 526

## 2  The Battle of the River Lech, 5 April 1632

Source: *Gustavus Adolphus crosses the Lech and pushes back the Count de Tilly*, engraving.

## 3  A 'Spanish square' army (left) formed up against a 'Dutch school' army (right)

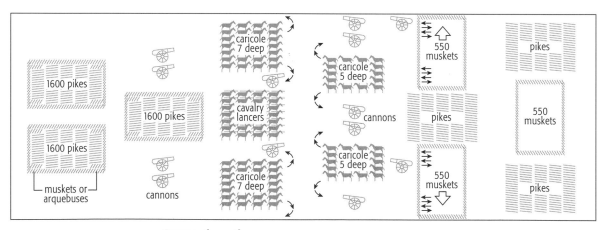

Source: the author.

### 4 The origins of enduring military tactics

This was the genesis of modern linear tactics, which remained basically unchanged – though constantly modified – until World War I. Even today, despite drastic tactical changes of two world wars and the advent of nuclear weapons, vestiges of Gustavus's linear concept remain in modern infantry doctrine.

Source: R. E. and T. N. Dupuy, *Encyclopedia of military history*, 1970, p. 526.

### 5 The basis of Gustavus's high reputation

Gustavus' objective was annihilation of the enemy, something very different from Wallenstein's gouty strategy, and still more from the siege warfare of Maurice . . . no other general of his age would have attempted the passage of the Rhine at Oppenheim, and still less that of the Lech, in the face of Tilly's entire army drawn up in a carefully chosen position.

Source: M. Roberts, *Gustavus Adolphus and the rise of Sweden*, 1973, p. 113.

## Historical-source questions A

1 Study Sources 1 to 3. Describe the battle shown in Source 2. What new tactics and weaponry were employed?
2 Source 2 was produced by the Protestant side during the war. To what extent does this lessen its value to military historians?
3 How significant was the contribution of the 'military revolution' to the outcome of the war? Use all sources and your own knowledge to answer this question.

## B The debate about the consequences of the war

This document set focuses on secondary sources. A lengthy extract from Wedgwood (Source 2a) has been included as this is the only text that gives a sense of the impact of destruction on a local scale. To create this depth of detail Wedgwood did not hesitate to use every chronicle available. Therein lies a problem for Steinberg.

### 1 The despairing reflection of a Bohemian exile

They have sacrificed us at the treaties of **Osnabrück** . . . I conjure you by the wounds of Christ, that you do not forsake us who are persecuted for the sake of Christ.

Source: Comenius, a Bohemian Protestant exile (in C. V. Wedgwood, *The Thirty Years' War*, 1938, this edn 1962, p. 526)

The Treaty of **Osnabrück** (1648) was one of the treaties that ended the war. The other was the Treaty of Münster, another town in Westphalia (also in 1648).

## 2a  The effect of military actions on civilians

At Magdeburg, Pappenheim had burnt what was left of the town when he evacuated it in the spring of 1632, and the Swedish troops who came in shared [with] the few survivors living in cellars and dug-outs among the ruins. The Alsatian town of Hagenau, three times occupied in eighteen months, lamented: 'We have had blue-coats and red-coats and now come the yellow-coats. God have pity on us.' At Frankfurt-on-the-Oder pestilence bred of the rotting bodies of the dead had overwhelmed the survivors. At Stettin and Spandau the Swedes had left the plague; at Bamberg the bodies lay unburied in the streets, and on both banks of the Rhine there was famine . . . The harvest of 1632 promised well, but in Bavaria and Swabia the passing troops trampled it down; in Bavaria there was neither corn left to grind nor seed to sow for the year to come; plague and famine wiped out whole villages, mad dogs attacked their masters, and the authorities posted men with guns to shoot down the raving victims before they could contaminate their fellows . . .

## 2b  The conflict as an example of the futility of war

The war solved no problem. Its effects, both immediate and indirect, were either negative or disastrous. Morally subversive, economically destructive, socially degrading, confused in its causes, devious in its course, futile in its result, it is the outstanding example in European history of meaningless conflict.

Source: Wedgwood, 1962, pp. 329–30, 526

## 3  Misleading sources

The traditional concept of the Thirty Years' War is based on two main groups of sources: deliberate official propaganda and unwittingly one-sided private records. [The first] reflected the opinions of the victorious powers . . . [The second] reflected the opinions of the educated middle class which was hit hardest by the economic upheaval of the time . . . The ruinous effect of the war years . . . has been very much exaggerated. War is by its very nature destructive . . . But all the campaigns of the period 1609–1648 were of short duration and the armies themselves were of very small size.

Source: Steinberg, 'The Thirty Years' War: a new interpretation', *History*, no. 32 (1947) (in T. K. Rabb, *The Thirty Years' War*, 1964, 2nd edn 1981, p. 42).

## 4 The result of local study research projects

Neither of [Steinberg's] arguments can be substantiated . . . Almost all the local studies dated the start of a decline, or intensification of decline, from the time when troops first appeared in an area, and not from 1619 or 1623 . . .

Although the armies were small, they could be most destructive, even if they did not stay long in one area.

Source: Rabb, 1981, p. 77.

## Historical-source questions B

1 Why did Comenius (Source 1) hate the peace settlement?

2 (a) Why did so much death result from the war? Refer to Source 2a.

(b) Why, according to Source 3, should the historian be careful about trusting an account like Source 2?

3 Study Sources 2 to 4. To what extent is Steinberg's claim that the middle classes were the war's main economic victims supported?

4 Account for the different views expressed in Sources 1 to 4. Which view most closely corresponds to your own? Give reasons.

## Summary questions

1 (a) During the period 1629 to 1648, the Habsburgs failed to maintain their early successes. Explain any *two* factors that particularly affected the development of the war during this period.

(b) Which one of these factors was the most important in the development of the Thirty Years' War after 1629?

For discussion or full essay:

2 How successfully did the peacemakers deal with the issues that confronted them at the end of the Thirty Years' War?

3 Devise a new, more descriptive title for the 'Thirty Years' War'. Argue your case.

# 10

# The European witch-hunt

## Focus questions

◆ Why was there a European witch-hunt in the first half of the seventeenth century?

◆ Who were the accused and who the persecutors?

◆ What are the different views taken by historians on this topic?

## Significant dates

**1486** Two Dominican friars, Krämer and Sprenger, publish *The hammer of witches*. Their 'research' on demonology is widely read.

*c.***1520** Secular rather than religious courts are increasingly used to try cases of 'bewitchment' after this date.

*c.***1560** Beginning of most intense period of witch persecution in Europe.

*c.***1580** Start of Catholic Counter-Reformation.

*c.***1640** End of main thrust of Counter-Reformation.

**1648** End of Thirty Years' War. General economic crisis.

*c.***1650** End of worst period of witch persecution.

**1691** Attack on belief in demonology is published : the Dutchman Bekker's *The world bewitched*.

## Overview

Between *c.*1560 and 1650 at least 50,000 women, men and even children were executed for the imagined crime of demonic possession. Most were judicially killed simply for being 'witches'. By and large women were the principal victims and men the main persecutors. Many of those trapped by the judges seem to have been no more than women out of step with their local communities. Mass hysteria, torture of suspects and fear fuelled the witch-hunts. Witch persecution had almost stopped by the end of the seventeenth century. What gave the persecution such momentum for so long was the virtual unanimity of academics, clerics and the general public that demonic possession was real. Study of the activity of witches was given the status of a branch of science.

# Why was there a European witch-hunt in the first half of the seventeenth century?

## From tolerance to persecution

The superstitious idea that people could be and were possessed by the agents of the 'devil' – the basis for the prosecution of people for the alleged crime of bewitchment – only became common currency after the appearance in 1486 of *The hammer of witches*, a highly influential book written by two **Dominicans**. Hugh Trevor-Roper pointed out in *Religion, the Reformation and social change* (1967) that belief in witchcraft was 'not a lingering ancient superstition' but a 'new explosive force'. There was no intense and widespread witch-hunt before the late sixteenth century although in almost every village there were those who practised folk medicine, sometimes using 'magical' remedies. The Emperor Charlemagne (742–814) decreed the death penalty for anyone burning supposed witches, declaring it a 'pagan custom'. In the eleventh century the laws of King Coloman of Hungary disregarded witches 'since they do not exist'.

The **Dominicans** were an order of missionary friars, also known as the black friars, with a reputation for being stern. They were the religious order most closely associated with the Inquisition.

Tragically, these sensible official attitudes changed in the fourteenth and fifteenth centuries, partly as a result of the influence of Krämer and Sprenger's book. *The hammer of witches* brought together material that claimed to describe a complete hidden world, the world of demons – the 'devil's agents' – and their human servants, the witches. From then onwards, it was used as the supreme guide for witch-hunters as it was full of useful tips about the recognition and interrogation of witches. This highly influential work was an encyclopaedia of prejudices and superstitions paraded as facts. The authors introduced the idea of a diabolical pact. It followed in law that people accused of witchcraft were not merely the victims of the devil but had voluntarily entered into a pact with him.

How did Krämer and Sprenger's book change the way witchcraft was viewed by the authorities?

Between 1589 and 1602 witch-hunting encyclopaedias were published in Germany, France and England, and were accompanied by an increase in persecution. These books were the work of serious scholars who insisted on the reality of witches, 'the devil's assistants on earth'. They pleaded for a tough line to be taken with what they described as a growing international threat from a rapidly multiplying host of witches. The witches must be burnt!

According to Krämer and Sprenger, a night in the life of a witch began with the possessed person covering themselves with devil's grease made out of the fat of murdered toddlers. Greased in this way, the witch slipped through cracks and up chimneys, riding on broomsticks, goats or spindles on the way to a witches' sabbath. In every country there were said to be hundreds of places where sabbaths were held. At the sabbath the witches met scores of demons. These were their 'paramours', their illicit lovers, to whom they were

A sixteenth-century engraving by J. Ziarnko shows a witches' sabbath. From Pierre de Lancre, *Book of the untrustworthiness of bad angels and demons*, 1613.

What appears to be happening in the engraving of the witches' sabbath?

bound by a devilish pact. What followed was in many ways a mockery of the Catholic mass.

The master of ceremonies was the devil himself. He often appeared as a black, bearded man, or as a stinking goat or huge toad. All those present joined to worship the devil, dancing naked around him to music made with horses' skulls or human bones. The witches kissed the devil in homage – under the tail if they were dealing with a goat, on the lips if he were a toad and on the buttocks if in humanoid form. Sexual orgies and feasts of vile cold dishes followed, ranging from cold turnips in Germany to roast or boiled unbaptised children in Savoy, exhumed corpses in Spain and fried bats in Alsace. Between sabbaths, witches occupied themselves by having sex with the devil; suckling familiar spirits in the form of weasels, moles, bats or toads; procuring death amongst their neighbours and generally causing havoc with nature.

Today we might conclude that Krämer and Sprenger's assertions were no more than the sadistic fantasies of two disturbed, sexually repressed Dominican friars. Some of the pictures produced in anti-witch propaganda border on pornography (the one shown on the top left on page 145 is a mild example). In their own time no one, so far as we know, saw it in this way; the friars were 'normal', the witches 'disturbed'.

What was the purpose of pictures of witches and witchcraft?

Stages in a witch's path to evil-doing. *Top left:* Subjection to the devil (woodcut, 1625). *Bottom left:* Having taken on animal form, witches cast their spells (woodcut, 1626). Both from F. M. Guazzo, *A compendium of evil doing*, 1629. *Right:* Death of a stable-hand by witchcraft, from H. B. Grien, *The witches*, 1510.

### Why was there a witch-hunting craze in the period *c.*1560–1650?

In the period *c.*1560–1650 witch persecution reached its height. This was the era of the witch-hunts, when tens of thousands perished at the hands of witch-finders who were often backed by the heads of state. Though many records have been lost or destroyed, most scholars agree that between 100,000 and 200,000 people were officially tried for witchcraft and about half that number were executed between *c.*1500 and 1700. Some estimates put the figures much higher. Most were killed in the period around 1560–1650.

Persecutions on a large scale began in the fifteenth century. The greatest were in the 1560s, the 1580s, the 1590s and the 1620s. Though the connections must not be exaggerated, the climax of witch-hunting was linked to the fiercest episodes of Reformation and Counter-Reformation missionary activity and persecution. Although most of the prosecutions and executions were carried out by **secular courts**, this was often in conjunction with or at the

The increasing use of **secular** (non-religious) **courts** after about 1520 led to more prosecutions and more death sentences.

behest of the religious authorities. The 1560s was a decade when Calvinists were particularly active making conversions in northern and central Europe. The last twenty years of the sixteenth century were times of intense Counter-Reformation activity. The 1620s was a decade of Catholic success in reconquering Bohemia and south Germany during the Thirty Years' War. In Catholic states witches were classed as heretics and therefore had to be rooted out. In 1590 Philip II of Spain declared witchcraft the scourge and destruction of the human race. Witch-hunting increased in intensity in areas of Counter-Reformation 'reconquest' – in Flanders and the Rhineland in the 1590s and in 1627–29 in Germany.

Ironically, the religious authorities in Calvinist states campaigned with equal vigour against their witches. At all times inclined to be harsh and demon-filled, sermons during witch-hunts were often directed specifically against witches. In Russia, even though workers of 'magic' were as widespread as elsewhere, in the absence of the bitterly fought battles of the Reformation there was no mass persecution of witches. In western and central Europe, princes keen to show their loyalty to a particular brand of religious faith lumped together all those who could possibly be described as religious rebels – including known witches, those with a poor record of church attendance and those with an inclination towards non-Christian practices. Some of the more active witches organised themselves in the same manner as a religious cult. Their local affairs were managed by a body of elders, the coven, a clear parallel with Calvinist church practice. Some of the accused witches displayed a passion for their activities and even embraced their terrible fate.

There was no automatic tie-up between Counter-Reformation reconquest and increased witch-hunting. The persecution of Huguenots in France, for example, was not accompanied by increased harassment of alleged witches. Economic factors may have been just as important as the power and influence of the organised churches. The 1580s, one of the worst decades for persecution, was also a time of general economic depression and plague. Witch persecution was particularly bad when the fabric of society was torn by famine, plague or the divisiveness and destruction of war. The uprooting of villages in Germany in the 1620s, during the Thirty Years' War, led to an increase in the number of vagrants and transients. This in turn threatened feelings of community. The resulting lack of neighbourliness turned out to be a bonus for the witch-finders. People were all too willing to seek out scapegoats. The identification of a common enemy might serve to restore a sense of community.

## Why did it end?

**Cyrano de Bergerac** wrote in the 1650s as if the European witch-hunt were a thing of the past, and in Calvinist Geneva the last witch was burnt in 1652.

> To what extent was witch persecution linked to religious persecution?

> What were the other main events and developments in the decades when witch persecution was most intense?

**Cyrano de Bergerac** (1619–55) was a soldier renowned for fighting in duels and for his enormous nose. His written works are noted for their vigour and wit.

Twenty years later, **Colbert** abolished the charge of sabbatical sorcery in France.

Attitudes took much longer to change. For centuries, even during the height of the persecution, there had been a few scholars who had expressed scepticism about the prosecutions. In the fifteenth century, Pomponazzi of Padua University had argued that men 'possessed by the devil', were simply depressives. He argued that all the marvels attributed to demons could be explained by other influences, such as celestial bodies and hidden powers. One superstition was substituted for another, but at least without deadly consequences. **Montaigne**, in the late sixteenth century, remarked that 'it is rating our conjectures highly to roast people alive for them'. Slowly the tide of opinion began to turn against witch persecution, yet as late as 1738 the dean of the faculty of law at Rostock demanded that witches be eradicated by 'fire and sword'. In the eighteenth century, cartoons featuring lame harmless devils appeared; it is evident that fear of the devil and of his power to do harm had declined – at least among Europe's social elite.

However, persecution did not end just because some university academics changed their minds. The decline of witch-hunting remains something of a puzzle. A variety of factors was involved, ranging from economic recovery to the decline in the influence of religion and legal embarrassment. Witch persecution had reached its peak in the first half of the seventeenth century, a period of widespread (though not universal) economic and political turmoil in Europe referred to by some historians as a 'general crisis'. When economic depression and rebellion subsided after the middle of the century, so did the worst of the European witch-hunt. With the progressive elimination of plague and the appearance of other elements of social security – such as fire and personal insurance – a different climate of opinion started to take hold in the early eighteenth century.

The persecution of witches is to be seen alongside that of Jews, Moriscos and Christian minorities, which also reached its height in this period. Trevor-Roper argues that these groups – unorthodox women and ethnic minority groups – were convenient scapegoats for society in Europe, then going through a long and painful period of 'introversion and intolerance'. The main pressure leading to persecution, he argues, came from the missionary orders and local Puritan leaders.

Sometimes persecutions in conquered territories were halted for largely practical reasons. The French in Lorraine and Franche-Comté, the Swedes in Mecklenburg, Franconia and Bavaria put a stop to witch persecution in these conquered territories during the Thirty Years' War. Rather than out of any deeply held objection to the practice, they did so largely because the witch persecutors were backed by the enemy state authorities, whose authority they

**Jean-Baptiste Colbert** (1619–83) became chief financial minister to Louis XIV. He carried out successful financial reforms and improved the civil law.

**Michel Eyquem de Montaigne** (1533–92) was a fearless critic and philosopher. As a 'humanist' he believed that rulers had an obligation to avoid conflict and religious dogma, looking after all their subjects.

Why was there a more secure and stable feel to life for the masses in the early eighteenth century?

The two anti-persecution books of the 1630s were **Friedrich Spee**, *Cautio criminalis*, 1631 – written anonymously but published by a 'friend' – and **Benedict Carpzov**, *Practica rerum criminalium*, 1635.

Why did the European witch-hunt come to an end?

were displacing. A few rulers did object on principle. Sweden's Queen Christina, a lady whose ideas were influenced by Descartes, gave explicit orders to suppress witch-persecution in Germany. As soon as the Swedes left Germany the persecution resumed.

The discrediting of confessions produced by torture undermined the reputation of the judicial authorities. Some of those involved in the persecution turned against it because of their disgust at the torture they had witnessed. The Jesuit **Friedrich Spee** was one. He was a confessor of witches in the witch-hunt at Würzburg, an experience which is said to have turned his hair prematurely white. He became convinced that all confessions were worthless because they were based solely on torture. Not a single witch he had led to the stake had, he said, been guilty. In 1631 he published a book anonymously to set the record straight. In another book in 1635, **Benedict Carpzov** admitted that torture had led to thousands of false confessions.

## Areas where persecution was fiercest

Some of the fiercest witch persecution was to be found in upland rural areas: the Pyrenees and the states on the higher foothills of the Alps such as Savoy and Bavaria. There were several reasons. Sovereigns were increasing their authority over their dominions. Bavaria, for example, was a region where the authority of the state was weak before the sixteenth century but much stronger by the end of it; pockets of discordance and opposition were rooted out. Rural poverty made people vengeful and eager to find scapegoats. The climate was extreme in these areas. When electric storms broke and snow avalanched, thoughts ran on miracles and magic. If death and destruction resulted, it was assumed that there must be an evil agency at work. If some were saved and others carried away, that was all the more evidence of a devilish selection and the handiwork of witches.

Christianity had hardly penetrated in some remote mountainous regions, and where it had it proved hard to sustain. Pre-Christian beliefs and rites, often connected to the fertility of humans and animals rather than crops and often involving worship of a god incarnated in a man, woman or animal, survived more vigorously in these areas. There were some connections to pre-Christian fertility cults. Works such as *The hammer of witches* and the well-publicised evidence of witch trials gave rise to a copy-cat culture of black magic. Recent research puts less emphasis on linking the highland aspect of some rural areas to witchcraft and its persecution. These studies simply stress that, whether '**white**' or '**black**', witchcraft was a largely a rural phenomenon.

Far away from centres of population, writers could allege truly fabulous witch phenomena, such as that at Hendaye in the far south-west of France, where 12,000 witches would assemble for special conventions five times a

A distinction is often made between '**white**' witchcraft, which was essentially folk medicine with an emphasis on magical remedies, and '**black**' magic, which employed evil tokens, curses and spells to harm others.

week! For the same reason, UFOs are rarely spotted above the city of London or monsters seen in the Thames. Finally, in the rural outback, the persecutors could more easily get away with murder, dressed as judicial execution. In the great cities levels of education tended to be higher (that was no guarantee of scepticism about witchcraft, but it was a help) and suspicion of miscarriage of justice more likely. Very few witches were burnt in Rome, Amsterdam or London in the whole period of the witch-hunts. City governments like those in Cologne and Nuremberg, in spite of being in the middle of regions of rabid witch-hunting, resisted the mass executions. The Paris parliament upheld almost 40 per cent of the appeals of those accused of witchcraft.

Nevertheless, witchcraft and some degree of witch persecution was to be found almost everywhere in Europe and city people were not above belief in the necessity of eliminating witches. Witchcraft and its persecution was common in low-lying and well-populated Orléans, Normandy and Flanders. Here, religion was the big issue. These were areas where pockets of strong Protestant faith existed alongside a majority culture following a different faith. They were identified as dangerous areas of dissent and potential rebellion by the authorities. In Switzerland the Calvinist cities made war on the Catholic countryside and hunting witches was just a part of this. In southern France the Catholic city of Toulouse was a witch-hunting centre acting against the neighbouring Protestant regions. If the practice of witchcraft was a largely rural phenomenon, cases of demonic possession were more frequently brought in the towns.

However, what seems to have mattered more than anything else was the attitude of the prevailing authorities. The city of Nuremberg was safe for witches while the nearby cities of authorities of Würzburg and Bamberg, independent bishoprics only forty miles away, hounded them. Even then the danger was extreme only during the rule of certain princes and prince-bishops.

For what reasons was witchcraft and its persecution frequent in remote upland rural areas?

Why was persecution more intense in some parts of Europe than in others?

## Who were the accused and who the persecutors?

### The accused

Of those accused of witchcraft, 75 to 80 per cent were women. However, the largest witch-hunts included **men** and **children** amongst the victims. All were victimised in the sense that, whatever harm they may or may not have done, the punishment was grossly out of proportion. Only if they really had committed murder and constituted a continuing menace to public safety, might their punishment be considered just. Since, with the exception of a tiny minority, they were not murderers, their punishment was unjust even by the harsh laws of the time. Typically, witches were accused of bringing on illness, infertility or accidents. Generally, they were tortured and burnt to death

In some regions up to 30 per cent of the accused were **men**. **Children** were a much smaller minority.

because of who they were, not for what they did. The witch-hunters said that the demons had to be found and exterminated.

Some of those who were persecuted were rebels against moral puritanism, whether of the Catholic or Protestant variety. The same impulses which led the religious authorities to stress the sacredness of marriage, the inviolability of the sabbath, absolute regularity in church attendance, and the wickedness of incest, rape, prostitution and abandonment of babies, led them to victimise 'odd' women. Some of the accused were elderly prostitutes, cut off from the rest of the community. Others were poor, elderly spinsters who practised folk medicine to earn a meagre income. **Wise-women**, the amateur doctors of rural societies, were often accused of mixing magic potions and creams. Acts of petty revenge against neighbours could lead women into danger. The legal powerlessness of women made them vulnerable. A man could take someone to court, a woman could not. Instead, she resorted to scolding, cursing or, if she knew how, casting spells.

Many of the accused were widows or spinsters. Unattached women were suspect in the eyes of their neighbours. During the sixteenth century, with an increase in both age at first marriage and the number of people who never married, there were more single women. Sometimes the older unattached women inherited property, or were likely to do so, making them prey to envious relatives and neighbours. If a woman's second husband died, she might well find herself in the difficult situation of living in the house of a resentful step-child. Accusations sometimes came from step-children.

Those most often accused of witchcraft were older women with a reputation for healing, scolding or working both good and bad magic. Again, it was women's misfortune in this period that traditional female occupations involved connections with the possible causation of illness and death, whether through preparing food or tending little children, the sick, or pregnant women. Many of those accused were midwives, who were generally older women. The authors of *The hammer of witches* singled out this group of women for special attention. It was also the white witch's misfortune, though it is doubtful that she saw it like this, that the currently favoured beliefs about medicine and astrology tended to support the authenticity of 'magical' remedies. This encouraged some unsafe or unhelpful remedies and made female healers more open to accusations of magical pacts and crimes. In this period there was no knowledge of germs and the importance of hygiene, and no understanding of epidemic disease or the numerous causes of serious illness and death.

A common accusation against accused women was that they had attended witches' sabbaths. Another was that they had had sexual intercourse with the devil. Although it could not be proved that so-called possessed women

The original Anglo-Saxon meaning of the word 'witch' was '**wise-woman**'.

Why were women, and 'wise-women' particularly, vulnerable to the accusation of devilish bewitchment?

flew through the night to attend sabbath assemblies, neither could it be conclusively disproved. Since the witch-hunters' encyclopaedias said these phenomena did exist, the prosecutors had proof enough if they could obtain a confession referring to someone having 'given themselves to the devil' or having attended secret meetings. A common accusation was of sexual intercourse with the devil. Frightened and suggestible children could be induced to talk of going in their mother's arms to the witches' sabbaths (see Historical sources B). For the final proof the prosecutors invented a number of supposedly scientific tests. Witches were stripped and searched for the 'devil's mark', said to be a spot where the woman did not feel pain. They were pricked all over until inevitably a mole, wart or birthmark was found which blunted nerve sensitivity.

The experts' stress on the importance of the witch's 'pact with the devil' – which began with Krämer and Sprenger's book – went alongside a number of crucial changes in the law and the handling of cases of witchcraft. After about 1520 state courts rather than specifically religious ones were widely used to prosecute witches. Statute books (the laws of the country) increasingly included witchcraft as a felony (a punishable crime). Two French scholars, **Jean Bodin** and Nicolas Rémy, wrote at length about the nature of proof required to demonstrate witchcraft. They concluded that the witches were so cunning that the normally strict rules of evidence ought to be relaxed in order that the cunning devil did not prevail. Germany at this period was moving to Roman law, involving an inquisitorial rather than accusatorial procedure. Under the latter system a false accusation could leave the accuser in a lot of trouble. They could face trial themselves for perjury (lying). Under the new inquisitorial system, the legal authority itself brought the case, not a private individual, and there was no jury. This tended to make people more willing to accuse others, knowing that there was little chance that the law would be likely to turn against them if they lied.

Inquisitorial procedure often involved intense questioning with torture. Torture produced the most bizarre confessions – though occasionally these emerged from psychologically disturbed individuals without any torture. Most of those who died in the great witch-hunts were the victims of false confessions extracted under torture. Johannes Julius, a town official at Bamberg, was a typical victim of the mass prosecutions. Under torture he confessed that he had renounced God, given himself to the devil and seen twenty-seven of his colleagues at a witches' sabbath.

**Common law** systems were still in frequent use outside Germany and it should be borne in mind that these could be as dangerous to the interests of the accused in witchcraft cases as **Roman law** systems. Although in theory fairer to the accused, trials by this system tended to end up appeasing the local

**Jean Bodin** (1530–96), legal expert and Calvinist political philosopher, is best known for *Six books of the republic*. A major work of political theory, this included 'proofs' that women were inferior to men.

**Common law** is built up over the centuries. Every case is examined on its own merits. Judgments are usually based on the precedent of judgments reached in similar earlier cases, but may themselves set a new precedent.

**Roman law** was based on the laws and commentaries of the Roman Emperor Justinian in the sixth century.

community, which was often passionately in favour of capital punishment – 'lynch law' prevailed.

Torture was widely used to extract confessions in continental Europe, where belief in demonic possession was stronger than in England. Johannes Julius wrote to his daughter that 'they never cease to torture until one says something' (see Historical sources B).

Though there were official restraints on the use of torture it seems that these were widely ignored and there is evidence that the worst tortures were often reserved for witches. Great inventiveness went into the devising of instruments. A torture chamber was made specially for witches by Gottfried Johann Georg II Fuchs von Dornheim of Bamberg. It was here that Johannes Julius was tortured. Thumbscrews, 'witch-racks', 'witch-pricking' and sleep deprivation were favourites. Once a confession was extracted, the witch was encouraged to denounce their associates. Often crazed with pain and terror and with nothing more to lose, the victim would name several acquaintances at random, who themselves would be brought to the torture chamber and name more people. From one flimsy case scores of people could thus be brought to their deaths.

The punishment for diabolic witchcraft (involving worship of the devil) in many parts of Europe was execution, usually by burning. Parts of western and central Europe were the most severe. In France and some of the principalities of the Holy Roman Empire, the legal method was either burning alive or burning following garrotting. The courts of the Spanish and Roman Inquisitions were less severe than the secular (non-religious) courts, being more likely to send a woman accused of witchcraft home again with a warning and a religious penance (such as confession and prayers) unless they were convinced that devil worship was involved. Even when found guilty of diabolic witchcraft, Spanish punishments fell short of execution, public humiliation such as whipping or standing in the **pillory** being more common.

## Persecutors

The persecutors broadly fitted into one of two categories: those in the local community who initiated or supported an accusation of witchcraft and those in authority who directed the witch-hunts. The second group numbered some of the most notorious witch-finders. Without the insistent drive of these witch-finders, persecution would have continued only at the low level of the medieval period. In Sweden and eastern Europe, where the demonic concept of the witch never took hold, only occasional small-scale witch trials occurred.

Prompted by the judges, local villagers accused witches of all manner of offences, typically of causing death and sickness, harming children, causing impotence, spoiling bread or curdling milk. Often the inquisitor then invited

The **pillory** was a wooden framework with holes for the hands and head. It was put in a public place to expose the offender to ridicule.

their neighbours to add to the list of complaints. In this way villagers took part in the witch-hunt. Those making the accusations were often living close to the accused, either as servants, employers or neighbours. Tensions over property rights or the improper public behaviour of a relative or in-law were frequent. Often the resentment and the victim's evil reputation were built up over a long period and the incident that prompted the charge was not the first. Once an initial charge was made, the accuser often thought back over the years and added a list of things the accused had done in the past.

The witch-finders were typically from outside the community concerned, usually churchmen from the middle and upper classes. Those territories which saw the most fearsome 'hunts' were small ecclesiastical states within the Holy Roman Empire such as the archbishopric of Würzburg and the bishopric of Bamberg. In these places a bishop or archbishop was head of both church and state. Persecuting witches was a way of demonstrating Christian piety. In 1602, the prince abbot of Fulda gave permission to his minister, Balthasar Ross – self-styled 'witchmaster' – to conduct a 'travelling inquisition' round his principality. In the best tradition of government inspectors, he made it his business to call unexpectedly on villages. Ross was paid by results and in three years he made good money out of his 250 victims. An ambitious judge could enhance his chances of promotion and sometimes they too had a direct financial interest in witch trials. Half a million florins belonging to those killed were confiscated in Bamberg. Trier was another notorious blackspot. In 1581 Johann von Schoneberg, archbishop of Trier and friend of the Jesuits, systematically rooted out Protestants, Jews and witches. In 22 villages, 368 witches were burnt between 1587 and 1593. In the eight-year reign of Philip Adolf von Ehrenberg of Würzburg, between 1623 and 1631, nine hundred people were burnt for witchcraft. These included his own nephew and children as young as 7, who were accused of having intercourse with demons. Gottfried Johann Georg II Fuchs von Dornheim of Bamberg oversaw the burning of six hundred witches in his ten-year reign, 1623–33.

> Who were the persecutors and how did they work?

The largest of the witch-hunts numbered men and children amongst the victims, something which was to help end the persecution. Some people began to say that the prosecutors was getting out of control. Men, seeing men as victims, felt that this was definitely going too far! In general, particularly in Sweden and Germany, the men accused were wealthier than the accused women and they were more often defended successfully by friends and family. They were rarely charged with activities such as night-flying or intercourse with the devil.

> Why did the torture of males accused of 'witchcraft' help to end the worst period of persecution?

If the majority of those accused of the crime were women, all of the witch-finders – whether sovereigns, judges or writers – were men. Some were undoubtedly misogynists, which means they hated women. Krämer and

Sprenger (quoted in M. Weisner's *Women and gender in early modern Europe*, 1993) argued that 'for the sake of fulfilling their lusts [women] consorted even with devils'. It is likely that men such as these, in strict religious orders and deprived of women, expressed their hostility to sexuality as a general hatred of women. Many of the prosecutors seem to have had a similar distaste for women; older women received harsher sentences than younger ones. B. Ehrenreich and D. English have suggested (in *Witches, midwives and nurses: a history of women healers*, 1973) that the witch-hunts were driven by male doctors trying to take over control of medicine from the 'wise women', the traditional healers. Older women were considered more lustful than younger ones and therefore more likely, especially if widowed or single, to engage in sex with the devil. Since semen was thought to be the same thing as brain tissue and bone marrow, impotence was often blamed on excessive sex and therefore on witches, who by their devilish appetite and power destroyed male potency. Male demons ('incubi') were said to use the semen drawn out by the female demons ('succubi') for intercourse with female witches. In the process demonic children were fathered. Such details help us to obtain a picture of the psychology of the witch-hunters.

What were the motives of the witch-finders? Why were women their main victims?

## What are the different views taken by historians on this topic?

The exotic activities of witches and the equally fantastic story of witch persecution have understandably attracted a lot of interest. Interpretations have changed greatly. Modern historians tend to see the persecution, rather than any activities of witches, as the main subject for research and explanation. Eighteenth- and nineteenth-century studies, based on literary accounts and descriptions of trials, tended to put the emphasis on 'witchcraft' itself.

Wallace Notestein in his *History of witchcraft* (1911) for the first time put as much emphasis on the persecutors as on the accused. Ten years later Margaret Murray, an Oxford anthropologist, caused a stir with her *The witch-cult in Western Europe*, subtitled *A study in anthropology*, in which she claimed that her research had revealed witchcraft as 'an organised religion . . . the ancient religion of western Europe'. **Anthropology** was a new subject then and academics were excited by its possibilities. It offered new kinds of explanations, leaping across continents, cultures and time. Murray based her research on British evidence, with selective support from French and Flemish sources. She believed more of the details of witch activities from trial evidence than is usual today. Her views were far removed from feminism and she concluded that 'the witches had a fair trial according to the methods of the period', a view which has recently had something of a revival.

**Anthropology** is the study of mankind through the comparison of societies and customs.

No historians now support Murray's theory that witchcraft was a survival of a fully developed pre-Christian religion, a hostile rival to Christianity. Cult organisation applied only to a small minority of those accused of witchcraft. However, the anthropological approach to the topic has continued. Influenced by anthropology, Keith Thomas, in his *Religion and the decline of magic* (1971) and Alan MacFarlane in his *Witchcraft in England* (1970) tend to be similarly non-judgemental about the persecutors and the persecuted. They draw comparisons with witch practices in present-day Africa, Asia and Central and South America.

Any explanation of the European witch-hunt must explain convincingly why scholars and judges were convinced that the power of evil was at work in the world and why that conviction ended. In advancing religion and sex respectively as the crucial factors, both Trevor-Roper and the feminist historians at least tackled that question head-on. In the process they aroused great controversy and have since been heavily criticised. Trevor-Roper's study of the witch craze (1967) put more emphasis on the persecutors and was more damning in its judgements, making clear links with the religious persecutions of the time. MacFarlane (1970), B. P. Levack (1987) and R. Briggs (1997) have criticised Trevor-Roper for making too much use of allegedly dubious nineteenth-century sources and for being unsympathetic to contemporary mindsets. Levack's view is that there was no model to explain witch-hunting that was applicable everywhere – no single-cause explanation. He argues for some empathy with the persecuting authorities, on the grounds that witches were genuinely seen as one element constituting a serious threat of social revolution. Torture and witch-hunting were carried out by understandably fearful local authorities. Local notables and judges used the secular courts to enforce law, order and conformity. They encouraged the presentation of witchcraft cases as a way of dealing with those who did not fit into local norms. Briggs, who points out that most accusations arose only after many years of building a case and that the mass persecutions were exceptional, refuses to use the expressions 'witch-hunt' and 'witch-craze' at all. Persecution, he argues, emerged all too readily from neighbourly disputes.

> What factors may have influenced local authorities to take a severe approach to the prosecution of alleged witches? Which were the most important?

Feminist historians consider the broad gender polarity between the female accused and male accusers to be crucial to our understanding of the whole phenomenon. They place more emphasis on the fact that at all levels of society men had much more power than women and it was men who carried out the persecutions. This is disputed by Briggs, who emphasises that 20–25 per cent of victims were male rather than that 75–80 per cent were female! When so much depends on the way in which historians present the evidence of those who have carried out the research, we can expect many more interpretations to emerge, for this is a topic that generates strong feelings.

# A  Anti-witch writers and preachers

The evidence that religious and witch persecution were closely linked is more than circumstantial. This document set begins with Calvin himself setting down his church's position in black-and-white terms and ends with an excellent piece of empathetic writing on the impact of Calvinist preaching. Scotland was one of those largely rural nations where the reformed faith took hold in the lowland cities and set itself against the barbarous practices of the highlands.

## 1  The biblical condemnation of witchcraft

The Bible teaches us that there are witches and that they must be slain . . . God expressly commands that all witches and enchantresses shall be put to death and this law of God is a universal law.

Source: Calvin, Sermon on the Witch of Endor, from H. Trevor-Roper, 'The European witch-craze of the sixteenth and seventeenth centuries', in *Religion, the Reformation and social change*, 1967, p. 37.

## 2  The wickedness of female sexuality

Proverbs 30 says there are three things which are never satisfied, but yea, there is a fourth thing which says not, It is enough; that is the mouth of the womb. Wherefore for the sake of fulfilling their lusts [women] consort even with devils . . . [Midwives] surpass all other in wickedness . . . no one does more harm to the Catholic faith than midwives.

Source: Krämer and Sprenger, 'The hammer of witches', 1486, trans. A. C. Kors and E. Peters, eds., *Witchcraft in Europe, 1100–1700*, 1972, pp. 127, 129.

## 3  The impact of Calvinist preaching in rural Scotland

The power of the [Calvinist] preachers on a simple rural population should not be underestimated – Sunday by Sunday they poured their fierce and eloquent sermons into the souls of their hearers – dreadful warnings and vivid descriptions of hellfire and the personal devil . . . It is not surprising that some of the congregation came to believe they were irretrievably damned, and being damned were the devil's own servants, and as servants became witches and learnt to imitate the rites which were so widely publicised by confessions at witchcraft trials . . . Some witch's confessions came from women who surrendered themselves voluntarily and poured out a rigmarole which sounded like the hallucinations of a mind that had cracked under Calvinist bombardment.

Source: T. C. Smout, *A history of the Scottish people, 1560–1830*, 1969, p. 202.

1   Explain the references underlined in Sources 1 and 2.
2   What are the similarities and differences between Sources 1 and 2?
3   To what extent does Source 1 support the argument of Source 3?
4   On what grounds did the authorities see witches as a threat? Use the sources and your own knowledge.

## B The use of torture against those accused of witchcraft

Those who believe that the camp guard or executioner is simply a hapless worker carrying out orders for fear of his own life should read Source 3. On the other hand, the 'structuralist' school of modern scholarship – represented in Source 5 – asks us to look below the surface of such an apparently callous statement. Did the victims of this hangman have a 'shared understanding' with him and did it lessen their pain?

### 1  A victim on the use of torture to produce confessions

Now my dearest child you have all my acts and confessions for which I must die. It is all falsehood and invention, so help me God. They never cease to torture until one says something.

Source: Johannes Julius, Burgomaster at Bamberg, in a letter to his daughter, c.1623–33, from Trevor-Roper, *European witch craze*, 1967, p. 157

### 2  The testimony of a child witness

At Lille Mme Bourignon founded a home for low class girls living like beasts. In 1661 she discovered that [some] were worshippers of the Devil . . . Bellot, aged 15, said that her mother had taken her with her when she was very young, and had even carried her in her arms to the witches' sabbaths.

Source: M. Murray, *The witch-cult in Western Europe*, 1921, p. 72.

### 3  The use of torture to produce confessions

I do not take you for one, two, three, not for eight days, not for a few weeks, but for half a year or a year, for your whole life, until you confess: and if you will not confess, I shall torture you to death, and you shall be burned after all.

Source: The hangman of the town of Dreissigacker in Germany, P. Carus, *The history of the devil and the idea of evil*, 1969, p. 331.

### 4 The abuse of rules regarding the use of torture

If the courts of Europe had adhered . . . to rules regarding the use of torture, then the adoption of this method of criminal investigation would not have led to innumerable miscarriages of justice . . . In particular the European witch-hunt would never have taken place . . . These rules were greatly relaxed and the system was grossly abused.

Source: Levack, *The witch hunt in early modern Europe*, second edn., 1995, p. 79.

### 5 Shared understanding between the torturer and his victims

[It was believed that] witches were women who could not feel pain as normal women could . . . A measure of physical pain, so the interrogators believed, was a process of the body which enabled the witch to free herself from the devil's clutches . . . The amount of pain had to be finely judged by the executioner, a scientist of the body . . . Torture was part of an understanding, shared by the witch and her persecutors, of the interrelation of body and soul.

Source: L. Roper, 'Early modern Germany', in *Witchcraft in early modern Europe*, ed. J. Barry, M. Hester and G. Roberts, 1996.

## Historical-source questions B

1  How do Sources 1 and 2 cast doubt on the reliability of the evidence brought forward in witch trials?
2  To what extent do Sources 1 and 3 support the argument of Source 4?
3  Source 5 argues that there was an understanding between the torturer and his victim. How far is this supported by Sources 1 and 3?
4  Use the sources and your own knowledge to explain why the issue of torture became a key factor in the decline of the witch-hunting craze.

## Summary question

1  (a) Explain how any *two* developments encouraged the witch-hunting craze in the period c. 1580–1640.

(b) Which factor was most important in bringing it to an end in Europe in the second half of the seventeenth century?

# 11

# The scientific revolution – fact or fiction?

## Focus questions

◆ How did science change as a result of both the contributions of individual scholars and broader developments in society?

◆ What was the balance of continuity and change in biology and chemistry? Why was less progress made than in physics?

◆ Was there a 'scientific revolution' in this century?

◆ Why have some historians preferred to describe the developments as a 'scientific movement' rather than as a 'revolution'?

## Significant dates

1538    Copernicus publishes first of two highly controversial works showing that the sun, not the earth, is at the centre of the solar system.

1609    Kepler publishes *New astronomy*, advancing an almost accurate elliptical theory of planetary motion. Galileo invents the first good telescope.

1632    Galileo publishes *Dialogues*, producing proof that the earth moves. The Catholic Church and the more extreme Protestant faiths condemn him.

1638    Galileo publishes *Two new sciences,* the most advanced work in physics until Huygens and Newton.

1656    Borellus invents one of the first good microscopes.

1660s   From this decade the earliest scientific academies are established (France, England, Prussia)

1687    Newton publishes *Principia* – the most advanced work on physics and maths until Einstein in the twentieth century.

1690    Huygens publishes the highly advanced *Treaty on light*.

## Overview

Dramatic advances in scientific understanding were made in this century, in spite of the fact that this was a period when there was widespread belief in supernatural powers, such as the devil working through demonically possessed people and animals. This was the age of Galileo and Newton, and of the telescope and the microscope. There were many levels of understanding of the natural world. That of Galileo or Newton was far removed from most amateur scientists and the uneducated (but sometimes technologically knowledgeable) masses. Great advances were made in physics, maths and astronomy, providing a new view of the universe and the physics of the earth much like our own (a true scientific revolution). However, biological and chemical theory failed to keep up with increases in pure observational knowledge. In spite of a growing realisation that people were simply animals in mechanical terms, it was also widely held that humans had a dimension in common with purely spiritual beings, namely angels (higher) and demons (lower).

## How did science change as a result of both the contribution of individuals and broader developments in society?

### 'The hall of fame' approach

This approach emphasises the way in which great leaps in scientific understanding were made by a small number of men, principally Copernicus, Galileo and Newton. To look at the history of science as if it begins and ends with the great names, the 'geniuses', has long been the chosen approach of scientists. It was also the interpretation favoured by most of the early historians of science and remains so among many of our contemporaries. The scientist Stephen Hawking, for example, claims in *A brief history of time*, published in 1988, that 'Galileo, more than any other single person, was responsible for the birth of modern science'. This approach highlights the revolutionary nature of changes in understanding in the early modern period. A completely new view of the universe and of humanity's place in it came from Copernicus, Galileo and Newton; God's special creations – man and the earth – were no longer centre stage.

Galileo was a bold thinker. He needed courage to make statements about the motions of planets, for these were not subject to practical experiments. He had contempt for the **Aristotelians**. In his *Dialogues* of 1632, Galileo produced mathematical proofs that it was possible for the earth to move. It was not immobile, as previously thought. The book gained a readership across Europe, meeting with a mixed, but generally favourable reception. Galileo had confirmed Copernicus's heliocentric system – Copernicus was the first to advance the theory that the sun was at the centre of the solar system. In later years Galileo moved away from astronomy towards more fundamental work on physics (*Two new sciences*, 1638). With his usual boldness, he applied maths to the natural world in a series of **thought experiments**. In some respects anticipating Newton, he demonstrated mathematically the laws which governed the speed of a falling body and the path of a projectile and gave some

A portrait of Galileo Galilei, (1564–1642), by Leoni (c. 1578–1630). An astronomer, mathematician and physicist, Galileo laid the foundations of modern experimental science.

The **Aristotelians** were scholars who relied upon the books of the Ancient Greek philosopher Aristotle and his disciples, instead of taking the trouble to apply logic and maths to examine new theories to explain nature.

**Thought experiments**
For example, an engineer designs a motorbike with enough theoretical power to go up the steepest of hills. For a practical experiment the assembled motorbike would be tested to see if it would go up such a hill.

consideration to particle theory and light. Galileo's experiments were nearly all 'thought experiments'. He was content to create conclusions from mathematical reasoning alone; others might, in the future, confirm his theories by observation and practical experiment. Though he remained a faithful Catholic, Galileo was too bold for the Catholic inquisitors of Rome. Above all, the church worried that his work might undermine faith in the sacraments, including the mass. They also resented his fresh evidence that God's special creations, earth and man, were not at the centre of the universe. The inquisitors sentenced him to house arrest and commanded him to renounce Copernicanism publicly.

If the hall of fame approach is over-used, the focus becomes too narrow. For one thing, chemistry, biology and applied science advanced very little. For another, there were subtler, more long-term developments in science and society that allowed the findings of the new science to acquire a permanent place. Finally, it is important to recognise that men like Galileo were not infallible geniuses. Galileo could and did make mistakes. The German astronomer **Kepler** devised a theory of the elliptical motion of planets that was essentially correct (*New astronomy*, 1609). In spite of the fact that it was published at the start of Galileo's career, Galileo rejected Kepler's work entirely, holding to the conventional view that celestial objects must move in a circular motion. The Italian was partly put off by Kepler's belief in magnetic mysticism as the means by which the planets were kept in orbit, but professional jealousy was also probably involved.

Even more remarkable work in maths and physics was just around the corner. In the late seventeenth century Huygens, Leibniz and Newton are the acclaimed 'greats'. They were professional scientists working in universities. Increasingly, the really significant advances were made by such academic professionals. By the end of the century, just as today, this kind of work required training in maths, physics and astronomy. Christiaan Huygens (1629–95), mathematician, physicist and astronomer, explained mathematically the polarisation, refraction and reflection of light. He also attempted to explain gravity. Gottfried Leibniz (1646–1716) of Prussia and the Englishman Isaac Newton (1642–1727) were rivals. Though, as a mathematician he was arguably the equal of Newton (both men independently developed the calculus), Leibniz was more philosopher than scientist and did not produce the spectacular advances in physics achieved by Newton. Newton went even further than Huygens in the application of maths to physical problems, demonstrating the universality of laws of motion. Newton showed that the same forces which applied to falling bodies and projectiles also affected planets.

An engraving of the German astronomer Johannes Kepler (1571–1630). He worked out three laws of planetary motion and also made discoveries in geometry and optics.

Why are Copernicus and Galileo considered to have been so important to a modern understanding of the universe?

## The 'social history' of science – less-familiar names and the wider context

One school of historians argues that the great scientific advances of the seventeenth century were the result of a much longer evolutionary process, stretching back to the work of engineers in the Middle Ages. The more figures who appear in the hall of fame, the less their independent achievements appear to be – more of an **evolution of scientific thought** than a scientific revolution. More names need to be included. Galileo and Brahe developed the ideas of Copernicus; they didn't start from scratch. René Descartes, the philosopher, was also a crucial figure (see page 167). Although many of his scientific theories were wrong, his logical, mathematical, mechanistic approach was the major influence on all the leading scientists of the late seventeenth century.

All the leading scientists, including Galileo, produced some theories that have since been shown to be wrong. Some would say the full history of science is the story of all those ideas, whether right or wrong. Modern science's theories are often less clear-cut and far more debated than non-scientists imagine. Three hundred years after Huygens's pioneering work on light, scientists still argue about whether it is transmitted in waves or particles or both. Much of the research into what we would now call biology and chemistry was moving in the wrong direction, but it was all part of the history of science. Progress in science has often been made by a 'two steps forwards, one step back' approach and if the greatest scientific advances were made by academic professionals, many lesser-known figures also made some progress.

The typical amateur investigator – usually an educated lesser nobleman, a clergyman or a doctor – was pursuing a hobby with his **observational research**. He cultivated rare plants or investigated strange local natural phenomena as just one of a very wide range of interests. Other interests often included art collection, local history or foreign travel. Some were particularly interested in the applications of science in architecture, music or war. Others developed mines or industries on their land. Many of the collectors and observers of natural phenomena exercised little discretion in their zeal and followed the lead of **Francis Bacon** in cataloguing using detailed observation and simple experimentation. This led to unverified, unscientific observations. Someone, for example, reported that gemstones were growing in Javanese caves – perhaps the result of confusion with limestone formations, which are sometimes spectacular. Someone else described how a woman had given birth to rabbits. Such isolated observations, usually unconnected to any sound theory, filled the pages of the early journals of science, such as the French *Journal des savants*. Even so, these researches helped to broaden science and subjects such as geology began to develop. It was the work of the amateur scientists that formed the backbone of the publications of the royal scientific academies that appeared in England, France, Prussia and Russia at the end of

**Evolution of scientific thought** The maths that Galileo used, for example, had its roots in the work of Renaissance scholars and late medieval terminal velocity theorists.

Much of this painstaking **observational research** had been undertaken by monks in the Middle Ages. The newer Renaissance tradition of letters and note-books (e.g. those of the artist Leonardo da Vinci) revived this earlier defunct tradition and spread such knowledge more widely.

**Francis Bacon** (1561–1626) was an English philosopher and statesman. He stressed the importance of experiment to interpret nature and gave impetus to scientific investigation.

What were the strengths and weaknesses of amateur scientific research in the seventeenth century?

the seventeenth century, academies that promoted science to a wider public and gave a platform for the 'greats'.

In several European countries science had gained a central place in elite culture by the end of the seventeenth century. It was becoming fully respectable and even fashionable in Britain, Holland, France, Prussia and Russia. Queen Christina of Sweden, Louis XIV of France, Peter the Great of Russia and King Frederick William I of Prussia took a keen interest. Such patronage helped to bring science in from the cold. In the sixteenth century it had more often been seen as a semi-magical hobby for clever and dangerous eccentrics.

By about 1700 there were more professional scientists and many of them were corresponding internationally. Both amateurs and professionals were supported by academies of science, botanical gardens and regional natural history books. However, science was still not granted a major place in the curriculum of either schools or universities. While Leiden University in Holland was a notable exception and some of the leading scientists worked at Padua, Pisa and Cambridge, universities functioned more as finishing schools for the teenage sons of the nobility than as places of learning.

A second important group of little-known figures who made a major contribution were the skilled craftsmen: engineers, industrial chemists and instrument makers. They produced a greater volume of technical writing in the seventeenth century than ever before. Instrument makers such as **Tompion**, on whose work the English scientist Robert Hooke depended, were sometimes highly knowledgeable and assisted in the discoveries often attributed solely to their masters. A gauger of wine casks, named Davy, corresponded with Newton on mathematical topics.

Marxist historians like Zilsel (in his paper 'The genesis of the idea of scientific progress', published in 1945 in *Journal of the history of ideas*) have argued that the close working relationship between many scientists and craftsmen that developed in the sixteenth century was the key to the emergence of the scientific revolution. While still accepting the view that there was a scientific revolution, this is at the opposite extreme to the hall of fame approach. Marxists stress the importance of advanced economic activity and politico-religious revolution to scientific progress. This may help to explain why science was so strong in economically advanced Holland and England in the seventeenth century. It may also be why mining, canals and agriculture were developed faster in England and Holland than elsewhere; and why rigidly Catholic Spain and Austria lagged behind in science. The Dutch were leaders in applying science to practical needs. Maurice of Nassau (see page 91) founded a school of engineering at Leiden and made use of its research in his innovations in warfare. Simon Stevin, the school's leading scientist, produced books on practical solutions to navigational problems, double-entry

> What were the indications that science had become a prestigious activity by the end of the seventeenth century?

> **Thomas Tompion** (1639–1713) was a master clockmaker who also made barometers. He was appointed clockmaker at the Royal Observatory in 1676.

> In which states was applied science pursued most strongly in the seventeenth century?

Willebrord Snellius
(1580–1626), Dutch
mathematician. He is
accredited with the
formulation of the laws of
refraction of light.

Which broader
developments helped
to promote flourishing
activity in science in
the seventeenth
century?

book-keeping and the superiority of decimal arithmetic over fractions. The Leiden Botanical Garden was designed for strictly medicinal purposes. It also helped the tulip industry, another commercial application of science. Botany, medicine and astronomy were encouraged, with other advances being made by Boerhaave in medicine and **Snellius** in physics.

Against the Marxist view, it has been pointed out that scientific advance was not exclusive to the more advanced economies or to Protestant states. Trade guilds and the often misdirected power of courtly favour limited innovation and technology transfer in both advanced and less advanced economies. Scientists came from all over Europe and science developed rapidly in Italy, France, Denmark and Prussia – all of them less economically advanced. Furthermore, by discouraging theoretical science, the practical-minded Dutch put limits on scientific advance. Arguably, the German Leibniz eventually did more for the practical use of maths (through the invention of calculus – used in all advanced mathematical problem-solving) than Snellius and Stevin did.

## What was the balance of continuity and change in biology and chemistry? Why was less progress made than in physics?

Mathematics, physics and astronomy were at the heart of the scientific revolution and have received a disproportionate amount of attention for that reason. What about the other sciences? In the seventeenth century scholars did not divide science into the three main branches we identify today, physics, chemistry and biology. At the start of it Bacon called the whole area of knowledge 'natural philosophy'. This was one of the ways in which continuity with the medieval period was more striking than change to the form of science with which we are now familiar. However, distinctions were made even in Bacon's time – between, for example, medicine and botany. Furthermore, such specialisation was clearer by the end of the century than it had been at the start. A new branch, geology, had emerged, while the pseudo-sciences of demonology, **alchemy** and astrology had declined in importance. The pseudo-sciences will not be looked at in detail, but it must be remembered that many people took them very seriously at the time, while some historians of science have argued that alchemy helped to advance modern chemistry and medicine.

Alchemy was the belief
that base metals could be
converted into gold.

What branches of
natural philosophy
were distinguished by
the end of the
seventeenth century?

### The state of knowledge at the start of the century

In the study of plants, animals and human anatomy, scientists in the early seventeenth century were no longer dependent on Aristotle, Pliny and Galen, the great compilers of scientific knowledge in Ancient Greece and Rome. They now took pleasure in studying plants afresh, whether in their own gardens, in herbals where they were laid out alphabetically, or in the growing number of botanical gardens. With the aid of the herbals of Fuchs (1542) and Zaluziansky (1592), they were able to identify many varieties. Inspired by Bacon and the discoveries of new plants in the New World, they attempted to discover and describe more varieties. Plants were appreciated and studied mainly for their usefulness as herbs for medicine and food, just as they had been by the monks in medieval times. Some scientists at the start of the seventeenth century were beginning to say that scholars should be doing less description and more categorisation of plants, perhaps according to their complexity (Zaluziansky) or by habitat (Cesalpino).

Gesner has done much the same thing for zoology as Zaluziansky had for botany with his *History of animals* (1551–58). Inspired not only by Bacon but also by the earlier research of Gesner and **Vesalius**, early seventeenth-century biologists felt they were making advances on the work of Ancient World scholars, simply by undertaking careful observational study. They were, but not as much as they thought. When it came to explaining how animals breathed, plants grew or humans reproduced, the new books were as incorrect as the old. Alchemy still had a lot of influence, on the whole of a negative kind.

By the start of the seventeenth century the alchemist Paracelsus (*c*.1493–1541) was a figure of almost legendary status for some scholars. Recently the work of Paracelsus has been reappraised and his reputation revived. Here, the argument runs, was someone who turned his back on traditional wisdom, concentrated on cures and developed the idea of treatment by synthetic drugs. Unfortunately, some of his cures were deadly. **Paracelsus** had made claims for alchemical productions of all kinds, arguing that all natural phenomena were of alchemical origin. Maintaining that fire was the origin of chemical and bodily action, he urged doctors to use chemical rather than herbal preparations, sometimes with fatal results. The chemistry of the body, he said, was managed by a spirit residing in the stomach.

Other unfortunate results of alchemical influence can be seen, for example in the continuing attraction of the theory of spontaneous generation to explain animal reproduction, a favourite of Aristotle. Many scholars said that insects, frogs and mice were generated spontaneously from the substances in which they lived. As for human reproduction, the idea that God's creation of Adam and Eve supplied the prototype for all mankind went unchallenged. The pseudo-science of demonology also benefited from acceptance of the idea of conversions of matter from one form to another (e.g. devil to animal form).

## By the end of the seventeenth century

Technological advances achieved in the first half of the century were beginning to make some impact on research in biology and chemistry. These were

Which old and new developments made botany a vigorous area for research in the seventeenth century?

Vesalius (1514–64) was a Flemish anatomist who described all the bones, muscles and nerves of the human body.

Paracelsus's claims for the medicinal value of mercury was the most spectacular element of his curative medicine. The metal is extremely toxic.

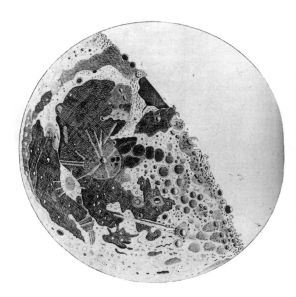

New sights: the moon from the telescope and spermatozoa from the microscope. The first is an engraving from Hevelius's *Stenographia*, 1647, and the second from Leeuwenhoek, 1677. Though the images were of low magnification, they were powerful demonstrations of the greater range of evidence opened up by the new observational instruments.

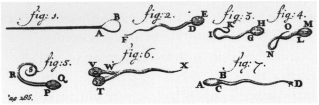

**Antony van Leeuwenhoek** (1632–1723) developed simple microscopes, with which he made some of the first observations of blood corpuscles, microbes and animal tissues.

the inventions of the microscope, telescope, thermometer, bubble-level and screw-micrometer. The microscope revealed the existence of previously unsuspected organic structures. In 1665 the English scientist Hooke saw box-like structures in cork magnified thousands of times. The Italian Malpighi used the microscope to study human organ tissues in the 1660s and in the next decade the Dutchman **Leeuwenhoek** observed red corpuscles in the blood and what he called 'animalcules' in drops of rain and pond water. Hooke, Leeuwenhoek and Malpighi were fascinated by these discoveries, but unaware of their significance. Hooke did not identify or understand cells, Leeuwenhoek did not know what the corpuscles were doing and Malpighi continued to hold wholly incorrect ideas about how muscles work. However, the collaborative processes of modern scientific investigation were being developed. Leeuwenhoek provided back-up proof, invited others to undertake the same observations and offered his own slides for people to view and provide their own explanations.

The microscopic observations were a little more productive in stimulating thought about chemistry. Once again, those with expertise in physical laws and properties (we would call them physicists) were in the lead in interpreting the new observations. The English scientist Robert Boyle hypothesised that oily liquids consisted of soft, round particles, but a hard metal like iron was made of firmly hitched particles. The general concept that the shape of the atom and the tightness of their links (density) determined the nature of the substance was grasped by Hooke, Newton and Huygens by the end of the century. Far ahead of most of his contemporaries, Newton even speculated that the proportion of solid matter was small compared to the volume of empty space, which we now know to be true.

Slightly influenced by the new microscopic observations and more by the work of the philosopher **Descartes**, biologists were beginning to see animals and even humans as assemblages of moving parts, machines moved by God. Descartes was now 'in' and Bacon 'out' – especially in France, where the English scholar was dismissed as a 'fact-grubber'. By the end of the century, building on Descartes' mechanical philosophy, a few brave scholars argued that the apple, the flea and human tissues could be considered in the same terms. Instead of believing that events were governed by spirits and demons, that the heavens moved in one sphere and our earth in another, leading scientists subscribed to the view that all things were controlled by the same laws of cause and effect. Newton believed that the world could be described mathematically and that God was simply the greatest of mathematicians.

However, the field of biology was a particularly tricky one for subscribers to Newtonian notions, because it forced scholars to confront the precise relationship of animals and plants to humans and the special purpose of each separate creation in God's scheme. So observations, for example, of remarkable similarities in the structure and systems of chimpanzees (then known as the 'pygmy') and humans were not taken to their logical conclusion. Faced with research such as that of **Swammerdam** (1669, 1675) scholars were prepared to concede that there were similarities in the anatomy and functioning of insects and mammals. Some even went too far, assuming that if they could see fleas in enough magnification they would see the fur, whiskers and teats of a mammal! Because Descartes had said so, they thought they would find the same internal, mechanical parts. A few dared to suggest that even plants might have souls. In spite of all this, the vast majority of scholars still maintained that, whatever the similarities, apes and humans must be fundamentally different from each other because God had so created them.

In spite of the constraints, observational and philosophical, there was real progress in a few areas of biology. In 1668 Francisco Redi disproved the theory of spontaneous generation by showing that meat would rot without producing maggots when shielded from flies. Finding convincing alternative explanations was the problem. Without sufficient magnification or knowledge of genetics, microscopic pictures of sperm seemed to confirm existing notions that the male developed the embryo and transmitted it to the female for cultivation. The old theories died hard, supported as they were by the full backing of the church. Many continued to believe in the theory of spontaneous generation into the nineteenth century. Mathematical approaches were far more easily applicable in physics and astronomy than they were in chemistry and biology. Animals and plants seemed bafflingly difficult to understand or to reduce to equations.

**Descartes** wrote in his *Principles of philosophy* (1644) that he had 'described the earth and the whole visible universe as if it were a machine, having regard to the shape and movement of its parts'. What was his influence on science?

A minority of French scientists supported Bacon in the 1640s and 1650s. Why did the others reject his approach?

**Jan Swammerdam** (1637–80), Dutch scientist. Using the microscope, he identified lymphatic valves and red blood corpuscles.

What factors were hindering progress in biology and chemistry? Why were these less of an obstacle in physics and astronomy?

# Was there a 'scientific revolution' in this century?

## The limited impact of the 'revolution'

The steam engine during the Industrial Revolution, computers today, have both had a widespread, penetrating effect on many aspects of life. We describe them as having a 'revolutionary' impact. Was the same true of the scientific revolution claimed for the seventeenth century? This period of development in science did result in some technological applications, though with a considerable time lag. The microscope, thermometer and barometer, when developed further, have had many practical applications. (The century even saw the invention of mechanical 'computers'. The calculating machines of Pascal (1642), Leibniz (1671) and Morland (1673) were a great advance on the abacus, anticipating the concept of a computer.) Historians now emphasise the increased capacity for further research that inventions like the microscope provided. However, this lay in the future, after the development of more sophisticated instruments and analytical procedures. This seventeenth-century 'scientific revolution' was overall very disappointing in technological appliance. Whether the sun orbited the earth or vice versa made no difference to the practicalities of day-to-day living. Though it may have been of great interest, the telescope's revelation of mountains on the moon was of no use to anyone. The microscope's revelation of cell structures in living tissues was, at that time, of no practical importance. For Leeuwenhoek and his colleagues science was primarily about increasing knowledge (of God's creation) and satisfying curiosity.

## Religion and belief in the supernatural

The fresh insights challenged, but did not overwhelm, religious and supernatural belief. Far from it; in the late seventeenth and early eighteenth centuries leading scientists and philosophers were able to accommodate the new science within their faith. It was to take evolutionary theory in the nineteenth century to encourage wider scepticism.

The first serious challenge came from Copernicus and Galileo, who offered a new explanation of the construction and operation of the world. Galileo himself was the most celebrated target of the later Catholic assault on Copernicanism. The heliocentric concept of the universe removed mankind and the earth from the central place accorded to them not only by Genesis, but also by **Ptolemy** and Aristotle. It demoted God's special creation of living beings to a corner of the universe. Pursued to one logical extreme, this way of thinking could lead to belief in an infinite universe held together by some kind of impersonal natural force. Further, by his fervent arguments in favour of observation and reason against the authority of books, Galileo challenged not

**Ptolemy** (living around AD 140) was a highly influential Egyptian astronomer and geographer. He placed the earth at the centre of the universe.

only Aristotle but the Bible (see Historical sources, p. 171). Lutherans were the first to attack Copernicanism and the Protestant restrictions on the new ideas were strongest in the early years – an interesting corrective to that point of view which associates Reformation politics with scientific progress. In his *Elements of physics* of 1549, the Protestant Melanchthon attacked the idea that the earth could move. The Bible said that the earth was still; end of story!

For what reasons was Galileo's research attacked by some Christians?

The supernatural continued to hold a secure place in the minds of many scientists. Joseph Glanvill (1636–80), one of the leading lights of the English Royal Society, was also a believer in the likely existence of demonic powers and their agents, such as witches. As late as 1722, John Locke, the prominent philosopher, wrote of the centrality of belief in miracles and spirits to Christian faith. At a popular level it has been shown that even in the Netherlands in the nineteenth century illness occasionally continued to be interpreted as the product of witchcraft. Challenge to religion and to belief in the supernatural came slowly. Certain phenomena, such as light, planetary orbits and reproduction, began to appear less magical. Every force and property could be described mathematically and attributed to 'natural laws' which worked in living bodies no less than on inanimate objects. In the face of these insights Christianity was not shaken. Neither was the faith of the majority of scientists, nor that of the masses. Faced with new facts and uncomfortable atheistic possibilities, science was adjusted to religion or even used to give it further support. **Archbishop Usher** acted in the spirit of the scientists by using the Bible to date creation to the year 4004 BC precisely. Arguing that biblical miracles were no stranger than the sudden appearance of comets, Locke and Leslie searched out convincing proofs that miracles like the parting of the Red Sea had occurred. **Ray** argued that the observations of microscopic biologists were a wonderful revelation of God's handiwork. There was nothing that could not be explained in biblical terms.

**James Usher** (1581–1656). Irish Calvinist and archbishop of Armagh. His famous '4004' chronology was accepted for well over a century.

**John Ray** (1627–1705) wrote in *Historia generalis plantorum* that the number of species in nature was fixed and limited and 'as we may reasonably believe, constant and unchangeable from the first creation to the present day'.

## Why have some historians preferred to describe developments as a scientific movement rather than as a 'revolution'?

A major trend in recent interpretations of this topic has been to describe the changes as a 'scientific movement'. Some historians have emphasised the 'social history' of science and argued that all attempts to further knowledge must be seen without inappropriate or unfair comparisons to later centuries. With these provisos they identify changes of profound importance, building on earlier advances. The status of scientific activity was raised. There was a growing acceptance of scientific 'proof'. Increasing numbers of scholars,

How can a change have a 'profound' but not a 'revolutionary' impact?

amateur and professional, were engaged in scientific research. The changes were complex, but few were, or could be, revolutionary, particularly in biology, chemistry and medicine.

## A genuine revolution, but not a popular one

Whatever else it was, the 'scientific revolution' was not a popular revolution. It neither affected the day-to-day lives of the masses nor entered their minds. Neither were there any truly remarkable changes in the fields of biology and chemistry. The stress on the authority of Scripture – the Bible – was even greater in the seventeenth century than it had been during the Renaissance. As the Bible was often the only book possessed by an ordinary family, this remained 'popular culture', not the findings of the new science. Some of those historians who wrote so enthusiastically about a scientific revolution (or the currently favoured scientific movement) were thinking exclusively about the educated elite. In respect of books, publishers were communicating less popular science to the general public by the late seventeenth century than they had in the sixteenth century. Newton's *Principia* (1687), for example, was notorious for being almost unreadable!

In spite of the current unfashionability of the concept, is it still possible to identify a seventeenth-century scientific revolution? Revolutionary changes in thought can happen without their being shared widely in the initial stages. This was the case in the seventeenth century, an era of deep social division. By the end of the seventeenth century, revolutionary ideas had transformed maths, physics and astronomy. The same emphasis on proof, observation and experiment was helping to nudge out the pseudo-sciences of astrology, alchemy and demonology. Biology, chemistry and geology, mostly products of the new emphasis on observation, had emerged as distinct areas of research, though restricted by obedience to the biblical version of creation. By 1700 science was a fashionable pursuit, followed by nobles and churchmen who corresponded by letter through scientific academies, rather as today's educated elite correspond through the Internet – actively with each other, but at a distance from the wider public. By 1700 something had changed radically and most of the advance had occurred in the previous century. Perhaps we should, after all – bearing in mind all these limitations – describe it as a 'revolution'.

# How seventeenth-century scientists saw their work

The concept of a 'scientific revolution' has been created by scientists and historians in the last century. Seventeenth-century people did not use the expression. Nevertheless, it is significant that scholars at the time certainly felt they were participating in something new and revolutionary, as we can see in the document study that follows.

## 1 Galileo's comments on Aristotle

How many propositions have I noted in Aristotle . . . that are not only wrong, but wrong in such a way that their diametrical opposites are true . . . [Man's understanding of the few mathematical truths perceived by God] equals the divine in objective certainty.

Source: Galileo, 'Dialogues on the two chief systems of the world', 1632, A. Rupert Hall, *From Galileo to Newton, 1630–1720*, 1963, p. 74.

## 2 Brahe's conclusions on comets

All comets observed by me moved in the aetherial regions of the world and never in the air below the moon, as Aristotle and his followers tried without reason to make us believe for so many centuries.

Source: Tycho Brahe, *'Astronomiae instauratiae mechanica'*, 1598, from M. Boas, *The scientific renaissance, 1450–1630*, 1962, p. 113.

## 3 The identification of distinct areas of study

It is customary to connect Medicine with Botany, yet scientific treatment demands that . . . theory must be disconnected and separated from practice, and the two must be dealt with singly . . . before they are united . . . In order that Botany may form a unit by itself before it can be brought into connection with the other sciences, it must be divided and unyoked from Medicine.

Source: A. Zaluziansky, *'Methodi herbariae'*, 1592, from Boas, 1962, p. 65.

## 4 Bacon on the pleasure of learning

The End of Knowledge . . . Men have entered into a desire of learning and knowledge, sometimes upon a natural curiosity; to entertain their minds with variety and delight; for ornament and reputation; to enable them to victory of wit and contradiction; and most times for lucre [profit] and profession; and seldom sincerely to give a true account of their gift of reason, to the benefit and use of men . . .

The Pleasure of Learning . . . far surpasseth all other in nature. We see in all other pleasures there is satiety. But of knowledge there is no satiety.'

Source: Francis Bacon, 'The advancement of learning', 1605, from *Francis Bacon selections*, eds. P. E. and E. F. Matheson, 1924, pp. 112–13

## Historical-source questions

1  What was new and bold about the claims made in Sources 1 and 2?

2  (a) Bacon (Source 4) said that some men wanted learning only for 'ornament and reputation'. Explain what he meant by this, in the context of the time.

   (b) What, according to Bacon, should be the main reason for increasing knowledge?

3  In what ways does Source 3 take an approach that is different from and more modern than Source 4 in regard to organising new knowledge?

4  Use the sources and your own knowledge to explain why some historians argue that there was a scientific revolution in the seventeenth century.

## Summary questions

1  (a) Assess the contribution of any *two* factors to scientific advance in the seventeenth century.

   (b) Which factor was most important to the 'scientific revolution'?

2  (a) Explain the importance of any factors restricting the impact of scientific advances in the seventeenth century.

   (b) Was there a 'scientific revolution' in the seventeenth century?

# Further reading

## Chapters 1 and 2: overview of political, religious and social history

D. H. Pennington, *Europe in the seventeenth century* (1989), is a clear and well-balanced account of the period. D. Ogg, *Europe in the seventeenth century* (1925), is a classic. Reprinted many times and considered old-fashioned by some, it is still one of the best general histories. Both achieve the difficult feat of combining a broad interpretative sweep with a wealth of detail.

Although Louis XIV is the main subject of J. L. Carr's *Life in France under Louis XIV* (1966), this includes an excellent introduction to the social structure of France. M. Weisner's *Women and gender in early modern Europe* (1993), is a detailed yet wide-ranging review, full of fascinating insights into economics, literature, witch-hunting and science.

## Chapters 3 and 4: France

R. Wilkinson, *France under the cardinals* (1995), is a lively and accurate overview. G. Treasure, *Richelieu and Mazarin* (1998), is a careful treatment of the subject, based on his researches over four decades. D. Parker's *The making of French absolutism* (1983) is less of a personality-driven interpretation and a good introduction to higher-level study.

## Chapters 5 and 6: Spain

J. Kilsby, *Spain – rise and decline* (1986), covers a tremendous amount of useful background. G. Darby, *Spain in the seventeenth century* (1994), is useful for a more detailed account.

## Chapter 7: United Provinces

K. H. D. Haley, *The Dutch in the seventeenth century* (1972), is a well-illustrated, clear introduction. G. Milton's *Nathaniel's nutmeg* (1999) enlivens English–Dutch rivalry in the spice trade with well-researched human interest stories. Bear in mind it is popular history.

### Chapters 8 and 9: The Thirty Years' War

S. J. Lee, *The Thirty Years' War* (1991), is a succinct account. T. K. Rabb (ed.), *The Thirty Years' War* (1972), contains an interesting range of primary and secondary sources.

### Chapter 10: Witchcraft

B. P. Levack, *The witch-hunt in early modern Europe* (1987), is well-researched. Both this and J. Barry *et al.*, *Witchcraft in early modern Europe* (1996), cover a lot of essential recent research. For the full drama of the topic either a stage production or the recent film of Arthur Miller's play, *The crucible* (1953), is worth seeking out. Bear in mind anachronisms.

### Chapter 11: Science

M. Boas, *The scientific renaissance* (1962), conveys the drama of the Copernican revolution, focusing on individuals, but without undue emphasis on Copernicus himself. J. Henry's *The scientific revolution and the origins of modern science* (1997), is a good recent introduction, with the modern emphasis on the social history of science.

# Index

Neri, Filippo, 30
Newton, Sir Isaac, 159, 160, 161, 163, 166, 167, 170
nobility, 8, 9–10, 21, 53; in Denmark, 25; in France, 35, 41, 45, 54, 58, 59, 60, 64, 66, 105; in Poland, 23; in Russia, 24; in Spain, 72, 81, 85, 87–8; in Sweden, 25; in the United Provinces, 98, 105
noble magnates, 41
Noni, Batista, 61–2
nu-pieds, revolt of the, 45

occupational structure, of France and the United Provinces, 104, 105
Olivares, Gaspar de Guzmán, count-duke of, 38, 39, 53, 68, 69, 77, 78–82, 83, 117; and the Catalonian revolt, 80, 84–5; character, 78–9, 82; and the colonies, 89, 90; compared with Richelieu, 79, 80–1; and the economy, 80, 87; policies, 79–80, 81–2, 84
Ormée (radical party in Bordeaux), 58, 59, 62, 66
Osnabrück, Treaty of (1648), 139; see also Westphalia, Peace of
Ottoman Empire, 5, 7, 20, 22–3, 24, 93, 94
overseas trade, 1; and the Dutch, 99, 100–2
Oxenstierna, Axel, 38, 39, 129

Papal States and the papacy, 22, 26, 112, 130
Paracelsus, 165
parliaments, 21
Paul IV, Pope, 17, 31
paulette tax, 66
peasants: in France, 35, 46; in Poland, 23; in Spain, 72; in Sweden, 25
Peter the Great of Russia, 104, 163
Philip II, king of Spain, 29, 39, 68, 69, 73–4, 92; and the colonies, 89; overcommitment in foreign policy, 74, 91; and the papacy, 112; and Philip III, 74; and the Portuguese, 93; and witch-hunts, 146
Philip III, king of Spain, 27, 68, 69, 74–7; and Lerma, 74, 75–7, 91, 92; style of government, 74
Philip IV, king of Spain, 27, 39, 68, 69, 78, 81, 83, 89; and the colonies, 90; personal rule by, 86, 92
physicians (doctors), 15
pillory, 152
plagues, 15; in Spain, 68, 71, 84, 88, 92; and witch-hunts, 147, 148
Poland, 6, 7, 24, 125, 128
Poland–Lithuania, 20, 23, 26, 94
Polisensky, The Thirty Years' War, 112
population: distribution, 3, 4, 104–5; effects of the Thirty Years' War on, 136; increases, 12, 14

Portugal, 19, 27, 51; colonies, 92–3; and Dutch commercial colonisation, 102; revolt against Spain, 69, 80, 83, 85, 86, 90, 93
poverty and poor families, 3, 8, 11–12, 14; and diet, 16; and ill-health, 14–15; rural poverty and witchcraft, 148
Protestant states, 19–20, 111, 114
Protestantism: Czech Protestants in Bohemia, 6, 113, 114, 116–17; in the Holy Roman Empire, 113–14; and the Reformation, 19, 20, 28–30, 145, 146; and the scientific revolution, 169; and sexual puritanism, 16–17; in Sweden, 24; and the Thirty Years' War, 130, 133; see also Calvinism; Huguenots; Lutherans
provinces, 28
Prussia, scientific development in, 164
Ptolemy, 168
Pyrenees, Peace of the (1659), 62, 64, 83

Ray, John, 169
Reformation, see Counter-Reformation; Protestantism
religion: Catholic states, 10, 19, 111, 114; diversity of, 5; Eastern Orthodox Church, 24; and ethnic minority groups, 6; in the Holy Roman Empire, 111; and ill-health, 15; Islamic faith, 12, 23, 25, 29, 73; Protestant states, 19–20, 111, 114; and radical groups, 53; religious allegiances, 25–6; and the scientific revolution, 163, 168–9, 170; and sexual puritanism, 16–17; and the Thirty Years' War, 114, 130, 133; in the United Provinces, 98, 100, 104; see also Catholic Church; Protestantism
religious festivals, 17–18
Rémy, Nicolas, 151
Retz, Cardinal de, 62–3
rich people, 3, 8, 9–10, 15
Richelieu, Cardinal, 21, 33–50, 52; and absolutism, 44–6; appearance, 38, 40; foreign policy, 42, 43–4, 46–7, 64–5; and the French economy, 34; handling of the plots against him, 41–2; and the Huguenots, 35, 42, 113; and Louis XIII, 39–40, 41, 45, 47–8; and Mazarin, 54, 55–6, 60, 63; motivations, 43; and the nobility, 8, 40–1; Olivares compared with, 79, 80–1; and the pursuit of war, 42, 43–4, 47, 49–50; rise to power, 37–8, 41; and the Thirty Years' War, 115, 128, 129, 133; titles, 39; and the United Provinces, 106, 108
Roman law, 151
Ross, Balthasar, 153
royal dynastic states, 26–7, 28
royal favourites, government by, 38–9
Rudolph II, emperor of Austria, 116

Russia, 19, 20, 24, 93; ethnic groups in, 7; mid-century revolution in, 52, 53; and Poland, 94; and the United Provinces, 102, 103, 104; and witch-hunts, 146

Saxony, and the Thirty Years' War, 128, 130, 131, 134
schools, 14
scientific revolution, 1–2, 159–72; in biology, 161, 164–7, 169, 170; in chemistry, 161, 166, 170; and the evolution of scientific thought, 162; 'hall of fame' approach, 160–1; Marxist view of, 163–4; and observational research, 162–3; in physics, 161–2, 163, 164, 170; and religion, 168–9; and royal scientific academies, 162–3, 170; and skilled craftsmen, 163; and technological applications, 168; and thought experiments, 160–1; and women, 12
secular courts, and the persecution of witches, 142, 145–6
serfs, 24, 25, 137
Sexby, Edward, 53
sexual attitudes, 16–17
Sherley, Antony, 84–5
ship-building, 104
Sigismund III, king of Sweden and Poland, 23, 27, 125, 128
Snellius, Willebrord, 164
social class, 7–12; in Spain, 72, 92, 96; in the United Provinces, 98
Spain, 19, 20, 21, 52–3, 68–96; agriculture in, 71, 87, 88; Aragon, 93; art in, 112; bullion trade, 72, 87, 89; Catalonian revolt, 69, 73, 80, 83, 84–5, 90, 93; Cortes (parliament), 79; decline and collapse of, 93–4; and Dutch maritime trade, 101; and the dynastic states, 26–7; economy, 71–2, 80, 84, 86–9, 92, 93, 94; emigration from, 88; empire, 21, 69–71, 73, 74, 80–1, 84, 86, 89–90, 92–3; ethnic divisions in, 7, 71, 72–3; expulsion of the Jews from, 72, 73; expulsion of the Moriscos from, 69, 72, 73, 77, 87, 88, 92; and France, 35, 37, 38, 41–2, 43, 46, 55, 62, 76–7; Granada revolt, 84; as a great power, 92–3; hidalgos, 72; and the Holy Roman Empire, 111; industry in, 71, 87–8, 92; Inquisition in, 72, 73, 112, 152; and the joint Habsburg Empire, 115; military power, 91, 93; Pax Hispanica, 69, 76; plague outbreaks, 68, 71, 84, 88, 92; political strengths and weaknesses, 71, 72; poor leadership in, 91–2; population decline in, 88; Portuguese revolt, 69, 80, 83, 85, 86, 90, 93; problems of governing, 69–72, 84–6; punishments for witchcraft in, 152;